T0390754

Disreputable Women

New Sexual Worlds

MARLON M. BAILEY AND JEFFREY Q. MCCUNE,
SERIES EDITORS

Featuring the most cutting-edge scholarship focused on racialized gender and sexuality studies, this series offers a platform for work that highlights new sexual practices and formations within diverse, understudied geographies. The dialectic of race, gender, and sexuality is central to the spine of all books in this series—rethinking the core questions of queer theory, gender and sexuality studies, and critical interrogations of race. With an interdisciplinary scope, authors draw on innovative methodologies, produce novel theories, and accelerate the study of gender and sexuality into new worlds of thought.

Disreputable Women

BLACK SEX ECONOMIES AND
THE MAKING OF SAN DIEGO

Christina Jessica Carney

UNIVERSITY OF CALIFORNIA PRESS

University of California Press
Oakland, California

© 2025 by Christina Carney

All rights reserved.

Library of Congress Cataloging-in-Publication Data

Names: Carney, Christina Jessica, author.
Title: Disreputable women : black sex economies and the making of San
  Diego / Christina Jessica Carney.
Other titles: New sexual worlds ; 3.
Description: Oakland : University of California Press, [2025] | Series: New
  sexual worlds ; 3 | Includes bibliographical references and index.
Identifiers: LCCN 2024031451 (print) | LCCN 2024031452 (ebook) |
  ISBN 9780520395084 (cloth) | ISBN 9780520395091 (paperback) |
  ISBN 9780520395107 (ebook)
Subjects: LCSH: Sex workers—California—San Diego—Social conditions—
  20th century. | Sex work—California—San Diego—History—20th century.
  | African American women—California—San Diego—Social conditions—
  20th century. | African American women—California—San Diego—
  Economic conditions—20th century. | African American women—Sexual
  behavior—California—San Diego—History—20th century. | Drag
  queens—California—San Diego—History—20th century. | African
  American lesbians—California—San Diego—History—20th century.
Classification: LCC HQ146.S275 C37 2025 (print) | LCC HQ146.S275
  (ebook) | DDC 306.74/2089960730794985—dc23/eng/20241122
LC record available at https://lccn.loc.gov/2024031451
LC ebook record available at https://lccn.loc.gov/2024031452

GPSR Authorized Representative: Easy Access System Europe,
Mustamäe tee 50, 10621 Tallinn, Estonia, gpsr.requests@easproject.com

34   33   32   31   30   29   28   27   26   25
10   9   8   7   6   5   4   3   2   1

To ADRIENNE, DENISE, and BUBBA
Who taught me to be nobody's darling

Contents

Illustrations

FIGURES

MAPS

Acknowledgments

It takes a village. Thank you to my parents, Adrienne and Victor, who always made sure I had plenty of books to read. Ruth, thanks for giving me my sweetness. Aunt Denise, you always validated my feelings and opinions, even when I was a young child—thanks for letting me know that I was *not* the crazy one. Cousin Dickie, your inappropriately funny Facebook posts brought me so much joy and laughter during my writing breaks; it has been so wonderful connecting with my elder gay cousin. My best friend since the fifth grade, Sydney, has seen so many versions of me and decided to stay on for the ride—thank you for creating a support system for me during the COVID-19 pandemic year in Chicago as I finished the book. And of course, this book would not have been possible without the amazing generosity I received from people I met and connected with in San Diego, in person and in the archives.

My professors and mentors at the University of Illinois in Urbana-Champaign and the University of California in San Diego have nurtured my intellectual curiosity in profound ways. Lisa Cacho's class "Race, Sex, Deviance" is the reason I decided to double major in women's studies and African American studies during my third year at UIUC. It was also Lisa Cacho who encouraged me to apply for the McNair Scholars Program, directed by Michael Jeffries and Priscilla Fortier. So much love to Dr. Ruth Nicole Brown, Chamara Kwakye, Claudine Taaffe, the girls of S.O.L.H.O.T for teaching me to *really* see and hear black girls—starting with myself. Fiona Ngô prepared me for the rigors of graduate school—every week she decided, in class, who was going to lead the discussion. You kept us on our toes! The Ethnic Studies Department at UCSD fostered an intellectual community like no other. My dissertation co-chairs, Yen Espiritu and Fatime El-Tayeb, your mentorship is unmatched. My wonderful committee members—Boatema Boateng, Dayo Gore, and Roshanak Kheshti. Graduate school was so much better because of "The Legendaries"—Kyung Hee Ha, Marilisa Navaro, Lila Sharif. R.I.P. Candice Rice.

Many thanks to the Departments of Women's & Gender Studies and Black Studies, and the College of Arts and Science, at the University of Missouri in Columbia (Mizzou) for their continued commitment to my success. Navigating the academy as a black woman can be scary, but I have been fortunate to have Lynn Itagaki, Sherri Marie, Stephanie Shonekan, April Langley, Linda Reeder, Srirupa Prasad, and Julie Elman to help me navigate this sometimes treacherous place. I am so lucky to have colleagues and friends who have taught me how to survive academia. Ultimate gratitude to the student activists at Mizzou, whose demands included the creation of my position as professor of Black (Queer) Sexuality Studies. Thank you to all the students who have taken my courses, especially Black Sexual Politics and Black Feminism—thinking and talking with students in these classes has given me so much joy.

The completion of the book would not have been possible without the support from the Institute for Citizens and Scholars, the

Black Midwest Sexuality Studies Writing Group, and a host of black queer and feminist collectives. Marlon Bailey, Jeffrey McCune, and Freda Fair consistently pushed me to lead with my own voice; you saw the potential (and finish line, ha!) before I ever did. I always knew she was a trickster, but both Kemi Adeyemi and Jillian Hernandez challenged me to think more critically about the great Maya Angelou—the chapter is so much stronger now because of your insights. Thanks to Terrance Wooten and Allison Reed for their feedback before submission and validating me during moments of deep imposter syndrome.

I cannot believe I wrote a book, or what a colleague called "a collection of related essays." I thought I was done. WRONG. Revising and editing is where the magic really happens. I have so much appreciation and respect for my editors. Colleen Jankovic is a developmental/copyeditor extraordinaire. The University of California Press editorial team, Jeff Anderson, Naomi Schneider, and Aline Dolinh, were incredibly patient and generous as I prepared *Disreputable Women*.

Lastly, thank you to Duke University Press for allowing me to republish as the first chapter of this book parts of my essay "'The Worse Element': Black Sex Workers, White Slavery, and Sexual Policing in San Diego," from the special issue "Troubling Terms and the Sex Trades" of *Radical History* Review, edited by Rachel Schreiber and Judith Walkowitz.

Introduction: Making "America's Finest City"

They would come through—take our hair off, take our water titties out. They did all that. Take us to jail; when we went to court, we had to go to court with just makeup on lookin' like a hot mess. They would parade us down the street and they would chain us together. We would walk from the jail down to the courthouse. And they would parade us down the street like that. We walked right down Horton looking like a fool.

GRANVILLE "BUBBA" OMEGA HUGHES

In this quote, Granville "Bubba" Omega Hughes (b. 1945, d. 2021)—my main interlocutor—richly narrates how municipal police would raid Silver Sands Café, a black-owned institution in downtown on Fifth and Market near Horton Plaza in the mid-1960s, and selectively arrest street-involved black drag queens who were made to look like "a hot mess" and "a fool." As the city embarked on a new redevelopment scheme for downtown, which began in the 1950s, some of the only places remaining for black queens to congregate were Robert Clay's Silver Sands Café and the adjacent Horton Plaza, a public square and park. Most of the queens labored as sex workers and performed in drag shows in downtown bars frequented primarily by US servicemen. However, to make the center core attractive for development and safe for suburban moms, certain forms of blight needed to be wiped from the landscape. In 1966, a year after Bubba arrived in San Diego, municipal police enacted Ordinance 9439 (Section 5619), which prohibited "in a public place, or in a place open to public view . . . apparel customarily worn by the opposite sex, with the intent to deceive another person for the purpose of committing an illegal act."[1] While most cities and towns had had cross-dressing ordinances since the mid-nineteenth century, San Diego did not enact one until 1966—after the US Supreme Court began ruling state and municipal vagrancy laws unconstitutional.[2] San Diego police claimed that "men posing as women" were targeting sailors by taking them to single-room occupancies (SROs) and hotel rooms to rob them.[3] The plaza queens were seen to pose a danger to (white) US servicemen.

Before the arrest of black queens in Horton Plaza in the 1960s, police began targeting disreputable women within this same interzone with "wholesale arrests of disorderly women, particularly negresses," as the city embarked on its first major military and imperialist project, the Panama-California Exposition.[4] Many of these vice districts overlapped into black, Asian, native, and immigrant communities, creating what Kevin Mumford names "interzones."[5] Under the guise of fighting white slavery, a sex-trafficking moral panic about interracial intimacy, local reformers spearheaded a campaign to eliminate more illicit forms of sex work. Based on arrest records and print media archives, black women were disproportionately targeted. In 1910, Keno Wilson "summoned a number of disreputable negro women" to his office, where they were told "to keep inside the lines of the redlight section as outlined by the police, or to leave the city."[6] Black women had a choice: either broker deals with the police to sell sex in specific places (not their rooming houses) or leave the town altogether. Black women who lived in rooming houses on H Street, later renamed Market Street, were some of the first targeted in the "clean-up." While twentieth-century politicians, reformers, and activists constructed black "disreputable women" and "plaza queens" *along with* the public and private places they congregated as menaces to society, this predatory sexual policing hinged on two key contradictions.

First: throughout the city's history, San Diego's (white) residents and visitors have relied on black bodies and spaces/places "around the corner" for sex, drugs, and other forms of labor but then violently disavowed them.[7] The city and its militarization could not function without providing sexual labor for its men—if the sexual labor were not there, the city would not be what it is. A 2016 report published by the United States Department of Justice revealed how San Diego's sex tourism industry brings in over $810 million annually for the city, second only to the US military.[8] Since the late nineteenth century, municipal police designated downtown as a place where vice should be *placed*. Police profited from the economies through graft and bribery and/or creating their own criminal syndicates.[9] The excess monies made from these informal economies found their way into the pockets of local and state politicians, since their campaigns for reelection were often financed by police unions or they owned properties in the larger red-light district. Police, politicians, and city boosters had much to gain from these informal economies—more so than the sex workers themselves.

Second: dominant society relies on places of marginalization being surveilled and rendered placeless in order to position itself as dominant. For dominant society, marginalized places represent both a problem and an opportunity, eliciting both pleasure and disgust. Space and place are not only representative of difference but also *produce* difference.[10] To reproduce a white heteropatriarchal status quo, certain bodies must be excluded. Red-light districts exist to physically separate and contain sexual deviancy from the view of respectable white women, whose virtue was a nation-building project. Within these zones, police disproportionately targeted black women, regardless of whether they were sex-working. This was not done to obliterate prostitution but rather to shore up support and an *imagined need* for police in urban areas. As Anne Gray Fischer argues, white women's sex work was essentially decriminalized, while municipal police across the United States ramped up the sexual policing of black women to "justify and expand . . . [their] discretionary power."[11] This also served the local economic and political interests by justifying the violent removal of a (criminalized) class of people from their homes and networks. This forcible displacement made way for urban renewal and gentrification efforts to make the city more welcoming and safer by funding an increasingly paramilitarized police force in the US-Mexico border town.[12]

Disreputable Women is a book about how sex-working black women navigate undesirability under white supremacy by crafting a politics of the disreputable that confronts and confounds the state—particularly the militarized city of San Diego. The criminalization of street-involved sex workers was central to how the state enforced racial segregation and managed the racial anxieties of the national body politic in the twentieth century, illustrating how sex-worker history is key to statecraft. In this book, I argue that homosexual/nonheterosexual and heterosexual, trans, and gender-nonconforming outlaws defied heteropatriarchal norms of white domesticity by using private space in black institutions for sex work in San Diego. These black queer subjects found clandestine and creative ways to escape surveillance and incarceration. In this book I map the disreputable zones and practices that black disreputable women create. I use *the disreputable*, a black feminist framework, to attend to the historical, political, economic, and epistemic shifts of black women's sex work and reproductive labor in twentieth-century San Diego. Using ethnography, archival methods, and literary analysis—always informed by a black feminist framework—I unveil how certain black women's practices toward sexual/individual freedom produce a new model of *liberative subjecthood*. While early twentieth-century local reformers and authorities described newly migrant black sex workers in the Fifth Ward of downtown as "disreputable," which assisted in institutionalizing processes of internal deportation, I instead use the term to illustrate how the disreputable black female subject was made, preserved, and contested.

The interplay between sex work, sexuality, and queerness enables me to think about the commodification of black women's labor and black women's different roles in sex tourism, how black pleasure and joy take place in spaces of sexual excess, and how gay, lesbian, and trans black bodies are involved in the making of a militarized space. I cull together and analyze newspaper articles, court cases, organizational records and journals, scrapbooks, ephemera, memoirs, oral histories, ethnographies, photographs, and state-funded research projects that reveal a discourse of racialized gender violence, alongside moments of black freedom that are understudied in dominant histories, literatures, and policies. This "scavenger methodology," coined by queer scholar Jack Halberstam, mirrors the scavenger methods black working-class sex workers deployed to create some semblance of freedom in the US border town, including reconceptualizing public and private space in inner-city black rooming houses, rural brothels, SROs, bars and restaurants, storefront churches, working-class fraternal orders, and civil rights advocacy organizations.[13] What I mean by *scavenger* is a person who out of necessity finds and makes use of discarded objects. This labor is anticapitalist, use-value oriented, ecologically sustainable, and often hidden. I gather these heterotopic objects to illuminate an archive of black people's continuous placemaking strategies in a cityscape where police and residents have perpetually advocated for their eviction. Rather than discard the disreputable subject, I embrace and animate her worlds, highlighting her epistemic resistance and taking seriously the performances, archives, and narratives often lost in the telling of urban histories and life.

Disreputability

Disreputability is a place-based act of refusal. As black geographer Katherine McKittrick rightly points out, "practices of subjugation are also spatial acts."[14] Prostitution is a quasi-state-sanctioned economy, but one with rules. These rules govern exactly *where* sex should happen, *with whom* you can have it, *how much* certain people should be paid for these services, and *when* those services are no longer needed. Some black women in San Diego defied these rules by using "place-based critiques, or respatializations" in the form of reconceptualizing the domestic sphere: using rooming houses and single-room occupancies for transactional sex, since racially segregated brothels restricted employment to white/white-passing women; using public space for sex work because of housing precarity; and queering seemingly straight black bars and fraternal orders in the few remaining black-owned spaces in parts of the city.[15] Even though black women were the matter through which urban renewal processes were realized, they were not passive victims; instead, they were active participants in transforming social relations and the physical environment.

Refusal, as a form of activism and practice of freedom, builds on existing interdisciplinary black feminist scholarship—a rich genealogy that maps this continuum across time and space. The "chorus" of black working-class women/girls and queers in the tenements of newly urbanized and industrialized cities of the early twentieth century have much in common with black queers and lesbians taking up space on the dance floor in a gentrified gay neighborhood in the twenty-first century.[16] They each defiantly take up space despite processes of urban development and dispossession. For Saidiya Hartman, the ghettos of New York and Philadelphia during Reconstruction and the Harlem Renaissance are places "where the poor assemble, improvise the forms of life, experiment with freedom, and refuse the menial existence scripted for them."[17] While reformers characterized this place, and the places within them, as sites of deviancy and decay, they were places where black women experimented with other ways of being. The tenement, for example, disrupted Victorian ideas and sensibilities—it was a place where differently gendered people formed alternative kinship structures and created moments of pleasure. Black intellectuals of that era, like W. E. B. Du Bois, failed to acknowledge their ingenuity and creativity. Kemi Adeyemi looks at the other side of development a century later, as places once occupied by marginalized folks are being redeveloped to make room for white middle- and upper-class hipsters. Instead of leaving neighborhoods that they have long called home, as developers hoped they'd do, black queer women stayed and claimed space despite the perils. As black women dance to the slowness of R&B tunes on a dance floor which is being infiltrated by white hipsters, they are also producing a politics and geography that challenge erasure and invisibility and instead create "alternative networks of communication, community, and movement."[18] These political spaces, such as the rooming house and dance floor, offer more to black women's sense of place and pleasure than formal political spaces.

In fact, black lesbian and queer activism (and feminism more generally) would not have been possible without black women's liberatory practices in disreputability. My analysis of early twentieth-century arrest records for vagrancy, a catchall statute used to criminalize non-normative behavior, illuminates the everyday practices of black heterosexual and queer sex workers who challenged the status quo. Women who dared to engage in nonmarital and interracial sex and reside in residential hotels with other women or without a male proxy, who drank, smoked, and talked back to authorities, were women whose behaviors the state remedied through surveillance, arrests, prosecution, and incarceration.[19] These are behaviors that some feminists, women, and queer activists of today take for granted.[20] The fact that black women and queer people continue to engage in sex work, despite other labor opportunities, points not only to its usefulness in terms of survival but more importantly to how disreputable women are *still* providing us with a template to think outside of normative economic, social, and cultural constructs.

Although considered labor, sex work is a form of antiwork politics, since for many women it is a less extractive and more pleasurable way of being in the world.[21] LaMonda Horton-Stallings's "transing of research on sex work" is useful in understanding sex work as a retreat from structural and institutional violence. In her engagement with James Boggs and Kathi Weeks, she points to how sex workers make us think differently about the very idea of work. "These sexual guerrillas, currently defined as sex workers, represent a radical spirit of revolt against antierotic, sex-negative, individualism, moral and health panics, and capitalism's deadly recycling of a Protestant work ethic."[22] Though money is the primary objective for black women sex workers, porn scholar Mireille Miller-Young argues that these illicit and disreputable economies also allow black women a sense of agency—many gain time to care for their elderly parents and children, for example.[23] Also, many women like and have fun at their workplace, as opposed to the often grueling and underpaid work environments that characterize twenty-first-century service labor jobs.[24] Even more, there is a constant conflation between sex work and sex trafficking. For example, a San Diego district attorney argued that there is "no such thing as voluntary sex work."[25] By contrast, antiwork sex work activists contend that work culture and capitalism perpetuate the demand for the trafficking of people, not sex work. Yet authorities and the national body politic still are invested in criminalizing sex workers and their clients.

The policies created to end sex trafficking, which constitutes a small percentage of all trafficking cases, mainly affect sex workers who have chosen sex work, not women who were forced by intermediaries into the trade.[26] Anti-sex-trafficking domestic and internal policies not only make marginalized women and queers vulnerable to arrest and caging but also strip them of agential power.[27] The racialized gender politics of early twentieth-century white slave (early anti-sex-trafficking) narratives share an eerie similarity with those of the antitrafficking discourse of the twenty-first century. Similar to efforts aimed at white slavery, "modern-day slavery abolitionism" (MDS abolitionism) supports aggressive criminal justice answers to human sex trafficking, promoting accountability for individual perpetrators and a rescue narrative for victims.[28] Funded by philanthropists, MDS abolitionism has overtaken the trafficking arena, replacing the long-standing NGOs that historically have taken a human rights rather than criminal enforcement approach to trafficking. By deploying an oversimplified, albeit popular, slavery narrative, MDS abolitionists create a moral crusade that deflects from broader institutional and structural causes of exploitation. Within this savior framework, state actors fashion themselves as emancipators instead of complicit actors in the engine that creates global inequalities and social and economic exclusions in the first place. As Siobhan Brooks notes, antitrafficking laws continue to unevenly affect black women sex workers. "Binary framings of debates about sex work—focusing on decriminalization versus criminalization, innocence versus guilt, or choice versus forced sex work—do not address the actual needs or political desires of sex workers, especially Black women. In fact, these binary framings do sex workers a political disservice."[29] Both conservative and liberal actors across the political spectrum have overwhelmingly supported these carceral policies—even including feminist and lesbian/gay activists.[30]

Disreputable Women also fills in a part of history about the buildup of the women's prison industrial complex in California, the world's leading carceral space. Since the population of black women, and black people more generally, in the state was quite small compared to those of white and brown people, most studies about black imprisonment in the state begin in the 1960s onward, which consequently overlooks how anti-blackness shaped discretion in policing and often was weaponized as a warning to other marginalized people.[31] In her examination of Georgia's prison system, Sara Haley demonstrates the "mutually constitutive role of race and gender in constructing subject positions, technologies of violence, understandings of the social order, and the construction and application of the law."[32] Though black women in San Diego's red light district numbered less than 200, black residences were the first targeted by state authorities during development processes in the early and mid-twentieth century. Black women in early twentieth-century California were not only disproportionately incarcerated, they were often imprisoned at men's penal institutions, like San Quentin State Prison. Black women were sent to men's prisons, while white women were seen as too "delicate" to be imprisoned—and were instead leased out as domestics to white employees, or if they were incarcerated, were not subject to harsher forms of labor.[33] Both white and black suffragists noted the inhumane and uneven treatment of black women inside these prisons—with black women inmates often tortured with rape at the hands of white guards.[34] Yet instead of arguing against imprisoning women in penal institutions, first-wave feminists spearheaded campaigns to create same-sex women's prisons, one of the very first forms of US prison reform.[35] This reform not only led to the current overrepresentation of black women in prison but continued violence against their bodies.[36]

Yet these carceral spaces were not only located or restricted to the prisons themselves but were also in the racially segregated neighborhoods where black people were placed by authorities. Rashad Shabazz's concept of "spatialized blackness" is useful here because it "underscores how mechanisms of constraint built into architecture, urban planning, and systems of control that functioned through policing and the establishment of borders literally and figuratively created a prison-like environment."[37] While Shabazz theorizes how it produced forms of racialized masculinity, Anne Gray Fischer, in *The Streets Belong to Us: Sex, Race, and Police Power from Segregation to Gentrification*, traces how the policing of black sex workers and interracial sex was key to gentrification processes in urban US centers.[38] In San Diego, black communities were ghettoized in downtown and then later segregated to the southeast of the city. In the early twentieth century, black people (including women) were placed on the outskirts of the police-protected vice district, as were indigenous, Chinese, and later Filipino laborers.[39] As antiprostitution legislation decreased the number of Chinese women in downtown rooming houses, black women began to occupy these dwellings. Since black women were restricted from laboring in Stingaree, the racially segregated police-protected vice district, they used rooming houses to perform sex work. When white (and black) Progressive Era reformers began to pressure the city to close Stingaree, authorities raided these rooming houses, while white brothels in Stingaree were largely left unmolested. Downtown continued to be a carceral space in the mid-twentieth century, but this time black queens and other gender nonconforming women became targeted by authorities. Authorities were the architects of these disreputable zones, which allowed them to both racially segregate vice and also criminalize these same people when political pressure mounted.

I also chart how mid-twentieth- and early twenty-first-century LGBT activists were not only complicit but also architects of disreputable zones. Christina Hanhardt's historicization of US gay neighborhood development was instructive to my understanding of safe space activism. Hanhardt points out in her groundbreaking *Safe Space: Gay Neighborhood History and the Politics of Violence* that LGBT politics and property politics are practically indistinguishable. Safe space activists condemned the sex-working black and brown drag queens in Horton Plaza to advance their quest to build and create a more sanitized gay territory in Hillcrest, a predominately working-class Latine neighborhood. Their tactics were not so different from those of the white first-wave feminists of the early twentieth century, who mobilized a moral crisis about sex work for their own political interests. Seemingly radical gay liberation activists, like Bernie Michels and Jesse Jessop, were complicit in the policing of the drag queens who often congregated in Horton Plaza. When black queens, like Bubba, were arrested, there was no outcry from safe space activists. Instead, homophile periodicals like the *Prodigal*, published by the Metropolitan Community Church of San Diego, instructed cis gay men how to avoid being conflated with drag queens, instead of fighting to remove the cross-dressing statute from the books. As Becki Ross and Rachael Sullivan argue in their research on antiprostitution gay activism in mid-1970s Vancouver, "the drive to expel prostitutes from the imagined gay community became part of the bargain made by (some) predominately white gay men to enhance their transition from lowly criminals and deviants to enterprising, morally upright citizens and community leaders."[40] Safe space activists were invested in property politics and establishing gay electoral power. Yet black queer women, like myself, remained invested in creating space in a place that practically got down payments to gentrify a working-class neighborhood into a family-friendly commercialized district.

Chapter Overview and Method

Changes in industry, such as the transcontinental railroad, the gold rush, US imperialism in the Pacific, US expansion in the West, and the buildup of the US military in California, were all pull factors that gradually increased the African American/black population in the state.[41] The black history of San Diego is similar to that of Richmond, California, located in western Contra Costa County, and of the East Bay community near San Francisco.[42] Unlike in other Californian cities, like San Francisco and Los Angeles, most of the black migrants coming to Richmond and San Diego came from the US South.[43] Spurred by the buildup of the US military in California, both the East Bay and San Diego experienced a dramatic peak in black migration for work in defense industries after the end of World War II. Despite a rich historiography, the field's attention to the unique history of blacks in San Diego is rarely interrogated.

San Diego largely has been insulated from the effects of economic crises and downturns, most (if not all) of which took place after major wars and contests over space. From the late nineteenth century, city boosters were determined to create a scheme for economic growth by courting the US military. The sale of indigenous land well below market value was the main reason the US Navy conceded to leaders in San Diego. The city's first major redevelopment and military project was the Panama-California Exposition of 1915. During World War II, through a partnership with Consolidated Aircraft, San Diego became a major aircraft defense production site. Currently, San Diego is home to the largest concentration of military assets in the region, contributing an annual $50 billion to the annual regional economy, which is 25 percent.[44]

The location of military bases, including servicemen and personnel, enabled black women to exploit the resources of the military for their profit, although this access was often uneven. Martial history usually is preoccupied with the mechanics of war, treaties, and policies, but my framing of militarism is more tuned in to how "the valorization of military life, values and solutions" is insidiously woven into the fabric of everyday life.[45] My framing of militarism is indebted to the field of critical studies of tourism and militarism led by indigenous feminist scholars who map histories of imperialism and its intersection with gender in the larger Pacific-Oceanic region.[46] In the introduction to the *American Quarterly* special issue "Tours of Duty and Tours of Leisure," Vernadette Vicuña Gonzalez and Jana K. Lipman challenge the field to think more critically about an "explicit gender analysis or focus on the politics of sexuality in tourism and militarism"; "explicit discussions of race"; "the opportunities and class mobilities opened up by militarism through travel"; how militarism "may hold out possibilities for stability, liberation, or even anticolonialism"; and how more attention is needed for histories prior to World War II. *Disreputable Women* is in conversation with the field of critical studies of tourism and militarism by showing how black sex workers have used militarism, since the turn of the twentieth century, not only for survival but as a resource to achieve social, bodily, and economic mobility.

Disreputable Women covers a vast time range, enabling me to use different methodologies, which, as a result, offer different perspectives on black queer life in twentieth-century San Diego. It is a critical engagement with archival knowledge. Because most documentary evidence is from civil, police, military, or business interests, or from reformers who partnered with them, the story of black San Diego is necessarily biased and disciplining. Black women historians have questioned the ethics *and* methods of historical methodologies (with their reliance on colonial archives) to tell counter-histories of the wayward, subaltern, and dispossessed. The partial history requires a framework for how we can think about issues of bodily autonomy, queer identity, pleasure, and fugitive identities. To do that, I interrogate analytical categories, such as "disreputable," "undesirables," and "floaters," that are often taken for granted as common sense. By interrogating these categories, I am interrogating the very project of knowledge production.

Chapter 1, "Disreputable Negro Women," is an exploration of disreputability and its historical meaning at the turn of the twentieth century—particularly examining how the Panama-California Exposition, first-wave feminist activism, the institutionalization of public health, and the popularity of eugenics contributed to a political and social context that led to the sexual policing of black and marginalized women in downtown San Diego. San Diego was a very different city than other California cities, as Caribbean and Central American black populations traveled there, often by ship. Additionally, the presence of large military bases and the US-Mexico border contributed to a unique racial-sexual geography of the city. The year 1909 was a turning point in the city, as San Diego embarked on its first major imperialist and military project, a world's fair—the Panama-California Exposition. The fair, and the state's official fair in San Francisco, was in response to the completion of the Panama Canal, which linked the Pacific and Atlantic Oceans. Using articles from the *San Diego Union* and *Chicago Defender*, San Diego probation records, California Supreme Court and appellate cases, and census records, I map a geography of black and interracial sex work in turn-of-the-century San Diego. Historical archives show how sex-working black women used rooming houses to exercise their citizenship rights to privacy by using the space for work, rest, and community. I also demonstrate how some black women used technologies of race and gender, like cross dressing, to escape sex work and participate in other informal labor fields.

The following chapter, "Are You in the Life?," combines literary and archival methods to explore how some black entrepreneurs eventually became intermediaries between police and sex-working black women, thereby ending an almost-decade of relatively pimp-free sex work in the downtown area. To get a more intimate picture of these intermediaries and the syndicates they created, I use Maya Angelou's sex archive, located in her memoir *Gather Together in My Name* (1972). This second volume of Angelou's autobiographical series documents her role as a pimp for two black lesbians that she meets at a black-owned bar called Hi Life Café in Logan, and her subsequent role as a brothel sex worker, where most of her tricks were Bracero agricultural workers. Though Angelou participated in disreputability, she, like the state, considered sex work a necessary evil and represented it as black women's ultimate defeat. I argue that her devaluation of black sex workers, including herself, enables her to become a hallmarked treasure in the national and international imaginary. Like the first chapter, this one also demonstrates interracial sex work, but this time with Bracero farm workers—many of whom crossed the US-Mexico border through San Diego.

In the last two chapters, I use ethnographic methodologies to link contemporary and historical struggles that were products of politicized sexualized economies of land ownership. In chapter 3, "We Were Just Negro Queens," I examine how *the* prominent gay organization of San Diego in the 1970s, the local Metropolitan Community Church (MCCSD), and safe space activists supported the criminalization of sex-working queens and gender-nonconforming people in downtown San Diego to advance their own political and economic aspirations. Bernie Michels, an active MCCSD member and cofounder of the Gay Center for Social Services, described how downtown was unsafe for white gays and lesbians. This argument was then used by safe space activists to fundraise to gentrify the neighborhood of Hillcrest. I use the oral history of Granville "Bubba" O. Hughes, my main interlocutor, to challenge this discourse of safety in downtown's gay ghetto. Her narrative also highlights an alternative faith community, Greater Johnson Missionary Church, a storefront church housed in a building owned by a group of black Masons. I argue how the church housed a certain sexual economy whose creation was a response to urban development, partly led by safe space activists, that led to the displacement of black people out of downtown to areas such as the neighboring Barrio Logan and other parts of southeast San Diego. While some black lesbians and gay men participated in safe space activism, and were even on the planning committee for the Center for Gay Services, oral histories by some founding members describe how sexism and racism played a huge role in the absence of black lesbian women in the new gay territory.

The final chapter approaches queerness and sex work in a more capacious way. "The Gathering" examines black lesbian activism in the last two decades of the twentieth century. Using organizational records and ephemera from two black social and political groups, Lesbians and Gays of African Descent United (LAGADU) and the Afrikan American Gay Women Association (AAGWA), I argue how members created a unique type of intersectional queer black nationalist activism through their work as playwrights, journalists, and community organizers of social events. I also use autoethnographic methods to show how black lesbian placemaking in Hillcrest has continued to be a contentious and complex matter. Interestingly, my own labor as a club promoter is very similar to that of the disreputable women and their intermediaries of the twentieth century, since I too have monetized black women's bodies and sexualities as a way to profit from the militarized tourism industry in San Diego.

In the pages that follow, I tell the story of disreputable women in a way that honors a legacy that speaks against dominant narratives of sex workers as deviants. Disreputability is a method of *being* that confounds state agents and discourses of respectability. Here, black women produce sexual cultures and economies outside of state surveillance and advance an epistemic world that is largely unconcerned with tradition, but rather is a radical refusal of the insignificance of sexual autonomy, sex work, and gender nonconformity as instrumental in the development of black community life. Whether through social hygiene campaigns by Progressive reformers at the turn of the early twentieth century or safe space activists in the middle of the century through the present, disreputability continues to be positioned as a threat that needs to be managed by citizens and authorities alike.

1 *"Disreputable Negro Women"*

Interracial Sex, Rooming Houses, and Social Hygiene

On the morning of December 19, 1920, thirty-four-year-old licensed hairdresser and beauty shop owner Irene Shepard was preparing her daughter for Sunday school when officers H. H. Kenney and Bernard Sotomayor came to her rooming house on 245 Seventeenth Street and told her that the "Chief of Police of the City of San Diego desired to see her."[1] Shepard lived with her husband, Asa Shepard, but it is unknown whether he was home at the time of her arrest. According to Shepard's written civil complaint, she accompanied Kenney and Sotomayor to the police station, where she claimed she was "immediately confined without being informed as to the charge against her" and was "humiliated, grieved and ashamed" during her "malicious prosecution" on a charge of keeping a "disorderly house" and being an "immoral person."[2] The former was for noncompliance with the Red Light Abatement Act, which prohibited occupants from using the premises for prostitution, while the latter fell under the vagrancy statute, an umbrella term that was often used to detain disreputable women.[3]

Soon after arriving at the local police station, Shepard was taken to the Mission Valley Isolation Hospital—a local military-funded detention facility for women suspected of carrying venereal diseases.[4] During Shepard's California appellate hearing on habeas corpus, the county health inspector, Dr. Alex M. Lesem, testified that she was "suspected of being infected with a contagious, infectious and communicable disease, namely, syphilis and gonococcus infection."[5] According to Dr. Lesem, two days before her arrest a vice detective went to Shepard's house and asked if she "would indulge in sexual intercourse with him for a consideration." Shepard allegedly agreed to the arrangement and was told by a vice officer that he would come later "to commit the act." Although Dr. Lesem claimed that "negro sailors" informed police that "there were some girls to be found at the residence of Mrs. Shepherd," neither the black sailors, the police, nor military authorities corroborated his testimony, implying that this story might have been fabricated. Although the judges concluded that there was insufficient evidence to continue holding Shepard, she was held for forty days following her arrest for "quarantine" due to the unproven suspicion of disease.

I start with this particular moment, which is representative of black women's mass incarceration and quarantine in post–World War I California, to illustrate how hygienists, the military, and municipal police disproportionately surveilled, arrested, and detained black women for disobeying racial, sexual, and gender norms. Shepard's arrest had an important spatial component—she was charged not only with vagrancy (for prostitution) but also with disobeying California's Red Light Abatement law, a 1914 state law that threatened property owners with forfeiture of their property for renting to prostitutes. Although Shepard claimed in her subsequent civil suit "having committed no crime or [misdemeanor]," she had broken a social taboo in the developing military town by being a black woman accused of prostitution. Regardless of whether she was a sex worker, a housewife, or a victim of sexual coercion and blackmail, Shepard could face serious consequences for disobeying local, state, and federal antimiscegenation and vagrancy laws, including sexual and physical assault, forced sterilization, loss of custody of her daughter, risking her husband's continued employment in the US Navy, and ultimately deprivation of her housing. Census records reveal that the Shepards moved numerous times after the incident and finally settled in southeast San Diego, the black-Mexican ghetto. Furthermore, it seems that Asa Shepard also lost his employment in the military, as a city directory listed him as working in the restaurant industry in 1935.[6]

The history and laws that created the conditions for Irene Shepard's incarceration and de-housing in San Diego began in 1909 when the city embarked on its first major military endeavor, the Panama-California Exposition. That year was a pivotal turning point for the city and county of San Diego, as it officially started to transform their reputation in the state of California from a "sleepy Navy town" to a military powerhouse.[7] While more modest than the official and heavily funded World's Fair in San Francisco, which opened the same year, San Diego's exposition shored up support for installing temporary and permanent military bases in the city. City boosters argued how San Diego would be an important national security location because of the construction of the Panama Canal.[8]

Leading up to the exposition, health officer Dr. Francis H. Mead instructed the plumbing inspector and self-declared social hygienist Walter Bellon to condemn downtown buildings and flag them for removal: "Walter, the town folks are talking about a World's Fair to be held here, and want to make the town attractive for the tourists who will come. The Board of Health wants the Stingaree district cleaned up, and also the waterfront."[9] During Bellon's tenure as plumbing inspector, he boasted about demolishing over 120 buildings and 500 rooms in downtown.[10] Prior to the state's housing abatement law, San Diego's Health Department and municipal police began to de-house people living in parts of downtown under the guise of public health and safety concerns. Yet the city attorney realized that his department lacked the power to implement "slum eradication" unless the health department could "present proof" that health was the factor, rather than mere social immorality.[11] As Bellon explained in his memoir: "Court action at times could drag on for years, perhaps very little accomplished, except the cost. But when health is the factor to be considered, the course is sure and effective, if properly handled, and executed, and if political pressure is held in check."[12]

Though Bellon seemed particularly fixated on Stingaree—the blocks bounded by First and Fifth, Market and K—and especially the neighborhood's Chinese community (see figure 1), the Health Department considered the red-light district to cover a 100-city-block area bounded by the waterfront, F Street on the north, and Sixteenth Street on the east. According to Bellon's memoir, many of the landholders of downtown institutions were prominent men, including a board member for the upcoming Panama-California Exposition.[13] However, Bellon and police chief Keno Wilson were at odds about the red-light district.[14] Since San Diego police created the police-protected vice district of Stingaree and profited from its vice networks, they had little incentive to obliterate prostitution. Bribery among the San Diego police had been reported since the late nineteenth century. For example, in an 1888 *Union* newspaper article, a beat reporter claimed that a "system of extortion . . . among prostitutes . . . [was] reported in Chinatown."[15]

FIGURE 1. Third and Island—Chinese District (circa 1912). Source: San Diego History Center.

Chief Wilson was also at odds with local reformers, many of whom were prominent white women of organizations like the Purity League, a wing of the Women's Christian Temperance Union (WCTU), an international but US-based feminist organization. In 1912, the *Union* reported on the efforts of the Vice Suppression Committee. Prominent leaders in this organization included Dr. Charlotte Baker, president of the Equal Suffrage Association, and Mrs. R.C. Allen, leader of San Diego's White Civic League, secretary of the Equal Suffrage Association, and the revered wife of the director for the city's upcoming world's fair.[16] The committee also included the Reverend Harbert, minister of the city's first black church—who opposed any "licensing [of] the social evil." He was quoted as saying, "The social evil will not be uprooted or killed by the closing of the Stingaree. Some of the women, those who [are] not too hardened, may be reclaimed, and those who are past reform can be driven out, and the place cleaned up."[17] Yet it was reported how the black minister was liked by San Diego police: "Rev. R. H. Harbert, who is regarded by the heads of the police department as one of the most practical and broad minded of the reformers." This ideological battle was capitalized on by the *Union*, which on October 13, 1913, reprinted letters from readers largely arguing for either a segregated district to house "the necessary evil" or a complete obliteration of prostitution.[18]

To quell reformers, generate some positive coverage about police in local papers, and divert attention away from corruption within the San Diego police department, Chief Wilson and the city council began their own campaign to selectively police sex resorts outside Stingaree, primarily targeting low-capital black women and white women who crossed racial lines. This predatory policing also affected non-sex-working black women who lived in the interzone of downtown where the police-protected red-light district overlapped into the Chinese neighborhood. This interzone was one of the few places where transient black women, many unmarried, could rent rooms.

In the eyes of local authorities, black women had no place in San Diego. The exhaustive work of historian Clare V. McKanna Jr. has found that although black women represented only 1.3 percent of the San Diego population between 1910 and 1930, they accounted for over 17 percent of the total arrests for prostitution and 24.8 percent of arrests for vagrancy; black women also paid more in fines per arrest compared with white women.[19] Print media from this period provide a mapping of San Diego's deeply racialized downtown interzones. These carceral geographies are accompanied by unsavory terms like "disreputable negro women," "strapping negresses," and "floaters," among many deplorable others that circulated with frequency during the white-slavery media frenzy of the late nineteenth and early twentieth century.[20] *She* was a trope that police, the local Purity League of the WCTU, black ministers and clubwomen, and other city boosters weaponized for their own political agendas.

"Do Not Molest the White Dives"

On February 10, 1910, the city council passed local Ordinance 3985 outlawing dance halls, also known as temperance saloons, where working-class people of all racial backgrounds gathered to partake in the local sex tourism industry. The new ordinance declared it unlawful to have a "house, hall room, or other place where drinks of any kind are sold . . . which is resorted by prostitutes . . . or by lewd and dissolute persons."[21] Those who violated the ordinance would be cited every day until they complied; individuals in violation would be guilty of a misdemeanor, punishable by a fine of up to $300 and/or imprisonment for 150 days.[22] Authorities claimed that prostitutes would meet customers at these institutions and then take part in transactional sex in nearby rooming houses.

Since the late nineteenth century, dance halls in San Diego had been long known as places of disrepute. Historical newspaper articles from this period explicitly illustrate how black, Chinese, and women sex workers and working men—and possibly queer men—crossed the color line. On Valentine's Day, 1895, the *San Diego Weekly Union* reported on a raid on dance halls that led to the closing of "two hell holes"—the Casino Theatre and Weeping Willow.[23] The article also included a published letter written about the institutions by J. W. Brenning, Esq., addressed to the chief of police of

San Diego. In it, he said that the places are "disreputable, disorganized and a disgrace to our city, and should not be allowed to keep open." In the same article, it was reported that Mayor William Carlson was witness to the subsequent raid. He described the scene:

> Both places were crowded with whites, blacks, women, and Chinamen. At the Weeping Willow on a rude stage were a couple of Mexicans with flour and red paint smeared on their faces, executing a war dance to the shriek of a violin and the groan of a place, while half-undressed and blowzy women, with faces that vied with those of the war-dancers, passed through the crowd and asked Tom, Dick, and Harry to set up the drinks. The air was redolent of Chinamen and other exotics. Fully 100 humans were packed into a room ten feet wide and thirty feet long. About 100 men were on the ground floor, and a number were in the upper boxes with the women, drinking and carousing.

Several years later, more parlors, rooming houses, and saloons with adjoining cribs newly opened. The red-light district area expanded with more sex resorts and stables on H Street. On February 18, 1888, a reporter for the *Union* described the following:

> On 3rd Street in a distance of two blocks, between H and J, there are 30 of these vile dens of vice. Around the corners on I and nearly 20 on 4th street and nearly a dozen on 2nd street. In this limited territory there are nearly 100 houses of prostitution each containing from 1 to 13 inmates. They are mostly of the lowest classes and of various races, at least a dozen negro and 30 Chinese women competing with their depraved white sisters on the nefarious

traffic. The houses which they occupy are for the most part cheap shanties but they are attractively furnished and glitter with tinsel and bright colors. In the midst of these low hovels on the corner of Third and I looms up the notorious Sherman House which assumes proprietors and pretensions of a maison de joie. Here are 13 girls presided over by Ida Bailey or "Red Headed Ida" who is always such a conspicuous figure in the front boxes of the Opera House. These are low down dives, but it must not be supposed that the terrible evil is confined within the narrow limits of the slums.[24]

These more public "low dives . . . of the slums" were depicted as the most atrocious, whereas exclusive (private) sex resorts and institutions, many of them patronized by affluent men, were rarely sensationalized in the media prior to 1909.

In fact, the emergence of dance saloons was the result of racial hierarchies within the local sex tourism industry. Upscale and racially segregated parlor houses catered exclusively to prominent white men who favored discreetness, while working-class white women and women of color rented rooms at cribs and stables to partake in transactional sex.[25] The parlors offered privacy to men who could afford it, while the stables were for lower-paying customers, for working-class men. Walter Bellon, the city's plumbing inspector, described the stables in his notes: "The Stables . . . resembled stalls. Built in a long row facing a compound, one opening leading to each a room from the outside and a door that gave seclusion. A wash bowl and pitcher served as plumbing, a bed, and a chair or two. Water was carried from a lone faucet that stood outside."[26] Daisy Jackson, a seventeen-year-old black female who lived in San Diego's Ninth Ward with her family, rented a stable in Stingaree. The *Union* reported how Jackson, described as "one of

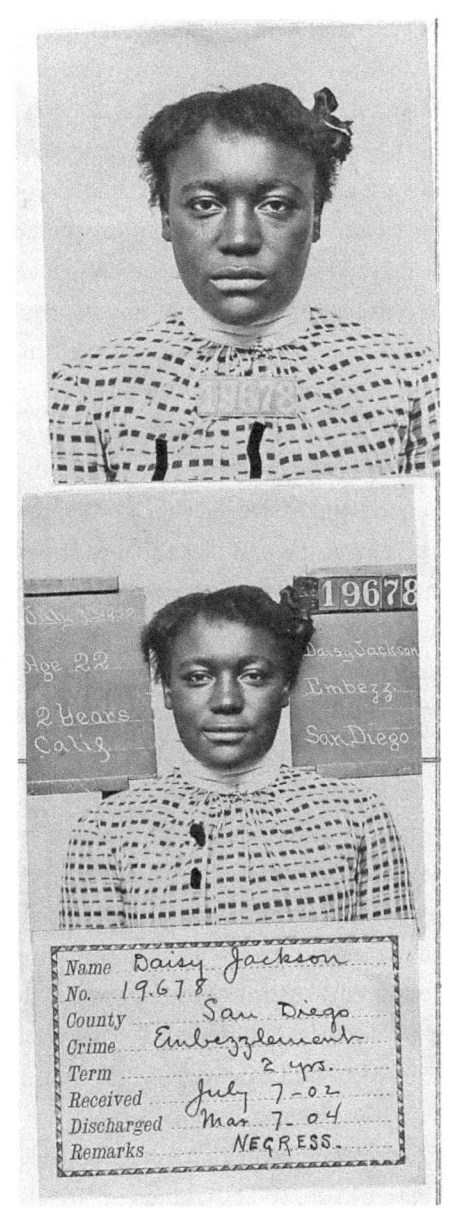

FIGURE 2. Mugshot of Daisy Jackson. Source: San Quentin Prison.

the colored lights of the local half-world," was "known at the stables."[27] In 1885 she pretended to hire a horse and carriage for local use, but instead drove to Los Angeles with her boyfriend. She was sentenced to two years at San Quentin prison for embezzlement (see figure 2).[28] Men who could not afford upscale parlor houses, or who were not white, met women and arranged sex in more public spaces (like the dance halls) and then relied on the women to take them to private spaces, like the stables or nearby rooming houses.

However, the ordinance was not trying to eliminate all prostitution, since police and politicians profited from prostitution—rather, only the interracial prostitution and sex work that the temperance saloons permitted. On March 5, 1910, the *Union* reported how "the notorious Parker House on Second and H streets, which is favored by negro women of low character was the *first* place that received a visit from the chief and the inmates warned to keep *inside* the lines of the redlight section as outlined by the police, or to leave the city."[29] Chief Wilson reportedly told reporters that "women living in up-town rooming houses must either seek a legitimate vocation in life, leave the city, or make the restricted district their home."[30] In other words, sex-working black women had to restrict their practices to the quasi-legal police-protected district—which meant they had to pay police and/or other intermediaries to continue to work there—or leave town. "If they persist in disobeying orders we will take measures to rid the town of them." Chief Wilson also prohibited men from "liv[ing] in or within the section of the city bounded on the east by Fifth street, on the north by H street, and by the west and south by the waters of the bay," and threatened proprietors with prosecution if they rented to known prostitutes.[31]

Looking at these mappings provided by print media alongside census data gives further insight into how black women creatively made place in a city intent on de-housing them. They provided each other with housing inside already-overcrowded apartments along H Street. The *Union*'s citation of black women as proprietors indicates that black women began to either buy, rent, or manage these properties to provide fellow black women with housing accommodations. While palace-like hotels catered to wealthy white businessmen and their families, rooming and lodging houses often housed transient unskilled and lower-paid workers.[32] The city's Young Women's Christian Association (YWCA) and other institutional residential hotels prohibited black women and other women of color, and dilapidated rooming houses built and operated by Chinese immigrants provided the only affordable living options.[33] Black migrants from the US South who did not live in the same quarters as their employers took up residence in racially segregated rooming houses, many of which were mixed gender. Rooming houses were usually built with up to eighteen rooms, including bath and laundry and other bedrooms created by dividing larger bedrooms and parlors.[34] Sometimes owners combined several houses together as a single rooming structure and rented to up to seventy tenants.[35] Many women lived with other women to share rent and for other communal support, since their salaries were too low for them to live independently in rooming houses like men.[36]

As the exposition neared and the city was motivated to expel black women from downtown, there was an explosion of articles about disreputable black women, particularly in the Fifth Ward, starting in 1910. Most of the articles represented black women as raucous outsiders by profiling arrests that involved disputes among tenants. In "Women Fight with Stones on Street," in the *Union* in 1910, it was reported that Leola Butler, Kate Jackson, and Clara White, "three buxom women of Ethiopia parentage," were fighting and "using language of a kind not countenanced by the best society" in front of the Parker Hotel.[37] Described as a "cheap lodging house," the Parker House sat at the corner of Second and H Streets.[38] The *Evening Tribune* also reported on the incident with the subheading "Leola Butler Talked Too Much" and explained the "disturbance" in more detail.[39] Butler, a "strapping negress," was fined ten dollars for "disorderly conduct" for "being too free in expressing her opinion of Mrs. Lulu Harper, another negress." According to the US Census, Leola Butler was actually *Leona* Butler, a twenty-three-year-old woman born in South Carolina, whose father was from Jamaica. Butler was a roomer at 12b H Street, presumably the "notorious Parker House."[40] Despite Chief Wilson's claim that the Parker House was a haven for disreputable women, only three roomers were reported as tenants in 1910. Besides Butler, the other two roomers were men—Louis Blanchesi and William Lubura. Anna Blanchesi, a sixty-one-year-old white woman from France, was listed as head of household.[41] The articles reveal how H Street, located in the Fifth Ward, was a place known for disreputable women—even though only eighteen black women were reported to have lived in the Fifth Ward in 1910, with only ten on C Street.[42]

The *Union* also sensationalized another area in the Fifth Ward, dubbed the "colored negro colony," comprising three places managed by Emma Samuel, Lucy Gibson, and Emma Henderson—all black women.[43] "Negro Women Have Trouble on H Street" reported on an alleged quarrel between a proprietor, Emma Samuel, "a negress," and her roomer Sally Jones, "a muscular woman of color."[44] The 1910 San Diego city directory listed Samuel as the proprietor of the Yokum, a room housing located at 1131 H Street.[45] The beat reporter for the *Union* described how Samuel had "the reputation of being inclined to resort to physical force when she fe[lt] it necessary to maintain her rights."[46] The two other black woman proprietors in the area were Lucy Gibson (1132 H Street) and Emma Henderson (350 1/2 Third Street). Fifty-two-year-old Gibson, whose occupation was listed as "boarding house," lived with her husband William H. Gibson, a longshoreman, along with three daughters, a son, and a granddaughter.[47] Her boarders were two black men, thirty-six-year-old Edward Jones and sixty-five-year-old Abner Hamilton. Henderson was a single thirty-year-old black woman whose occupation was listed as "proprietor" and her industry as "rooming house."[48] Her boarders were all unmarried black women (including an Afro-Mexican woman)—Verna McNeal, a twenty-nine-year-old housemaid from Tennessee; Adele Vaughn, a black seamstress whose parents' birthplace was listed as Mexico; and Fannie B. Hines, a twenty-nine-year-old divorcée and hairdresser born in Texas.[49]

Although Chief Wilson declared that "white prostitutes will be similarly dealt with," the *Union* reported how some white sex workers welcomed the selective policing. White madams and prostitutes believed that the interracial sex trade was bad for their businesses, since this economy was criminalized more harshly than white-only brothels and parlors.[50] A beat reporter wrote on how white prostitutes did not denounce the closing of temperance joints and the displacement of nonwhite sex workers, but instead stated how they were now "protected from the rougher foreign element, which has always been a menace to the peace and quiet of the district, and which was expected to make trouble when the men were compelled to leave the temperance joints."[51]

Horace B. Day, a candidate vying for a city council seat, took out an ad in the *Union* on March 14, 1909, titled "Horace B. Day's

Attitude on the Stingaree District," bellowing out how police "do not molest the white dives" and alluding to police corruption: "It is a matter of common knowledge that there are about 15 so-called 'temperance joints,' but in reality 'blind pigs,' and dives of the lowest kind, now operating openly in that district. The police are constantly on duty in that district but do practically nothing toward compelling these joints to obey the law. They make a show by raiding a poor old Chinese lottery joint, or a fan-tan game now and then, but do not molest the white dives."[52] Nevertheless, Chief Wilson continued to deploy similar tactics after the passing of the 1910 ordinance.

The interraciality of California's Chinatowns, where white, black, and Asian men sought out Chinese women for sex labor, alarmed antivice reformers and spurred calls to rescue immigrant Chinese women from "yellow slavery."[53] While this might seemingly allude to the protection of Asian women from sexual exploitation, these laws were actually anti-immigration laws which led to women's proximity to state violence. Chinese women migrated to San Diego beginning in the 1870s during the height of Chinese fisheries in the city, but their migration was curtailed five years later.[54] An 1873 law prevented "lewd or debauched" women from entering California; this was followed by the Chinese Exclusion Act (1882), a federal act which limited the annual admittance of Asian migrants in the United States.[55] Due to this curtailing of Asian migration, the number of Chinese people living in the United States plunged from approximately 107,000 in 1890 to 71,000 in 1910, alongside a further widening of the sex imbalance within Chinese American communities.[56] Anti-Chinese sentiment across the nation ultimately led to the migration of black women (and men) to the West. White employers in California put out ads in black newspapers, such as the *Chicago Defender*, advertising domestic work opportunities for black women.[57] While some black women had prearranged contracts before their departures, many traveled to California with merely a hope that they would find employment, and many opted to participate in sex work instead of being domestics in white households.

Anna Barnett, a twenty-three-year-old black woman from Texas, worked at an all-white male boarding house in the Third Ward and then moonlighted in downtown.[58] On Saturday March 26, 1910, the *Union* reported how Barnett, described as "a 200-pound negress," was arrested for allegedly assaulting and robbing Jack Osborne.[59] Osborne had met Barnett and an unidentified black woman at a saloon at Fourteenth and K Streets, and later invited them to his rooming hotel. While in his room, an argument arose. Osborne alleged that Barnett held him up and went through his pockets, stealing $10 from his wallet. When he tried to stop her, he alleged that Barnett stabbed him and another roomer, O. E. Storrs, who tried to aid him. While the other woman who accompanied Barnett escaped, Barnett was later discovered at a "shack on M street, near the Cuayamaca railroad station" and charged with assault with a deadly weapon. The *Union* reported that "little sympathy was shown to Osborne in the court proceeding, in view of his having frequented the society of negresses, and the admission he made that he had invited the women to his room." Osborne did not "endeavor to explain the presence of the two negro women in his room," which ultimately resulted in the postponement of the trial.[60] Instead of accepting a plea deal, like most women charged with vagrancy and prostitution-related offenses during this time, Barnett decided to go to trial. She was represented by attorney David R. Taylor, "who succeeded

FIGURE 3. Mugshot of Anna Barnett. Source: San Quentin Prison.

in having the charge reduced to assault."[61] A San Diego judge sentenced her to ninety days in the county jail.

Though authorities claimed that sex workers endangered the safety of men, often accusing them of robbing unsuspecting men, scholars and activists have pointed to the fact that street-involved prostitutes are the ones most likely to be victims of robbery and assault, usually at the hands of johns, pimps, and police.[62] People like Barnett doing sex work outside of the brothel system were easy targets because they were known to possess cash on them but were not protected by state or private intermediaries. Another way of reading Barnett is to imagine how she was forced to resort to violence to protect herself from being victimized by her clients. Her decision to fight back, especially as a black woman, was the act that most likely offended authorities. Prior to her stint in San Diego, Barnett was incarcerated in San Quentin Prison for assault with a deadly weapon (see figure 3).

Barnett's audaciousness did not end in San Diego. In 1933, she was charged a third time for assault—this time of her white employer Allan Crawford in Savannah, Georgia.[63] Although Barnett probably understood that she likely would be convicted by an all-male white jury or judge, she still exercised her right to due process by pleading not guilty during the arraignments and taking her chances at trial. Crawford was reluctant to face her in a Savannah courtroom and instead pleaded in a letter for the court to release the "honest and industrious" Barnett, who "had been in his emoly [family] for a great many years." He had no interest in disclosing the personal matter, and although Barnett made a statement on her own behalf, the cause of the conflict is unclear, since no transcript exists of her statement.

Barnett's San Diego court proceedings do reveal an interconnected system of entrepreneurial black women who created a system of kinship allowing them to profit from the city's illicit economies. The relatively small community of black informal laborers meant that the women had to pool together their resources to counter state violence. Both Ella Gates, a twenty-one-year-old married woman originally from Los Angeles, and Abbie Ramsey, age unknown, served as character witnesses for Barnett during her trial for the assault of Storrs in 1910.[64] Archives indicate that they were also informal laborers. Gates, a domestic abuse survivor and divorcée, was accused by police of being a vagrant and disobeying miscegenation laws.[65] In 1907, then eighteen years old, she was arrested for vagrancy on two occasions in January and then June.[66] Though I was unable to find concrete census data on Ramsey, San Diego newspapers, court transcripts, and city directories have her living in San Diego between the years 1910 and 1919.[67] Along with serving as a character witness for Barnett in 1910, she and her husband Alfred "Sunny" Ramsey were arrested in 1916 for "conducting a resort where opium and cocaine [were] sold" at 227 Twelfth Street.[68] The creation of these networks was a direct challenge to municipal police, who were the arbiters and creators of Stingaree.

To remove Barnett and Gates from the city, local authorities targeted them through eviction, arrests, and incarceration for nonviolent offenses. However, historical archives reveal that the women actively challenged these intrusions into their privacy. Though Barnett was routinely arrested and detained at the San Diego County jail, she continued to return to San Diego after her confinement. On November 8, 1910, authorities arrested her for "lewd" conduct, and she was released on $50 cash bail.[69] Two days later, on the tenth, she was arrested again after police discovered her in the room of George Russell, a black man. While Russell "escaped with a fine of $10," Barnett was sentenced to thirty days in the county jail. A year later, on April 2, 1911, Barnett again was sentenced to jail, this time for ninety days for "disturbing the peace."[70] Authorities claimed that she had assaulted Maggie Dangerfield, another black woman. Interestingly, Dangerfield had been arrested at least five times within a two-year time span, including twice for assaulting multiple police officers and smuggling opium from Mexico, but she never served more than sixty days in the county jail for her offenses combined.[71] Barnett's last arrest in San Diego was July 5, 1911.[72] She was arrested for vagrancy along with other black men and women. Barnett was fined $10, which she was unable to pay, and "was given the privilege of leaving the city instead."

Gates went through a similar process of de-housing. In 1908, the city council evicted her, along with her mother Sara Langley, from 12a Motor Avenue (Newton Avenue and Twenty-First Street); Willis Rice was listed as "head of household," but his relationship with the women is unknown. Their neighbors had written the city council that Gates and Langley were "keeping a house that [was] a shame and a disgrace to a respectable neighborhood."[73] The petition was very explicit about the interracial nature of their visitors: "they always have a congregation there of the very lowest class of people, and are the means of this low class coming into the neighborhood, consisting of white, colored and Chinamen." Gates reemerged in San Diego around 1910 after the owner of a property, B. L. A. Munroe, a "colored man," died and left her as executor of his estate.[74] According to his will, he left two lots and two houses to Gates. Munroe also named her as the executor of his will. He left the remaining property, two lots and three houses, to a daughter who lived "in the east." In all, the properties were reported to be worth around $4,000—which would be $132,866.32 in 2024. However, the San Diego Superior Court refused to allow Gates to serve as executor of the estate, citing the complaint from neighbors. P. J. Layne, representing the San Diego Public Administrator, claimed that Gates was "of immoral character and not a fit person to assume control of all the property." Gates challenged the decision, which went all the way up to the California Supreme Court. On September 26, 1911, the California Supreme Court affirmed the San Diego Superior Court's decision to disinherit her.

A deeper examination of the Supreme Court brief reveals how Gates's case overrode precedents set by the *Estate of Newman* (1904), *Estate of Gordon* (1904), and *In re Bauquier* (1906) court cases, all involving white women.[75] Citing the aforementioned cases, attorney Patterson Sprigg, who represented Gates, argued that there was no provision of law by which an executor could be removed except for "some mental deficiency or by proof dishonesty of purpose," and that "mere immorality is not sufficient to justify a court's refusal to appoint as administrator or administratrix one who is duly nominated for such appointment by will."[76] In 1904, the Superior Court of the City and County of San Francisco rejected arguments that a seventy-four-year-old was not competent enough to be executor of his sister's estate, despite objections from other family members.[77] In that same year, in the *Estate of Newman* case, judges sided with a widow who was initially disinherited because she "contracted a bigamous marriage."[78] In 1906, the California Supreme Court dismissed claims by Frank Bauquier, who refused to allow "Mrs. Rodes," his sister, to be executor because he was "prejudice[d] against" her.[79] These three legal precedents upheld laws that protected the rights of executors.

However, the California Supreme Court explained that the evidence provided against Gates was "much stronger" than in those cases.

The justices' claim that Gates was "not only immoral but *promiscuous*" pointed to a certain *type* of sexual non-normativity—nonmarital and interracial sex.[80]

> Here, according to the testimony, the woman was not only immoral but promiscuous; prone to disorderly conduct; once the consort of a man who in spite of difference in race lived with her at a saloon "in the lower part" of the city; had been arrested several times for vagrancy; and was living at the time of the trial in meretricious relations with one Ramsey. Sometimes such a woman may be one of "integrity" in the usual affairs of business, and if the court had granted her petition perhaps the finding in her favor would not be disturbed. But when the court had her before it, the judge having listened to the testimony and having observed her demeanor, found from the evidence upon which to based such a finding.[81]

George Pringle, a veteran of San Diego's police force, claimed to have known Gates for fifteen years, and within those years frequently saw her drinking in saloons. According to Pringle, "every time she got drunk she would hire a horse and buggy and would drive furiously through the streets."[82] An unnamed police officer stated that Gates lived with different black men and corroborated Pringle's claim that she lived "in a saloon with a white man in the lower part of the city of San Diego." Finally, William H. Wetherbee, another police officer, testified to the fact that Gates had been arrested three times for vagrancy. According to Judges J. Henshaw,

J. Lorigan, and T. L. Lewis, the overwhelming "disqualifying facts" presented by law enforcement officers proved Gates "to be incompetent." The scientific knowledge (eugenics) of the time concluded that most prostitutes were "feebleminded" and therefore not capable of making decisions.[83] They "placed the matter in exactly the same position as if it were one of intestacy," meaning the will was forfeited.[84]

As the exposition approached, local authorities continued in their attempt to thwart rumored black syndicates—as well as violate black people's rights to privacy. In 1912, authorities arrested two "negresses" and "a mulatto" as suspects of a "colored gang . . . selling cocaine and other drugs" at "an abode on lower Second street."[85] Although no illegal drugs were found on Tommy, Johnny, or Felix, they were still detained "pending an investigation" and likely faced vagrancy charges stemming from the gender (and racial) transgressions of the group. Although the authorities marked two of the suspects as "negresses," two of them identified themselves as "Tommy Johnson" and "Johnny Gordon." Johnson and Gordon evidently refused to give police their names assigned at birth, which prevented authorities from creating a gender-normative record in accordance with the Bertillon System of Criminal Identification—a criminal coding system based on race, sex/gender, height, and other physical descriptors.[86] The inability to accurately identify the "negresses" probably frustrated authorities, who were adamant about identifying disreputable women as a way of removing them from the cityscape altogether. The third suspect, Felix McCrome, who self-identified as a person of "Spanish descent," also proved difficult to identity. I could find no census records of anyone with that name residing in San Diego at that time. Authorities questioned his proximity to whiteness by describing him as "mulatto," thereby disputing Felix's claims of "Spanish" ancestry. Historically, people racialized as "colored" and "negro" routinely challenged essentialist notions of race, biological racism, and eugenics discourse by claiming to be "Spanish," "colored," "Indian," "mulatto," and other hybrid forms of racial identification in order to claim space and varying forms of autonomy.[87]

While one might interpret the data from the *Union* about Johnson and Gordon as an example of early twentieth-century transgender identity or subjectivity, I want to resist this urge. As both Sara Haley and Riley Snorton argue, black people have transgressed legal and medical understandings of gender of their time to suit a variety of material needs and desires, including as a way to protect themselves from sexual assault in all-men's institutions or to pass as white and male in order to escape to freedom in the North during antebellum slavery.[88] While Gordon and Johnson might have engaged in cross-dressing as a way of publicly claiming a gender that did not correspond to the gender given to them at birth, there might have been more immediate and material needs that cross-dressing afforded them. As LaShawn Harris points out in her examination of black women informal laborers in early twentieth-century New York City, it was very rare for black businesswomen to work alongside black men. Men simply refused to do business with black women, because they did not see them "as individuals capable of leading successful business enterprises or delegating responsibilities to men."[89] In this group, the "negresses" outnumbered the lone male group member, which suggests that Johnson and Gordon might have held leadership positions. In other words, by cross-dressing as men, Johnson and Gordon were able to perform different jobs within informal economies besides sex work but might have been able to hold leadership positions foreclosed to them if they presented as women/feminine. Yet "the negresses" were still subject to surveillance because of their gender and racial transgression.

As the two fairs approached, the official one in San Francisco and the smaller one in San Diego, state legislators enacted two important laws in 1913 which were influenced by local campaigns in California, including San Diego. The first one was the Red Light Abatement law passed in April 1913, which took effect the following year in 1914. The Women's Christian Temperance Union and other women's organizations were the first to introduce the bill in California.[90] The first law of this kind had been passed in Iowa in 1909; it enabled the state to regulate the use of private property and made it possible for any citizen to file a complaint. If the courts could provide sufficient evidence that a person was running a "disorderly house," the premises could be forcefully vacated.[91] If police concluded that building owners were renting to women of "ill repute," or who were even suspected of engaging in prostitution, they could be fined and in jeopardy of losing their property.[92] Antivice authorities would raid homes without notice to investigate the complaint. At other times, authorities sent an informal notice to the owner indicating that their property was being cited for prostitution. As Peter C. Hennigan argues in his work on California's Red Light Abatement Act and its impact on private property, "progressive reformers would seize upon [the] erosion of common law principles to transform public nuisance law into a powerful legal weapon for controlling public and private property."[93] The American Social Hygiene Association (ASHA), founded in 1913, served as a "legal clearing house" for challenges to California's Red Light Abatement law.[94] The ASHA recognized early on that adherence to a model law could insulate the law from constitutional challenges.[95] Bellon, charged with condemning buildings for zoning violations, welcomed state support: "the Redlight Abatement Act came directly on the heels of the Health Department's sanitary crusade in the Stingaree [red-light district]."[96]

Later the next year, in October 1914, California lawmakers passed a law requiring hotel proprietors to be licensed, which again was already being implemented in San Diego. Black women's entrepreneurial and structural ingenuities were thwarted by a 1913 ordinance that required rooming house owners to obtain licenses, thereby limiting how housing was created and managed in the city. These licenses were hard to obtain, since the city required owners to equip the structures with modern plumbing, which most structures lacked. In his scrapbook, Bellon pasted an editorial from the *Tribune*, which explained how the measure affected San Diego. The 1913 article explained that Bellon had estimated that "at least 15,000 persons . . . inhabit hotels, lodging houses, and tenements." At the time of the article's publication, proprietors had a month to obtain licenses.[97] Out of the seventy buildings, 1,892 rooms, six hotels, forty-six lodging houses, eight tenements, and eight "combinations [of] lodging and tenements," Bellon reported issuing only thirteen licenses within the first month of enforcement, indicating how most housing structures in downtown were unable to immediately conform to the new regulations. Black women also lived in shacks near the harbor—which provided the last remaining housing for low-capital folks before Bellon set them on fire in 1915 (see figure 4).

By 1915, the year the exposition opened, some of the last remaining structures for demolition using the Red Light Abatement Act were near the waterfront. In "Police Enforce Abatement Law," authorities are said to have "rounded up thirteen negresses, three

FIGURE 4. View of squatter shacks at the waterfront at the foot of Broadway in about 1900. Source: San Diego History Center.

white women, an Indian woman, a negro and a white man in a raid on waterfront shacks" near Market Street in June 1915.[98] Rev. Robert C. Barton, "agent of the morals efficiency committee for Southern California," stated, "this is not a spasmodic attempt at enforcement of the law . . . but a systemic campaign and it is to be thorough." A local reformist was quoted as saying, "The aim is to get rid of the prostitutes by closing all the places to them. That is the reason for the direction of the campaign against the owners of the house. This will be a complete clean-up."[99] A month later, in July 1915, the health department burned down most of the structures along the waterfront.[100] In December 1915, police claimed that twenty-two black women, who lived in "cheap rooming houses and shacks on lower Market Street, were driven out of the city."[101]

As historian Catherine Christensen contends, many prostitutes in the West relocated to the Baja California region to escape new forms of anti-prostitution laws and spatial segregation, since prostitution was legal in Mexico.[102] However, most of the women who migrated and profited most from these Mexican economies were white women. Black and white women who were unable to travel across the border, either because they were discriminated against at the border or because they could not secure work in Baja, were forced to continue working in an increasingly hostile geography within the borders of the United States. Soon after implementing de-housing policies, local and state officials were now creating legislation that led to the *mass* incarceration of women for prostitution-related offenses. And again, officials in San Diego led the charge.

Quarantine

In 1917, Dr. A. E. Banks, health officer and superintendent of public health in San Diego, wrote a letter to Dr. W. A. Sawyer, the secretary to the California State Board of Health, outlining seven steps cities ought to take to eliminate vice: (1) reporting all cases of venereal disease among servicemen and military personnel to the city's public health department; (2) eliminating the "worse element" of prostitutes through the use of "prompt arrest under vagrancy charges" and being "anything but lenient" in prosecutions; (3) regulating the placement of bars; (4) prohibiting prostitutes from bars and restaurants; (5) specially training municipal police officers on how to successfully obtain evidence for prosecution; (6) developing guidelines for the "detection of diseased women"; and (7) cooperating with civilian doctors on reporting private patient information to the city health board.[103] At the end of the 1917 letter, Banks made an appeal to the state board to go so far as to approve the forcible quarantine of women as a tactic to ensure the health of US servicemen. Bascom Johnson backed up this call, speaking from his role as director of the Army Sanitary Corps and member of the Social Hygiene Association, declaring that given the threat of venereal diseases to military functioning, "treatment and quarantine of those infected [would] produce very remarkable results."[104]

In that same year, in May 1917, immediately after the declaration of war against Germany, Congress passed Section 13 of the Selective Service law, known as the Chamberlain-Kahn Act, directing the secretary of war "to do everything by him deemed necessary to suppress and prevent the keeping or setting up of houses of ill fame . . . within such distance as he may deem needful, of any military camp, station, . . . or mobilization place."[105] In a letter published in the *Journal of Social Hygiene*, it was noted how "Mr. Kahn was well informed regarding the pioneer work of the California State Board of Health in combating venereal diseases. He knew that the methods tried in his state could be applied effectively throughout the nation."[106] The bill was supported by the Commission on Training Camp Activities of the War Department, the Medical Department of the Army, the State Health Officers' Association of the United States, the United States Public Health Service, and the American Social Hygiene Association.[107] As Kristin Luker notes on the "double-edged sword of social reform": "New developments in penology meant that those convicted of this newly redefined crime of prostitution faced a very different institutional structure than had existed only a few years before. The first two decades of the twentieth century saw an expanded set of institutions, which, when combined with new ideologies about crime and criminals, meant that women guilty of the new crime of prostitution were likely to face both more differentiated treatment among themselves and more extended incarceration."[108] As Scott Stern acknowledges in his study of the US government's century-long project of detaining women on moral charges, "It was California's plan, after all, that first ordered the examination of 'persons reasonably suspected' and the incarceration of those found infected."[109]

This attack on black women in San Diego was also being implemented simultaneously on the global level in Panama. Toward the end of World War I, the US military began to systematically quarantine black Caribbean women in Panama. As Joan Flores-Villalobos examines in her book on black women's reproductive labor during the construction of the Panama Canal, the presence of seemingly unattached black women in the region troubled military officials, who insisted that black women should have "natural protectors" if they worked in Panama.[110] Black women who did not have male proxies were automatically assumed to be prostitutes. The Health Department of the Panama Canal, composed of both Panamanian and American hygienists, stated that "ninety per cent of the patrons of the prostitutes of Panama and Colon have been American soldiers, sailors, and civilians."[111] With the implementation of General Order No. 20 in 1918, landlords who rented to prostitutes were fined; only physicians were allowed to dispense drugs to treat venereal disease; officials made "all vice illegal"; and the governments increased funding for "medical officers" and "personnel of the health department."[112]

Many of these army and navy medical officials in Panama would later join the American Social Hygiene Association as health professionals, and then the Commission on Training Camp Activities (CTCA), the military's police force charged with protecting soldiers from venereal disease.[113] In 1916, Charles Eliot, president of Harvard University and honorary president of the American Social Hygiene Association, declared, "If the civilization of the white race is to survive, it must be saved through the diffusion and adoption of sound policies in regard to social hygiene, carried enthusiastically and persistently into action."[114] The scientific discourse about disease and gender posited black women as particularly sexually perverse, evidenced by their higher rates of venereal disease.[115] Lloyd Thompson and Lyle B. Kingery, both doctors of the United States Army Medical Corps, argued that in 1619 enslaved Africans had "spread this plague [of syphilis] in the New World."[116] Their study cited a French scientific journal in which a doctor claimed to have "never examined a negress over fourteen years of age who was a virgin." These medical researchers concluded that "women of the race indulge in sexual intercourse as much as the men, and it would naturally follow that they contract syphilis as frequently," and that "negro women are more often infected than [black] men."[117]

Black men were also targeted by the rhetoric of social hygiene. The CTCA viewed African American troops as incapable of conforming to the organization's "white, urban, middle-class image."[118] As Nancy K. Bristow explains, MPs in the Commission for Training Camp Activities surveilled the sexual behavior of servicemen in public and private spheres, and "members of the CTCA maintained that the constructive programs of supervised recreation and social hygiene education for soldiers and civilians were the heart and soul of CTCA design." Unlike white men, black soldiers were compulsorily quarantined and received prophylactic treatments when coming back from tour.[119] However, women overwhelmingly represented the majority of those detained and quarantined. While MPs would internally discipline troops, women were turned over to municipal police. Bristow notes, however, that "Black women were twice condemned as criminals by the CTCA."[120]

By 1918, reports of vagrancy in printed news media included commentary on the antivice unit of the military, the CTCA, and the new Mission Valley isolation hospital, which opened in 1917. In that same year, the *Union* reported that military and civilian police were called to a brothel at 1746 N Street, where federal and municipal authorities found soldiers in the house and "turned over" the servicemen to military officials. Ella Hubert was charged with "running a disorderly house," while Inez and Hora Grayson, "both negresses," were held on vagrancy charges and then taken to Mission Valley for examination.[121] That December, Gertrude Salisbury, a "negress," was held for examination after a raid on a rooming house in "lower Sixth street."[122]

The military also helped finance this special hospital to hold women suspected of having a venereal disease. A *Journal of Social Hygiene* publication explained how San Diego County appropriated $10,000 from the federal government toward the Mission Valley venereal disease isolation hospital, which admitted both "Mexican and negro women."[123] It is unclear if white women were also housed here. Historians have noted how white women were usually sent to privately run reformatories, considered more "enlightened alternatives to jails," while nonwhite women were sent to some of the most deplorable detention centers—often lacking basic sanitation.[124] As historian Irma Victoria Montelongo notes, Mexican women were also disproportionately arrested and detained—with those with darker skin being held the longest.[125] A female inspector reported that the Mission Valley institution treated on average twenty-two patients daily, with a maximum of forty-eight. By January 1, 1921, three years after the hospital first opened, it had admitted a total of 810 patients. Under quarantine regulations, women were committed for the period of infectivity: "6 weeks for syphilitica, 12 for gonorrhea cases."[126] No men were admitted, and the institution did not provide statistics as to the number of patients admitted for having had "sexual relations with soldiers and sailors." By 1920, social hygienists spent over $1.5 million on forty-three detention homes nationwide, with as many as 30,000 women detained during World War I.[127]

As Bascom Johnson saw it, prosecuting prostitution was something San Diego had to do "to fulfill its obligations to the boys in khaki," particularly in exchange for federal funding.[128] In a 1917 report in the *Journal of Social Hygiene*, his description of San Diego as the "Mexican town of Tia Juana . . . a gathering place for gamblers, prostitutes, crooks, and every species of underworld character" points to sexual and racial diversity engendered by the US-Mexico border.[129] He continued, "These gentry pass through San Diego on their trips to and from; some of them try to make San Diego their headquarters from which to operate. They are often free spenders and, while they probably take out of San Diego as much money as they bring in, they give that city the appearance of a festive and hectic kind of prosperity during the racing season."

Johnson was particularly focused on maintaining the color line, especially between whites and blacks.[130] He forced the closure of the Creole Palace Café, a cabaret operated by George Ramsey, a black man. Ramsey was twenty-four years old when he arrived in the city as a valet for Herbert Snow, a wealthy amusement park owner.[131] In 1917, Johnson accused Ramsey's Creole Café of having "scantily clad" women dancing with both white and black customers.[132] Johnson petitioned to have the entire cabaret shut down on moral charges. Ramsey denied the allegations. Interestingly, a beat reporter was empathetic to the singling out of the Creole Palace despite the fact that the U.S. Grant, a white-serving establishment, held similar performances: "The colored café seemed to bear the brunt. . . . Creole Palace is not any worse than at the 'higher-toned' places like the U.S. Grant Grill."[133] In the end, the military designated the Creole Palace Café off-limits for servicemen, which ultimately led to its eventual closure.

The quarantining of "promiscuous" *women* on morality charges, officially called the American Plan, created a new gendered class of criminals—the prostitute. This engendered not only new criminal codes, misdemeanors, and felonies, but the creation of sex-segregated penal facilities. More importantly, it was wartime (military) policies that made prostitution a felony offense. Black women were disproportionately targeted, surveilled, and detained by local, state, and federal authorities. This criminalization was place specific in San Diego, with black-women-operated rooming houses and clubs operated by black men targeted by municipal and military officials. Interracial contact, not prostitution per se, was the most targeted. Black women were considered the worse element, with authorities representing them as inherently diseased and promiscuous. Their detentions were considered the most urgent. It is important to note that these geographies of incarceration were not only limited to the United States but also occurred in places like Panama—with US military authorities de-housing black women and subjecting them to quarantine. By

World War II, the de-housing and detention of women suspected of venereal disease was implemented nationwide, not just in specific municipalities as before—with authorities continuing to disproportionately target black women.[134] Though abatement laws and detention became more institutionalized, and bolstered by scientific and sociological knowledge, black women continued to resist by using clever and strategic ways to invest and control disreputable spaces and economies.

Trickster

While George Ramsey and, to a lesser extent, Robert Rowe have been heralded by historians as the financiers and creators of the historic Douglas Hotel and Creole Palace in downtown San Diego, based on census data and city directories it seems as though Mabel Ramsey (also known as Mabel Tyler and Mabel Rowe) held a more prominent role than acknowledged.[135] Her marriages to both George Ramsey and Robert Rowe were not about romance, but necessarily about business. Put differently, due to laws that restricted women's access to property ownership she used marriage (to men) to protect and control her financial assets. Although the Married Women's Property Act of 1839 granted women the right to be sole owners of property and conduct business, they still had to have their husbands' input, and single women were omitted from the act altogether.[136] While much is known about the male investors, little is known about Mabel Tyler/Rowe/Ramsey—and it seems that that was the way she wanted it to be. She played trickster when it came to her racial identity and romantic entanglements. A closer look at the archive reveals how Mabel Tyler/Rowe/Ramsey, a racially ambiguous woman from Indiana, used racial passing and informal/formal marriage to become the wealthiest and most powerful black businesswoman in San Diego during the early twentieth century.

With an expenditure of $100,000, the Douglas Hotel and Creole Palace was considered the largest investment for any business owner during the early twentieth century.[137] The building, which was completed in 1924, stood at the downtown corner of Second Avenue and Market Street, in very close proximity to Horton Plaza (see figure 5). It was the only major downtown hotel to provide accommodations to black visitors to the city. The Creole Palace nightclub was located inside the hotel and booked black stage and screen acts during the 1930s and 1940s, including Billie Holiday and Duke Ellington. The hotel also had a controversial history. Jaspar Davis, the second black officer on the San Diego police force, cited the institution as fostering illegal and illicit behavior, such as prostitution and gambling.[138] According to musician Jelly Roll Morton, Robert Rowe was one of the "sports" of Storyville and was a "kingpin of the [New Orleans] district" before migrating to California.[139] Shortly after arriving to San Diego, George Ramsey started owning and managing lodging houses, bars, and cafés. In 1917, Ramsey went into business with Anna B. Brown, a black madam who managed Yesmar Hotel (Ramsey spelled backward) and then later the Anita Hotel, both brothels in downtown San Diego.

According to city directories and census data, Mabel Tyler was unofficially married to Robert Rowe and then legally married George Ramsey after the death of Rowe, who died shortly before the hotel's grand opening. Mabel deployed technologies of race, by identifying as either white or black, for very strategic reasons. Her marriage to Rowe enabled her to retain some control of the Douglas Hotel after his passing. While census records listed her as white

FIGURE 5. View of the exterior of the Creole Palace, located at 204 Market Street. Hotel Douglas, an African American–owned hotel, was located next door at 206 Market Street in about 1932. Notable African American entertainers and musicians performed at the Creole Palace in the 1930s and '40s. Source: San Diego History Center.

during her cohabitation with Rowe, she was later identified as "negro" when she subsequently married Ramsey. Both Mabel Tyler (later Rowe and then Ramsey) and Robert Rowe passed as white, which according to historian Allyson Hobbs put them in a better position to obtain loans and social mobility in Jim Crow San Diego.[140] In the 1920 census, Mabel Tyler was listed as a forty-two-year-old unmarried white woman from Indiana who operated a "lodging house" at 405 Fourth Street.[141] The lodgers at the residence included Joseph Meyers, Charles Davis, Dennis Thompson, and Robert Rowe—all listed as white male laborers. Robert Rowe was listed as a forty-one-year-old white male "lodger" from Mississippi who was a waiter in the restaurant industry. While

FIGURE 6. Hotel Douglas Nite Club, with Al Ramsey, Mabel Rowe, and George Ramsey (circa 1930). Source: San Diego History Center.

Rowe was rumored to be involved in informal economies in Louisiana, Tyler was also a well-known madam of brothels in San Diego.[142] Four years later, in 1924, Tyler and Rowe made it publicly known that they were also a married couple, with the city business directory listing Robert Rowe as the "spouse" of Mabel *Rowe* in 1924—which presumably indicated that they obtained a municipal marriage license.[143] Her marriage to Rowe (whether official or unofficial) was beneficial since she, Mabel Rowe, was cited in the 1926 (revised) San Diego black business directory as part owner of the Douglas Hotel.

Yet her marriage to Ramsey in 1927, a year after the opening of the Douglas-Creole, might have been a way to further cement power over the operations of the hotel and club. Newspaper archives detail their turbulent personal and business partnership, up until their divorce. The 1926 (revised) San Diego Negro Directory, which was financed by the Rowes, characterized Mabel Rowe as a passive proprietor whose key role in the hotel was interior design.

> We at once engaged an architect to draft plans; after they were completed we turned them over to Mrs. Mabel Rowe, wife of Mr. Rowe, for her approval, and right here I want to say that she deserves as much credit as Mr. Rowe and myself. When things looked a little dark it was her kind words of encouragement that kept us in the go-gettem spirit. Her work in selecting and arranging the furniture, etc., and constantly on the job doing all that was in her power to make our dream come true.
>
> It was then that we summoned the contractor and offered him a bonus if he would rush things by putting on a double crew, which he did, and here is where Mrs. Rowe again played a very prominent part, by furnishing coffee and lunch to the men and keeping them all in good humor.[144]

Yet it seems that Mabel Tyler/Rowe/Ramsey was anything but passive. In 1929, Mabel appeared in the city directory as the wife of George Ramsey, and a year later the US Census listed Mabel Ramsey as the "negro" spouse of George Ramsey.[145] George Ramsey's divorce from Rena Saunders might have been caused by his business relationship with, and subsequent marriage to, Mabel Rowe. On January 14, 1926, the *Union* reported how Saunders was booked at the city jail on a charge of assault with a deadly weapon.[146] She accused the newly married Mabel Ramsey of "insulting remarks" and fired two shots at her. In response, Mabel returned with three shots. Neither Saunders nor Ramsey was hit, but Saunders was later picked up and released on $1,500 bond. Yet the couple, who married in 1927, separated several years later in 1931. A *Tribune-Sun* newspaper article on January 11, 1940, detailed some aspects of their divorce suits. Mabel Ramsey was awarded an "interlocutory decree of divorce" based on her cross-complaint of George Ramsey's infidelity.[147] In her suit, she claimed that George tried to "kill her by striking her," while George's suit claimed that she "nagged him, struck him and 'raged' at him." Apparently their "joint interests in the hotel and nightclub" were settled out of court—with George agreeing that his wife could obtain a divorce. According to oral histories and newspaper accounts, Mabel Ramsey ran several of the properties as brothels, which at times were subject to "staged" police raids.[148] Though her two marriages ended in tragedy and divorce, marriage enabled Mabel to become a powerful player in San Diego's downtown economies. George Ramsey died in San Diego in 1963 at the age of seventy-five; however, the whereabouts of Mabel Ramsey remain unknown. Her last known residence was in San Diego in 1944, but she continued to own properties in the downtown area well into the 1950s.[149]

The Douglas Hotel was eventually demolished during mid-twentieth-century urban renewal processes, yet a few black-operated rooming houses still stand and operate as low-cost single-room occupancies (SROs)—most under different names, including Mountain View Estates (formerly Anita Hotel, Yesmar Hotel, and Rolland Hotel), Bottom Line (formerly Pacific Hotel), Modern Hotel (formerly Western Hotel), and the Clermont Hotel (see map 1).[150] The Clermont was the only hotel designated for historical preservation (see figure 7).[151] The remaining three structures were operated by black women (and men).[152] The

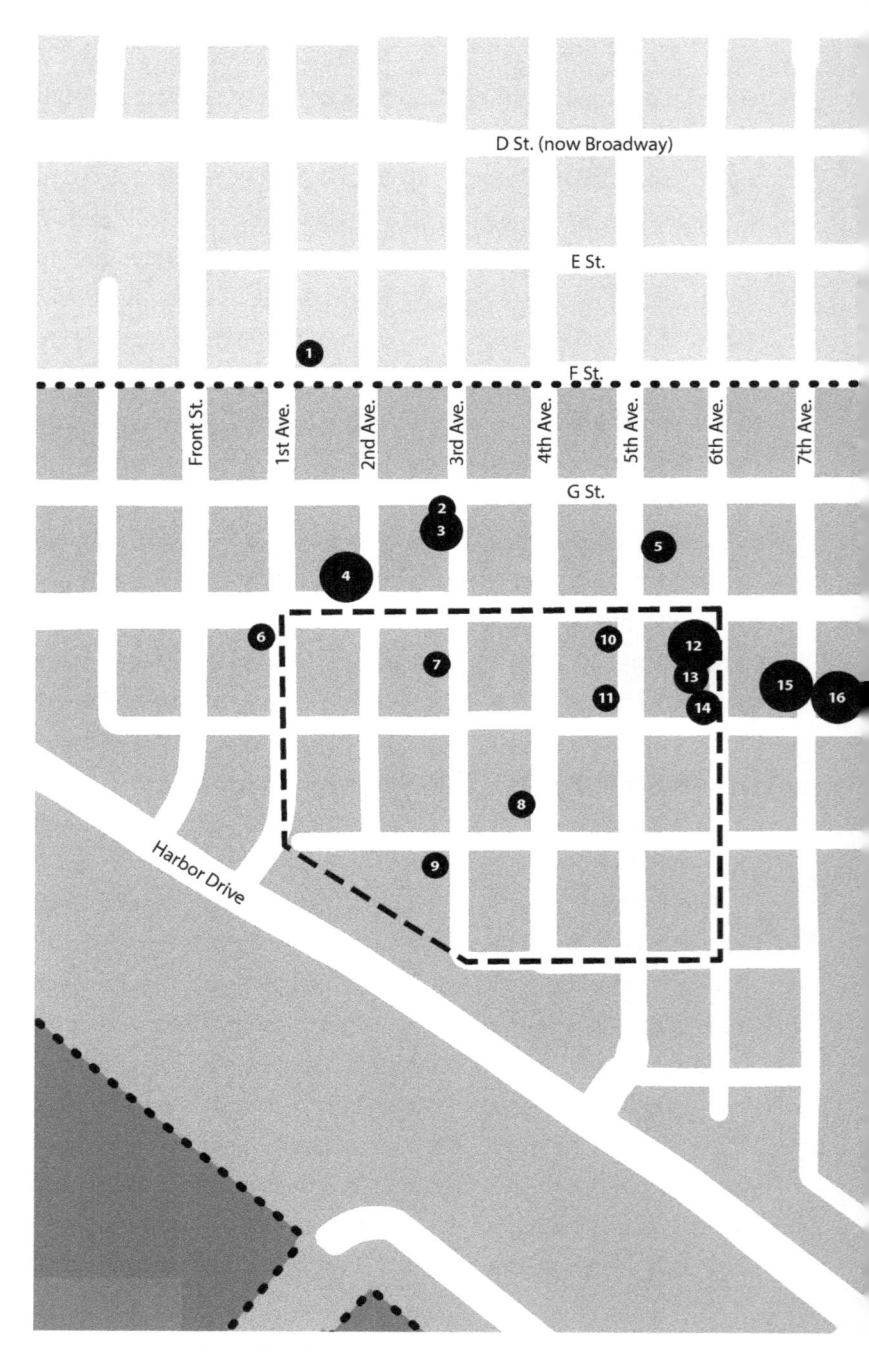

MAP 1. A mapping of black residential hotels in downtown San Diego (Kumeyaay Nation) during the twentieth century, along with two vice districts as defined by the police

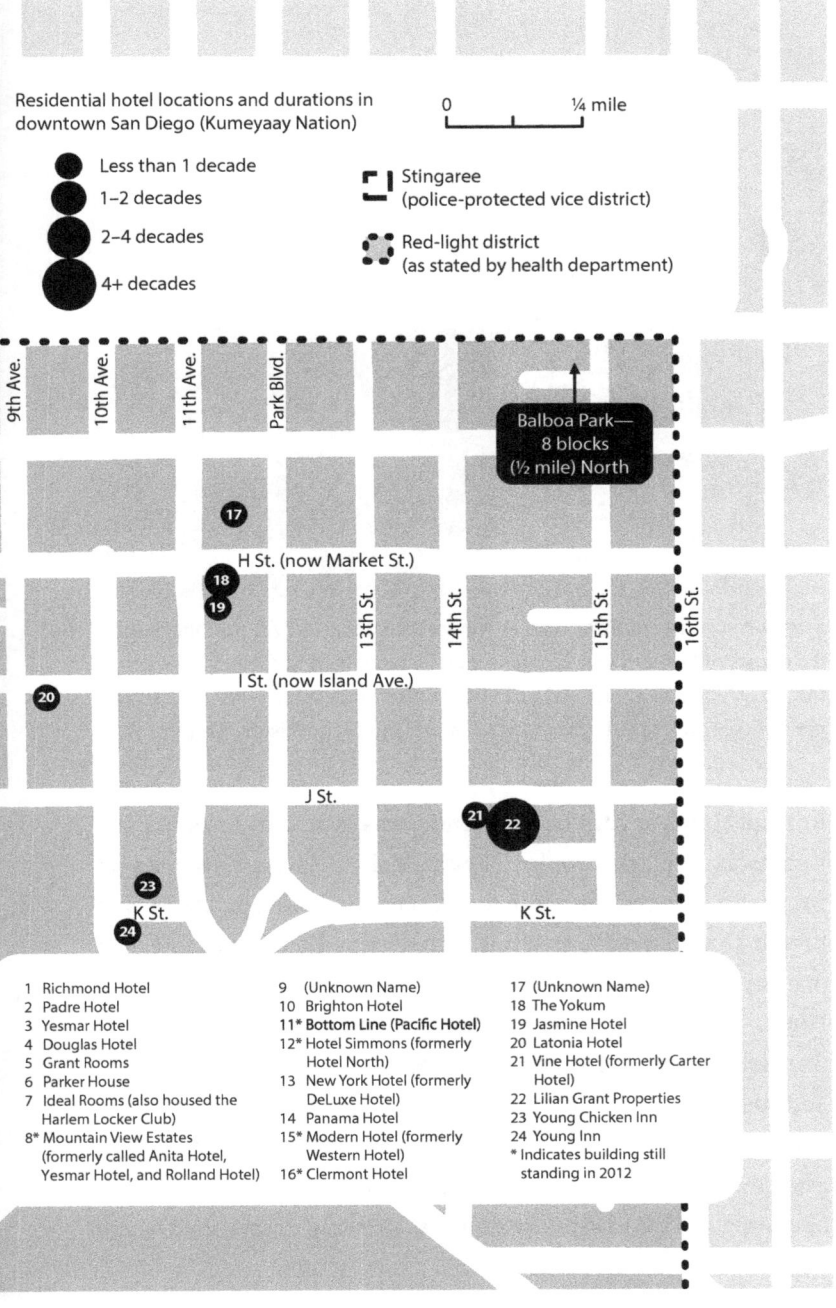

Residential hotel locations and durations in downtown San Diego (Kumeyaay Nation)

0 — ¼ mile

- Less than 1 decade
- 1–2 decades
- 2–4 decades
- 4+ decades

Stingaree (police-protected vice district)

Red-light district (as stated by health department)

9th Ave. · 10th Ave. · 11th Ave. · Park Blvd. · 13th St. · 14th St. · 15th St. · 16th St.

Balboa Park— 8 blocks (½ mile) North

H St. (now Market St.)

I St. (now Island Ave.)

J St.

K St.

1. Richmond Hotel
2. Padre Hotel
3. Yesmar Hotel
4. Douglas Hotel
5. Grant Rooms
6. Parker House
7. Ideal Rooms (also housed the Harlem Locker Club)
8* Mountain View Estates (formerly called Anita Hotel, Yesmar Hotel, and Rolland Hotel)
9. (Unknown Name)
10. Brighton Hotel
11* **Bottom Line (Pacific Hotel)**
12* Hotel Simmons (formerly Hotel North)
13. New York Hotel (formerly DeLuxe Hotel)
14. Panama Hotel
15* Modern Hotel (formerly Western Hotel)
16* Clermont Hotel
17. (Unknown Name)
18. The Yokum
19. Jasmine Hotel
20. Latonia Hotel
21. Vine Hotel (formerly Carter Hotel)
22. Lilian Grant Properties
23. Young Chicken Inn
24. Young Inn
* Indicates building still standing in 2012

and health departments. Five structures out of the twenty-four are listed as still standing as of 2012. Balboa Park is located eight blocks (½ mile) north.

FIGURE 7. Exterior three-quarter view of the three-story Clermont Hotel at the corner of Seventh and Island (originally I Street). The view is from across the street, and a bicycle is parked in front of the hotel. A hay-and-grain store is partially seen at the left (circa 1905). Source: San Diego History Center.

Rolland Hotel, at 422 Fourth Avenue, was owned by Joe and Belle Robinson, a black couple. They sold it to George Ramsey in 1915, who changed the name to Yesmar Hotel and operated it as a brothel from 1915 to 1921. It was then renamed the Anita Hotel and operated as a brothel by Anita B. Brown up until 1924. The Pacific Hotel, 506 Fifth Avenue, operated between 1926 and 1941 and was listed in the 1936 colored directory, and then was bought and operated by Asian proprietors. In the 1920s, the Western Hotel had many black occupants, but it ceased renting to black people after the 1930s. Excluding the Clermont Hotel, most buildings operating as SROs are in constant risk of being demolished as the city develops new ways to bring more capital investment to the downtown center.

Conclusion

As this chapter demonstrates, black women's bodies became battlegrounds for maintaining the "color line" in San Diego during the early twentieth century. Black clergy and first-wave feminists targeted "cheap amusements" for working-class black laborers in the city, such as saloons and dance halls.[153] Nevertheless, black women not only made space in the city for work and pleasure, they also challenged Jim Crow laws through formal and informal ways—including demanding rights to privacy in municipal and state courts, establishing black-owned businesses, and creatively deploying technologies of race and gender. Some of these same structures still serve as low-cost residential units. As I will demonstrate in chapter 3, these same SROs became occupied by low-capital queer and gender-nonconforming sex-working people, including black queens, well into the 1990s. Starting in the 1940s, downtown San Diego became known as the gay Tenderloin, which depended on the disposable income of transient servicemen.

Yet the 1940s were also a turbulent time for black people and communities in downtown San Diego, because the city was in what was the initial stages of its second major redevelopment campaign, which systematically began pushing black people out of downtown to the more isolated Imperial Avenue region.

The Zoot-Suit Riots of 1943 might have been the last straw for many remaining black residents in downtown. In June 1943, white servicemen attacked black residents and businesses in downtown as well as Logan Heights along Imperial Avenue. The Douglas

Hotel and Creole Place were especially targeted by the white mob. The *Chicago Defender* reported:

> Conversations with colored sailors revealed that for some time trouble has been brewing, but that white Navy men expect Negro Navy men to stick with them regardless of whether they are right or wrong, but in this situation the Negro soldiers and sailors are behind the Spanish element and the Negroes 100 per cent, because the trouble has been aggravated by the whites.
>
> Civilians help to agitate the movement, white women deriding, from passing cars, Negroes dressed in modern style and accusing them in overtones of being "zoot-suiters." The Chinese Village, 632 Third Avenue, which has a habit of refusing service to Negroes, at times, was placed out-of-bounds by military authorities early Thursday morning following many violent scenes occurring in front of the establishment, in the heart of the Negro neighborhood but largely patronized by white sailors and marines.
>
> The Creole Palace and the Douglas club, corner Second and Market streets, were literally besieged with a combination of white sailors who were only dispersed when jeeps loaded with marine police, shore patrolmen and military police surrounded the four blocks leading to the Negro business place and finally barricading it from all outside trade.[154]

The military later placed the Douglas Hotel/Creole Palace off-limits for military personnel.

These Zoot-Suit Riots were not restricted to San Diego but were a national phenomenon. As Luis Alvarez discusses in *The Power of the Zoot: Youth Culture and Resistance During World War II*, Mexican Americans, African Americans, and other minoritized others used zoot suits as a form of resistance against white supremacy.[155] The San Diego riot happened the same year as the zoot suit riot in Los Angeles, which is well documented. In both cases, Mexican and black servicemen created solidarity as they faced off against white mobs. San Diego's leadership turned a blind eye. San Diego Race Relations, founded in 1924, whose members included Walter Bellon, met with the then mayor, Harley E. Knox. Knox, however, blamed black parents for "juvenile delinquency" and "bad press"; he claimed they were "frequently responsible for racial friction."[156] Obviously, the mayor had no interest in appealing to black residents.

The ghettoization of black people toward areas closer to the southern US-Mexico border region, and farther from the city center, engendered new black formal and informal economies. By the 1940s, Logan Heights emerged as the hub of African American life in the city.[157] Black-owned businesses lined Imperial Avenue, the primary business corridor, along with National Avenue, Logan Avenue, and Ocean View Boulevard. In the following chapter, I use Maya Angelou's literary and sex archive to get a more intimate glimpse into the lives of sexual economies in the post–World War II San Diego black ghetto. As a pimp and sex worker, Angelou not only participated in disreputable economies as a means of survival but then used this sexual knowledge to become one of the most recognizable figures in US history.

2 "Are You in the Life?"

Maya Angelou's Sex Archive and the Role of Black Intermediaries

I had not finished recovering their chits and was about to turn to the cabdriver when a drunk, half-dressed white sailor stumbled through the bedroom door. He had nothing on below the blue middy. There was a moment's hush when the women and Hank looked at me. I was hypnotized at the man's nudity and couldn't take my eyes from his white, soft, dangling penis. In those seconds I became a child again. Unreasoning rage consumed me. The low-down sneaky bitches—I had told them to have the place cleared before I got there. They had probably had tricks there every night and I hadn't even questioned them. I could have gone to jail or worse. After all I'd done for them, their whorish hearts were so ungrateful that I had been subjected to looking at the sickening aspect of a white man's penis.

MAYA ANGELOU, *Gather Together in My Name*

This excerpt, taken from Maya Angelou's second autobiographical volume, *Gather Together in My Name* (1974), recounts the moment she discovered that Beatrice and Johnnie Mae, an unhoused sex-working black lesbian couple, had been letting tricks stay past assigned work hours at Angelou's brothel in southeast San Diego. They did this to make more money for *themselves*, since Angelou (their pimp) reaped most of their profits. While Angelou is best known to the public as a celebrated poet, autobiographer, and maternal figure within black/African American communities, it is less publicized that she also documented how she was once a pimp and brothel worker. In fact, her understanding of sexual capitalism took root in San Diego. While some have celebrated Angelou's disclosure of her sex work as an example of female and pro-ho empowerment, I complicate and challenge this framing by showing how Angelou also internalized racial hierarchies and, not unlike the state, exploited sex-working black women.[1] Though she discloses her participation in illicit sexual economies, the Maya Angelou iconography becomes a fortress that extracts ho-ness and mammifies Angelou by way of producing a commercialized and digestible figure for the American public. However, there is a violence in this process of disarticulating and reinventing her past. What happens when we do not pay attention to all the ingredients that have gone into making Angelou the revered black political and cultural figure? Examining dis/reputability in *Gather Together in My Name* means attending to parts of San Diego's history that are overlooked, while also reexamining other creative practices by Angelou herself.

I use Angelou's second autobiographical volume as a case study in disreputability because it tells an intimate story of a migratory black sex worker in post–World War II San Diego. This text is not necessarily about Angelou per se, but about the larger predicament of black women in San Diego and California. Since black San Diegans were relatively left out of the defense industries, and black veterans were systematically denied GI Bill benefits after being discharged, disreputability became some black folks' only option.[2] After finding herself locked out of formal economies, Angelou decides to capitalize on the sexual needs of servicemen at the newly constructed Camp Pendleton in San Diego County. She starts her journey into disreputability in San Diego as a pimp for Beatrice and Johnnie Mae. When servicing the needs of white servicemen becomes too risky, she migrates to the San Joaquin Valley. Here, she is a brothel worker whose patrons are Mexican men in the Bracero program, many of whom are arriving in the United States via the San Diego County international border. Since there is less of a moral crisis regarding black and Mexican interracial sex, the "wild west rhythm" of the San Joaquin Valley becomes a place where black sex workers do not have to worry too much about state surveillance (141). However, this comes at a cost. Angelou must now split her earnings with her pimp/boyfriend along with the madam of the brothel. In an ironic twist, the former pimp is now being exploited in a similar way to how she herself exploited Beatrice and Johnnie Mae.

In this chapter, I argue that Angelou's use of disreputable tools is profoundly profitable and problematic, while also being a precursor to her entrance into the world of more reputable cultural productions. Here, through Angelou's narratives, I explore how women's mobility in public and private space was severely curtailed due to Progressive Era antiprostitution legislation. Sex workers relied on male intermediaries—pimps, taxi drivers, bouncers, and bar owners—to help secure their safety from state authorities. Intermediaries, using their networks and experience, were complex participants in a system of exploitation and racialized hierarchies, for profit. As a pimp, Angelou exploits the housing precarity of Beatrice and Johnnie Mae by creating a system that includes renting the women an apartment, hiring security, and employing a white cab driver to solicit servicemen. The women (combined) retained 35 percent of the profit, while the rest was split between Angelou, Hank the security/doorman, and the taxi driver (unnamed in the book). As a pimp, Angelou is shielded from the risks Beatrice and Johnnie Mae face, since sex-working women were far more likely to be arrested than procurers or madams.[3] More importantly, black sex workers—who because of racial capitalism are not able to charge as much as white women for sexual services—are hit especially hard. Black women, like Angelou, understand this predicament and try to circumvent this uneven playing field by working as intermediaries to access social and economic mobility.[4] Angelou's role as an intermediary needs to be placed within a certain historical and economic context. While her role as pimp was problematic and exploitative of other black women, it was also a means through which she not only survived San Diego but thrived. For Angelou, disreputability was a necessary part of her success, carving a world of profit inside a structural world where "sex worker" was always already a specter and an occupational reality.

While some critics have questioned the validity of Angelou's claims, literary critic Selwyn Cudjoe contends what is most important is her "attitude toward the facts."[5] The individual ethos in *Gather Together* is radically different from the collective ethos in the volumes that preceded it. For example, she writes: "I had managed in a few tense years to become a snob on all levels, racial, cultural, and intellectual. I was a madam and thought myself morally superior to the whores. I was a waitress and believed myself cleverer than the customers I served. I was a lonely unmarried mother and held myself to be freer than the married women I met" (63). Even after Angelou herself becomes a brothel worker in the San Joaquin Valley, she still holds contempt for her fellow comrades, calling them "hardhearted whores" (72). Yet I, like Cudjoe, am reluctant "to accept in an unquestioning manner her interpretation of what these events meant to her life."[6] Instead, I find disreputable ways into her narrative, to uncover her wayward ways and draw connections between the literary persona and her own public preservation of a reputable self.

The second part of my argument for this chapter is that to understand Maya Angelou and her trajectory, she must be understood as a producer of literary and sexual worlds. In my perspective, as black feminist thinkers we cannot afford to single-mindedly perform literary analysis of Angelou's work but must also engage with her lifeworld through ethnography, referring to her memoirs, unpublished writings, and poetry. Unveiling her social world through interviews, personal correspondence, and letters to gain a more complex understanding of how black women cultural figures were under pressure to uplift the race is a necessary endeavor.[7] Black iconography, meaning dominant narratives about her and also her own autobiographies, has not allowed room for both Maya Angelou the sex worker and Maya Angelou the mother, or Maya the pimp and Maya the poet.[8] However, before I enter Angelou's world in *Gather Together*, I must spend some time thinking with literary critics as they assist in illuminating the politics of disreputability as it makes its way into her work, the "literary autobiography"—a genre that carves out a particular lifeworld that would circulate as a kind of *truth* about Maya Angelou. We must reckon with Angelou as a character whom readers fictionalize and one who is also fictionalizing as well. Angelou is a *trickster* who produces a text that is not all about her. As a literary scholar, she masterfully uses trickster devices so that readers think these stories are real; she is producing truth through the trickster figures. Yet what an ethnography of Marguerite Annie Johnson's (Angelou's birth name) life reveals is that she herself is trickster we will never fully know. This, however, is not a shortfall but instead a black feminist practice in disreputable writing and performance—where one writes about the complexity of the black female experience but chooses not to reveal the inner self. This limited interiority access becomes an asset for Angelou as she transitions from disreputable to respectable—becoming a mainstream cultural icon, literally hallmarked on US currency. Angelou knew what to sell—whether that was pussy or Hallmark greeting cards.

"This Will Be Something Else"

In an interview with Sheila Weller in 1973, before *Gather Together* was published, Angelou discussed how she was creating a "fictional" character for her second autobiographical volume.

> SW: Can you tell me something about the book you've been working on?
>
> MA: It's called *Gather Together in My Name*. It's really a continuation of *Caged Bird*. But what I'm really trying to do is something new. *Caged Bird* is autobiography. This will be something else.[9]

Angelou was explicit on how *Gather Together* would diverge from the more traditional autobiography genre. In the interview, she disclosed how she wanted to create a story about "the woman who didn't escape"—a woman who made choices that were apparently different from the choices Angelou herself made.[10] "So the book will deal with my life from the birth of my son—which is where *Caged Bird* leaves off. At that point, I made a choice. And she makes a different choice."[11] When Weller asked Angelou to elaborate on "this fictional character, this alter ego," Angelou described her as "a vicious bitch . . . the worst of all to write"—admitting that this *bitch* emerges in her other writings, including "Getting Up Stayed on My Mind," a story about a black woman junkie.[12] Angelou told Weller that she was unsure if it would work—and if not, she would "try something else." Although the content of the narrative is quite different, the final published version of *Gather Together* is similar to *Caged Bird*—Angelou remains the central protagonist. It is unclear if or how much of this "fictional" character is still (if at all) existent in *Gather Together*. Is the vicious bitch present in the final version? Is Angelou the bitch—the cunning madam of a brothel in San Diego? Did her attempt at creating "something else" engender a hybrid mix of "truth" and "fiction"? Is Vivian Baxter, her mother, the bitch? Is she the one who "didn't escape"? It remains unclear. This uncertainty (or ambiguousness) is not a form of deception; instead, it is a practice characteristic of a particular literary and autobiographical tradition.

Angelou's writing practice is indeed ethnographic, but it follows the typical conventions of African American autobiography and literature, which (1) prioritizes the telling of an African American *collective* struggle over adversity *and* (2) uses literary paradigms to achieve this end.[13] As Selwyn R. Cudjoe contends, "the Afro-American autobiographical statement emerges as a *public* rather than a *private* gesture . . . and superficial concerns about *individual subject* usually give way to the *collective subjection*."[14] The writer of the African American autobiography, whether Linda Brent or Frederick Douglass, is tasked with explaining how black people overcame "pain, humiliation and powerlessness [and] refused to be crushed by the burdens [they] bore."[15] Angelou follows in this trajectory by illustrating the unique violence at the intersection of being black, female, and from the South. Despite the barriers, she, like black people before her, musters up "the strength of her individual will" to persevere. In Angelou's case, disreputability was a way black women were able to survive and thrive in post–World War II California. Françoise Lionnet, in "Con Artist and Storytellers: Maya Angelou's Problematic Sense of Audience," lists the various traditions Angelou draws from—eighteenth- and nineteenth-century English narratives, black vernacular and folk traditions (Br'er Rabbit), along with what he argues is the third element of "strong women," akin to the protagonist in the fictional autobiography of Moll Flanders. Though these literary and autobiographical texts are mostly geared toward a white audience, Lionnet contends that Angelou "succeeds in gesturing toward the black community, which shares a long tradition among oppressed peoples of understanding duplicitous uses of language for survival."[16]

Vivian Baxter, Angelou's mother (and a character in *Gather Together*), is a perfect example of this black vernacular/folklore tradition—Angelou constructs her mother, a disreputable character, by inverting black religious tropes and the fictional autobiography of Flanders. Lionnet explains, "So, on the one hand, we have a religious style that allows us to insert Angelou's work back into the black *religious* context. On the other hand, we have a textual figure, Vivian, who is a model for the narrator and who embodies the free style of improvisation (with variation on and repetition of a single basic pattern) in black *music*: jazz and the blues. The link between these two poles is the literary tradition, which relays Richard Baxter, by means of Defoe's *Moll Flanders*, to the twentieth-century black female writer. The biological mother, Vivian Baxter, has a fictional counterpart in Moll, whose 'autobiography' could be seen as the matrix that allows Angelou to produce and reproduce her own narrative discourse."[17] In an interview with Rosa Guy,[18]

Angelou even admitted that seeing her mother "as a character . . . she would read about" became essential to her success as a writer. Baxter is a sexually liberated woman, even if it comes at the expense of her children. Angelou fails in her attempt to emulate her mother's individualism, instead becoming unpopular as both a pimp and a sex worker. Still, the lives of Baxter and Angelou paralleled.

As intergenerational sex workers, Baxter and Angelou used disreputability to achieve respectability. Angelou does not come right out and say that her mother is a sex worker, but instead she hints at the possibility—allowing the reader to come to their own conclusions. In the first instance in *Gather Together*, she gestures toward Baxter as a sex worker during a contentious moment as a young teenager living in her mother's boarding house in San Francisco: "Maya, you disapprove of me because I am not like your grandmother. That's true. I am not. But I am your mother and I am working some part of my anatomy off to pay for this roof over your head" (16). What exactly is this "anatomy" Baxter is pointing to? And how is this tool different from the one her grandmother uses in Stamps, Arkansas, to sustain their standard of living? We can speculate. Angelou continually makes references and connections to Baxter and sex work/prostitution. Before Angelou leaves San Francisco and ultimately settles in San Diego, her mother gives her her "blessing" and then proceeds to tells her, "Be the best of anything you get into. If you want to be a whore, it's your life. Be a damn good one. Don't be chippy at anything. Anything worth having is worth working for" (31). Baxter again gestures toward sex work in the latter half of the book. This time, it is after Angelou learns that her application for the WACs has been accepted and she has been scheduled for a physical exam—a requirement before enlistment.

"I'd gladly have settled for syphilis and gonorrhea. If the Army could take care of my teeth, a couple of injections would cure the diseases." Before Baxter goes off on a "date," she tells Angelou, "Remember if you decide for the Army, I'll support you. If you decide to be a whore, all I can say is, be the best. Don't be a funky chippie. Go with class" (101). The fact that Baxter repeatedly mentions sex work is indicative of sex work as a realistic, plausible, and perhaps beneficial occupation. We can also think about sex work more capaciously—Baxter is also a sexually disreputable character because she engages in both nonmarital and nonmonogamous sex. Interestingly, Angelou chooses to frame herself as the opposite of her mother—as an unhappily liberated woman who is in so much shame about being a sex worker *and* mother that she quits the disreputable way of life. Yet she is not nonagential.

By positioning *Gather Together* as historical writing, a black/lesbian pulp genre fiction, I am able to understand how Angelou playfully uses *trickster-troping* as a way to make visible queer desire in a way that strategically escapes censorship or surveillance. L. H. Stallings explains trickster-troping: "the intersection of folklore, vernacular, myth and queerness becomes one alternative practice that Black female writers and performers exploit to represent and convey their desires without the damaging repercussions and impediments from the rhetoric of sex or the discourse of race."[19] One of Angelou's "unacknowledged techniques" is her creation of the sex-working "bulldaggers" Johnnie Mae and Beatrice. In *Gather Together*, Angelou becomes titillated by the idea (and assumption) that the women were trying to "seduce" her (60). Instead, Angelou gets tricked. Beatrice and Johnnie fool her into thinking they are playing by their pimp's rules. Angelou becomes the fool, who must then retreat—enabling Beatrice and Johnnie

Mae to take back their economic, bodily, and sexual autonomy. The sex workers, like Br'er Rabbit, "[draw] attention to the king's nakedness and [satirize] the accepted norms of a social order."[20] In *Gather Together* Angelou does this with playfulness and humor, which Lionnet notes is a "sharp contrast to the seriousness of Richard Wright," a black novelist whose prose takes a darker and more pessimistic tone.

Angelou taps into this playfulness by also using the melodramatic and exaggerated prose typically found in black pulp fiction, a popular genre consumed by working-class black people during the 1960 and 1970s—as well as lesbian pulp.[21] As a respite from their realities, "in black pulp fiction readers also found confirmation that their lives as marginalized subjects possessed a value of its own, and that their day-to-day struggles opened up new ways of 'being black' amid the blight of the inner city."[22] Kinohi Nishikawa, author of *Street Players: Black Pulp Fiction and the Making of a Literary Underground*, notes that "while mainstream society seemed to turn a blind eye to how these problems were destroying inner-city communities, readers turned to black pulp fiction for the imaginative resources that would help them reflect on their social reality."[23] Angelou was quite the fan of pulp, often reading the *Street and Smith* pulp magazine as a young adult.[24] *Gather Together* was written and published during a time of political and cultural disillusionment. Dr. Martin Luther King Jr. was assassinated, nonviolent political action grew unpopular, and despite the gains of the civil rights movement, black people found themselves underresourced, living in poverty, and highly surveilled by state actors. Though lesbian pulp was written and consumed by primarily (white) men, some readers see it as affirming, healing, or therapeutic—despite the fact that the genre often characterized lesbians as "often abusive, or alcoholic, or otherwise unable to live happy lives."[25] Yet Beatrice and Johnnie Mae are not easily tricked. Through the use of trickster-troping, Angelou is actually making fun of the pimp, breaking down these dichotomies while also profiting from disreputability.

Literary scholars, even in their close reading, fail to understand how Angelou subversively embeds desire and queerness into her writing. In 2002, the year Angelou's Life Mosaic collection debuted with Hallmark along with the release of her sixth autobiographical volume, literary critics John McWhorter and Hilton Als took aim at her entire literary canon to date. In "Saint Maya," published in the May 2002 edition of the *New Republic* (and then later republished in 2014 following Angelou's death), McWhorter describes Angelou's characters as "chocolate icons gliding through a vaudeville version of black history. . . . The people in these flamboyant tales—the narrator included—have a pulp-novel incoherence." To McWhorter, Angelou becomes "simply a caricaturist." Two months later, in July 2002, Hilton Als wrote an article for the *New Yorker*, rearticulating similar concerns. Angelou included the newspaper clipping of Als's article in her papers that are housed at the Schomburg Center for Research in Black Culture in New York City; the article's title is circled with an unintelligible note that includes the name of a close friend and confidant, Rosa Guy. For Als, Angelou is one of the early "pioneers of self-exposure" whose "questionable exploits . . . have evolved . . . to document the ups and downs of [Angelou's] own life." For Als, Angelou's own desire for a respectable life, that is, motherhood, monogamy, and marriage, prevents her from attaining a certain "level of self-knowledge."[26] While Als's analysis of Angelou's texts—that is, as akin to an incoherent pulp novel—is flippant, the irony is that it actually points to how she uses the genre of pulp fiction to creatively employ a method of trickster-troping in a text quite different from all of her other autobiographical volumes.

In the section that follows, I perform a sort of disreputable reading and writing practice alongside Angelou. I engage her literary world while also narrating other tales of disreputability in San Diego. As an unhoused migratory sex worker, Angelou had to perform both reputability and disreputability in order to get employed in formal labor fields and access child care, for example. This mirrors other black San Diegans' efforts to achieve economic and social mobility as well.

"Are You in the Life?"

Though Angelou does not say exactly why she decides to relocate to San Diego in 1946, she is aware of the city's vibrant transnational sex tourism industries well before her arrival. She details her brief visit to San Diego in her first autobiographical volume, *I Know Why the Caged Bird Sings*. In 1943, she travels to National City, a town located in San Diego County fifteen miles from the border, to visit her father, Daddy Bailey. While there, she becomes her father's wingman during a joy trip to Ensenada, Mexico, a city in Baja California. She drinks alongside her father's friends at a bar while Daddy Bailey speaks fluent Spanish to Mexican prostitutes. There, she observes a well-established local vice economy in which black men play an active role. "In the Mexican bar, Dad had an air of relaxation which I had never seen visit him before. There was no need to pretend in front of those Mexican peasants. As he was, just being himself, he was sufficiently impressive to them. He was Black. He spoke Spanish fluently. He had money and he could drink tequila with the best of them. The women liked him too. He was tall and handsome and generous."[27] For Daddy Bailey and other black men, Mexico was a place where they could wield their newfound social and economic power over Mexican indigenous communities, that is, "Mexican peasants." In "Tijuana and the Borders of Race," Josh Kun explains how Tijuana, and Baja California more generally, starting in the 1920s became "an invaluable South of the Border hub of blacks in the American West."[28] Black musicians from Los Angeles traveled to Tijuana to play for the numerous cantinas and saloons. Because of its proximity to the US-Mexico border, San Diego became a popular layover city for entertainers as they traveled to Baja California. The oral histories of black musicians from San Diego document how black musicians were still traveling to Tijuana well into the mid-twentieth century for "jam sessions."[29]

During Angelou's trip to San Diego to see her father, she becomes unhoused. In her telling of the story in *Caged Bird*, Delores, Daddy Bailey's Mexican girlfriend, violently assaults her out of jealousy and anger stemming from their trip to Baja. After Delores assaults her, Daddy Bailey takes Angelou to a friend's house to get her wounds treated, but then he leaves. She decides to wander the street, where she happens to stumble across a junkyard that is tenanted by a group of black, Mexican, and white unhoused teenagers. Before mustering up the courage to call her mother in San Francisco for help, Angelou lives in the junkyard for a month with her new comrades, learning to dance in contests for money and drive a car. For Angelou, the intimacy she shared with this interracial group was something that profoundly changed her. "The unquestioned acceptance by my peers had dislodged the familiar insecurity. Odd that the homeless children, the silt of war frenzy, could initiate me into the brotherhood of man. After hunting down unbroken bottles and selling them with a white girl from Missouri, a Mexican girl from Los Angeles, and a Black girl from Oklahoma, I was never again to sense myself so solidly outside the pale of the human race. The lack of criticism evidenced by our ad hoc community influenced me, and set a tone of tolerance for my life."[30] As insightful as this statement is, Angelou does not elaborate much on the experience.

A year after visiting her father in San Diego, sixteen-year-old Angelou becomes pregnant, and her life is suddenly thrown into a crisis. Although she graduates from high school, she is unable to access high-paying positions. Black women's marginalization in formal labor fields often forced them into low-paying positions. While white women's representational power made them ideal candidates for higher-paying sales positions and receptionist work, black women were relegated to low-paying work as domestics and cooks, which often reinforced positions historically designated for them. And though her mother and stepfather tell her they will babysit her young son while she attends college, Angelou declines. Hoping to escape the confines of her mother's house and independently sustain herself and her son, she applies to become a telephone-company receptionist. She passes the examination, but the white female interviewer lies and tells her that she failed. Angelou demands to take the test again, but the interviewer refuses, instead informing her of another opening she could apply to: "bus girl in the cafeteria" (10).

As a teenage single mother Angelou knows she has to perform reputability to attain even menial labor opportunities. She learns this firsthand when she applies for a cook position at the Creole Café after being turned down as a telephone operator. To portray a level of respectability, she lies and tells her potential employer, Mrs. Dupree, that she regularly attends church.

> "Can you start on Monday?"
>
> "I'll be glad to."
>
> "You know it's six days a week. We're closed on Sunday."
>
> "That's fine with me. I like to go to church on Sunday."
>
> It's awful to think that the devil gave me that lie, but it came unexpectedly and worked like dollar bills. Suspicion and doubt raced from her face, and she smiled. Her teeth were all the same size, a small white picket fence semicircled in her mouth.
>
> "Well, I know we're going to get along. You a good Christian. I like that. Yes, ma'am, I sure do."
>
> My need for a job caught and held the denial. (11)

After hearing that Angelou regularly attends church, Mrs. Dupree becomes less guarded, "a small white picket fence semicircued in her mouth." Angelou, the "good Christian," establishes a commonality between the two of them—their shared faith—affirming her trustworthiness.

When Angelou asks her mother's friend and tenant Papa Ford to teach her how to cook in preparation for her new position, he insists she not take it: "Colored women been cooking so long, thought you'd be tired of it by now. . . . Got all that education. How come you don't get a goddam job where you can go to work looking like something? Get married, then you don't have to cook for nobody but your own damn family. Sheeit" (14).

However, Angelou feels extreme guilt about living in Baxter's boarding house while unemployed: "Here I was in her house refusing to go back to school. Not giving a thought to marriage (admittedly, no one asked me) and working at nothing. At no time did she advise me to seek work. At least not in words, But the strain of her nights at the pinochle table, the responsibility of the huge sums which were kept in the bedroom closet, wore on her already short temper. She was not annoyed with me; she was playing the hand life dealt her as she had always done. And she played it masterfully." She decides to chart out a new path for herself after her brother encourages her to leave their mother's house. Baxter gives Angelou her blessing: "Be the best of anything you get into. If you want to be whore, it's your life. Be a damn good one. Don't be chippy at anything . . . Anything worth having is worth working for" (31).

Angelou travels to Los Angeles to meet her maternal side of family, hoping they will take in her and Clyde. However, she is disappointed. They quickly usher her from their house on Federal Avenue, which she describes as "a model of middle-class decorum" (33), to the train station so she can continue her journey to San Diego, where her father lives. "I congratulated myself on having absolutely the meanest, coldest, craziest family in the world" (36). She continues her journey to San Diego knowing that she cannot depend on her father.

San Diego had become a different city from the one she visited in 1942. Post–World War II San Diego was experiencing an economic downturn. By 1944, Convair, an aircraft manufacturer based in San Diego, had laid off most of its employees; between 1944 and 1946, its military sales sank from $644 million to $14 million. But despite the outflux of jobs, the city's African American population increased from 4,143 in 1940 to 13,136 in 1946, accounting for 3.6 percent of the population.[31] Angelou was part of the 1946 wave.

In this decade, Logan Heights emerged as the hotbed of black social life and commerce, due in large part to racial covenants (see map 2). Though it was a predominately Mexican/Mexican American neighborhood, black people started to move there in larger numbers during the 1940s.[32] Imperial Avenue, National Avenue, Logan Avenue, and Oceanview Boulevard served as important areas of commerce. The California Negro Directory of 1941 points to black-owned businesses in southeast San Diego, including the Bethel Baptist Church (Twenty-Ninth and Clay Avenue); Drug Store (Thirtieth and Imperial); Harris Mortuary (2601 Imperial); NB Studio (2912 Clay Avenue); Dr. C. L. Surgeon (3110 Imperial Avenue); Tony Smither Real Estate (3056 Imperial Avenue); black fraternal orders such as the Fidelity Lodge (3007 Logan Avenue) and Elks Lodge (6 Hensley Street); the United Service Organization (USO) Club on Imperial Avenue and Evans; and the YWCA (2905 Clay Avenue).[33] Since black servicemen and women were not allowed to stay on base, many lived in rooming houses in Logan Heights. The *San Diego Union* newspaper revealed two rooming houses located in southeast San Diego in 1950, at 2701 Imperial Avenue and 3137 Webster Avenue. Another notable place was the YWCA Clay Avenue Branch, the first community/civic organization to provide housing and employment opportunities for black women in the early to mid-twentieth century. Angelou might have sought their services once she arrived in the military town.

The visual archive also documents how black people ventured out to clubs possibly patronized by their Mexican neighbors. Around 1950, Norman Baynard, a local professional photographer who took nearly 12,000 images of black life in mid- to late twentieth-century Logan Heights, took a picture of a group of black people at the El Morocco Club (Federal Boulevard and Euclid Avenue)

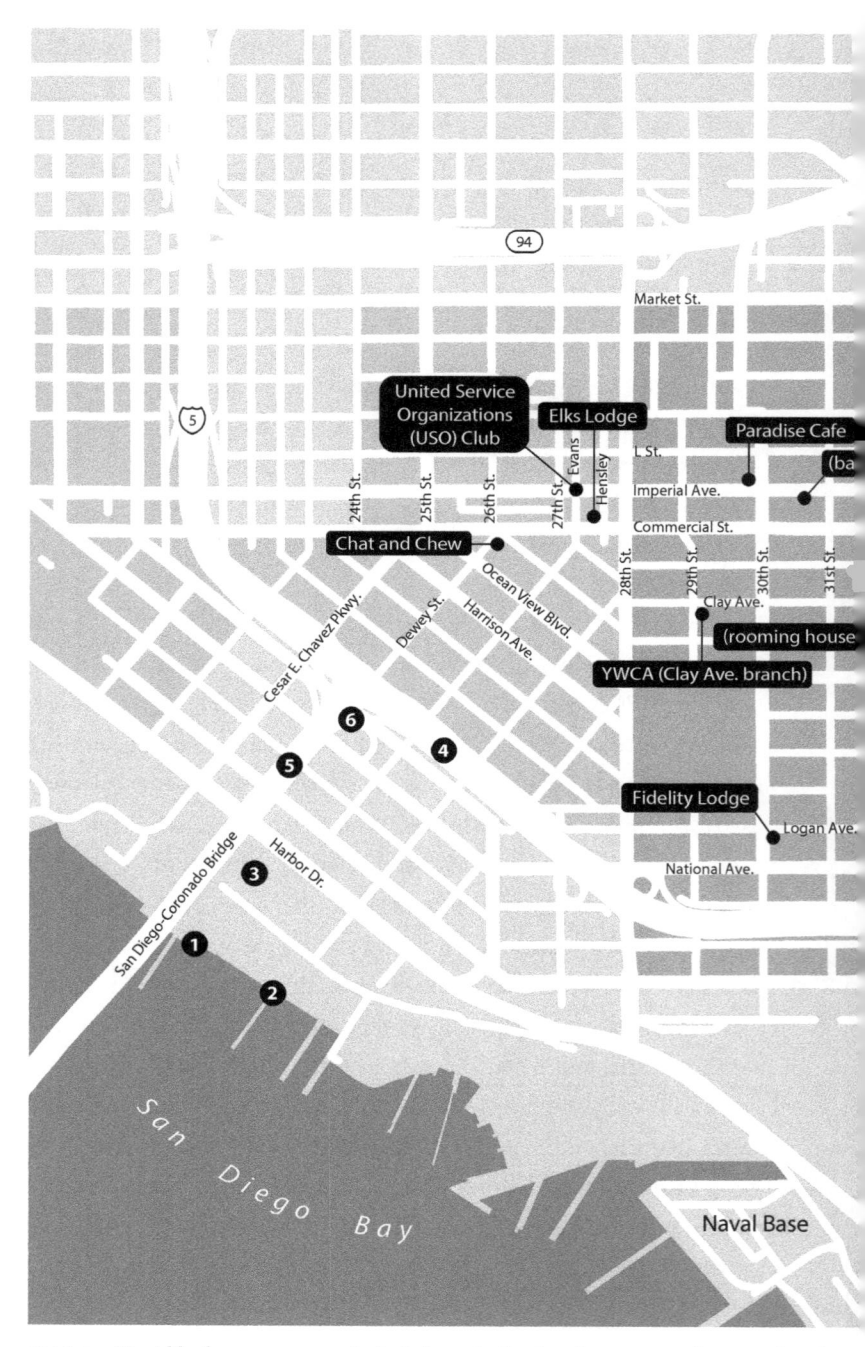

MAP 2. Most blacks were concentrated closer to the I-15 freeway, on the east. Starting with World War II, militarized urban renewal, highway development, and rezoning fundamentally changed the spatial borders of Logan.

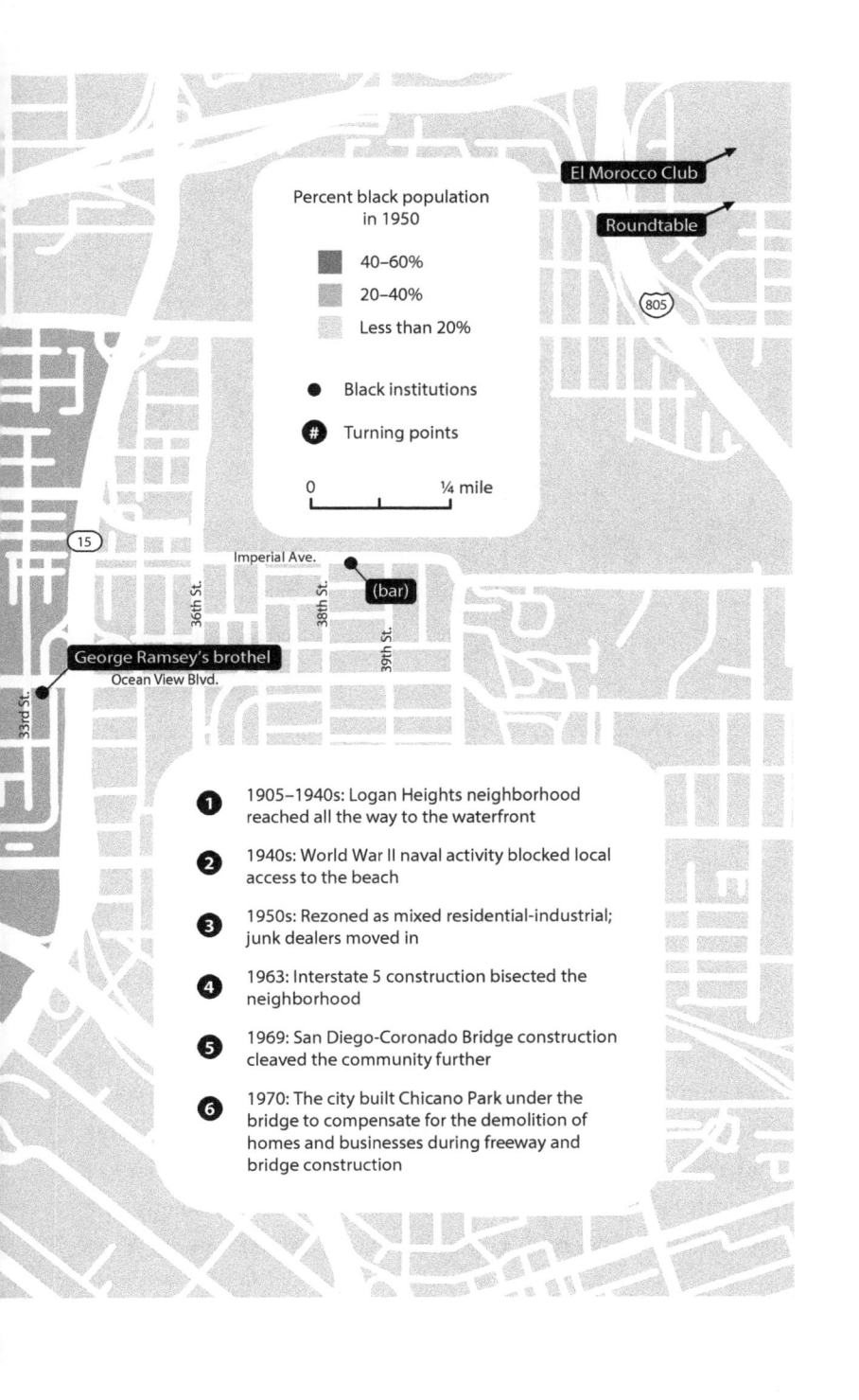

Percent black population in 1950

- 40–60%
- 20–40%
- Less than 20%

● Black institutions

Turning points

0 — ¼ mile

El Morocco Club

Roundtable

805

15

Imperial Ave.

36th St.

38th St.

39th St.

(bar)

George Ramsey's brothel

Ocean View Blvd.

33rd St.

1 1905–1940s: Logan Heights neighborhood reached all the way to the waterfront

2 1940s: World War II naval activity blocked local access to the beach

3 1950s: Rezoned as mixed residential-industrial; junk dealers moved in

4 1963: Interstate 5 construction bisected the neighborhood

5 1969: San Diego-Coronado Bridge construction cleaved the community further

6 1970: The city built Chicano Park under the bridge to compensate for the demolition of homes and businesses during freeway and bridge construction

FIGURE 8. Five people seated at a table and booth in the El Morocco Club.
Source: San Diego History Center.

(see figure 8). The five people are seated around a table in a club. Everyone seems to be in a celebratory mood—possibly celebrating Cinco de Mayo. The man to the right has on a *traje de luces* matador (or bullfighting) costume, while the woman on the other end of the group is wearing a traditional Mexican *folklórico* skirt and holding maracas (a musical instrument). The other two women are also dressed in a festive manner with small sombrero-like hats—with one of the women having a drawn-on mustache. The ambiguously gendered person is donning gear worn by *lucha libre* wrestlers (Mexican fighters). Though this photo could read as simply an appropriation of Mexican culture by black settlers, it might also demonstrate black people's efforts to integrate into the predominately Mexican American neighborhood.

Oral histories recorded by the San Diego History Center also point to disreputable black-owned spaces in Logan as far back as the 1920s. Mr. Owen Alonzo Fitch and Mrs. Sylura Fitch (later Sylura Richardson Barron), influential and prominent political leaders and business owners in San Diego's black community, owned two liquor stores on the 2900 and 3000 blocks of Imperial Avenue in the 1920s.[34] In a 1993 oral history, Sylura explained how they and a local bail bondsman created a scheme to get black sailors arrested so that they could then pocket part of the bail money:

> He [Owen] convinced me to let him build something for the Navy people 'cause he used to be the Navy man, you know. On the weekend, instead of them goin' staying places, they'd come down and stay free or somethin' like that, you know, and relax—for the Navy people. . . . Then he got in with the bail bondsman down in town. . . . He'd give [sailors] free liquor and then he would call the police department to pick 'em up goin' back . . . in the bill he'd get with the bail bondsman and tell him that the police had picked 'em up and then the boys wouldn't have no money. . . . Then the bail bondsman asked the Navy boy, "Do you know Mr. Fitch?" And the boy said, "Oh, yea, he's a good friend of mine." "We'll bail you out and then you can pay us afterward." And then he would split the money with my husband. Isn't that something?

Barron probably used the profit from those businesses to open other businesses. After she remarried William Barron, a carpenter in the navy, Sylura opened a barbershop, beauty shop, restaurant, and a "dine and dance exclusive" called Barron's Topside. In 1948, she was the first black woman delegate to a major political convention. She also ran for the San Diego City Council in 1951 and founded the Democratic Women Power Club in 1972. While she was known as the lady for "hauling voters to the polls," she also disclosed how she got her start as a disreputable business owner on Imperial Avenue in Logan.

A state-funded report, "Special Crime Study Commission on Organized Crime in California, 1945–1954," noted that George Ramsey, owner of the Douglas Hotel and proprietor of other downtown institutions, was running a house of prostitution on the 3400 block of Oceanview Boulevard in southeast San Diego.[35] A photo taken by Baynard alludes to Ramsey's investments in the neighborhood (figure 9). In the photo, George and Mullen Ramsey (presumably a family member) are standing on a lot for a groundbreaking on Thirtieth and Imperial. Ramsey already owned several brothels in the downtown area. This report was then used to criminally prosecute Charles Eugene Berry, State Board of Equalization chief administrative officer for San Diego and Imperial Counties, for bribery and conspiracy.[36] Obviously, state investigators tied Ramsey's businesses to the larger corruption engine of San Diego. Black newspapers documented Ramsey's very close relationships with officials on the board. For instance, in February 1937, the *Defender* reported how he served as a "host" for an influential group of visitors to the city: George M. Hatfield (lieutenant governor of California), George Stout (chief of the State Board of Equalization), and M. N. Munson (chief of the Liquor Administration of San Diego and Imperial County).[37] Angelou worked at one of these black institutions.

Before Angelou begins work she has to find child care for Clyde. She does not reveal how she meets Mrs. Cleo Jenkins, her son's

FIGURE 9. Mullen and George Ramsey standing in a vacant lot with a shovel. Records indicate this is the groundbreaking at Thirtieth and Imperial (circa 1950). Source: San Diego History Center.

babysitter, but her initial encounter reveals how she again has to perform reputability.

"Are you in the life?"

The big black woman could have been speaking Russian. She sat with her back to the window and the sunlight slid over her shoulders, making a pool in her lap.

"I beg your pardon?"

"The life. You turn tricks?"

"No. I do not." How could she ask me such a question?

"Well, you surely look like a trickster. Your face and everything."

"Well, I assure you, I'm not a whore. I have worked as a chef."

"Well." She looked at me as if she'd soon be able to tell if I was lying. (36)

This question from Mother Cleo is indicative of not only surveillance but also the particular gendered constraints placed on working-class women. Angelou's heavy makeup and lack of a wedding ring signal to Mother Cleo the possibility of her being a sex worker—"in the life."[38] Angelou leaves Clyde for a week at the home of Mrs. Cleo and her husband, Mr. Henry Jenkins, visiting him every day. While she does not reveal where she lives during that week, Mrs. Cleo then allows her to live with them: "I see you a good girl coming over here to see your baby every day and all, so my husband and me, we ready to let you live here with us" (43). Angelou can now, at least, sleep with her baby at night.

"Stupid Bitches"

In *Gather Together*, Angelou names the bar she works as the Hi Hat Café, which might be the Hi Ho Club, a place designated in the city-funded study on the history of Barrio Logan. She gives us a thick description of the Hi Hat:

The Hi Hat had too much atmosphere. Music blared and trembled, competing with customers' voices for domination of the air. Neither won, except that for a few seconds during the lull between records, the jukebox sat quiet up against the wall, its green and red and yellow lights flickering like an evil robot from a Flash Gordon film. The customers came mostly from the underworld, though there was a scattering of young sailors among them. They all jockeyed and shifted, lifting glasses and voices in the thick air, which smelled of Lysol and perfume and bodies, and cigarettes and stale beer. The women were mistresses of decorum. They sat primly at the bar, skirts tucked in, voices quick or silent altogether. On the street they had been as ageless as their profession, but near the posturing, flattering men, they became modest girls. Kittens purring under the strokes. (41)

Obviously, the Hi Hat was a disreputable black institution where drinks were not the only things being bought and sold.

In addition to the "mistresses of decorum" at the bar, Beatrice and Johnnie Mae, a black lesbian couple who always ask for Angelou to wait on their table, are also looking for tricks. "The fact that pimps and panders didn't harass them, bespoke the tolerance in the black community for people who chose to lead lives different from the norm," Angelou notes (41). While a disreputable space, clear boundaries and hierarchy exist between patrons and staff. After Beatrice and Johnnie Mae invite Angelou over to their house dinner, a fellow waitress warns her to steer clear of them.

> "You'd better be careful." She sent a hostile glance to Johnnie Mae's table.
> "Why?" I wanted to hear her say it.
> "Those women. You know what they are?"
> "Bull daggers." She smirked with satisfaction at saying the word. (46)

After the waitresses' comment about the fears of being "turned out," Angelou feels the need to return to their table to publicly declare that she is not a lesbian.

> "Listen. I'm not a . . . not . . . not a lesbian, and I don't want to be one. Is that all right?"
>
> Their faces closed. Johnnie Mae asked, "Is what all right?"
>
> Suddenly I was ashamed. "I mean, I wanted you to know that . . . that I don't go that way." (46)

The women are also taken off guard. "Is what all right?" Johnnie Mae asks. Angelou disrupts the ensuing awkward silence with, "I'd like your address. . . . What time on Sunday?" "Two o'clock. When we come from church." Obviously, Angelou is not too fearful. We can read this as a moment of curiosity on her part. The forbiddenness excites her.

Angelou becomes especially aroused when she visits them on Sunday, after they arrive back from church. As the women cook dinner for her, she interprets their displays of affection as a secret plot to "excite" her: "I hated their stupidity, but more than that I hated being underestimated. If they only knew, they could strip buck naked and do the Sassy Sue wiggle and I would continue to sit, with my legs crossed, sipping the Dubonnet." "I held the glass of thick sweet wine as protection. Thinking she would hesitate to pounce on me if there was a chance I would spill the wine on her furniture, I kept it in front of me like a shield" (51).

Beatrice served in the Women's Army Corps (WAC) as a corporal, but after the war she was unable to find employment outside of domestic work.[39] Once discharged, Johnnie Mae started working as a housekeeper, where she met Beatrice, who worked as a cook

(46, 54). As a way to escape domestic work, the couple take "two all-night tricks apiece once a week" (52). According to Beatrice, the money they earn is enough to meet their basic needs and more. However, their landlord is in the process of evicting them because, as they claim, "his son is a faggot" who goes "around wearing women's clothes." Angelou is apparently startled and bewildered at this fact: "Lesbian Prostitutes! Did they trick with women? I ached to know. How did they pick them up? I had never heard of women hustling other women, but surely they didn't go to bed with men. I fished for a way to put my question." She describes Johnnie Mae and Beatrice as "embarrassingly ugly . . . nasty things [who] . . . had no idea that they were so strange-looking" (57). For Angelou, their lesbianism is connected to their undesirability—even though she herself is titillated by their alleged advances toward her.

Although similarly situated, Angelou takes advantage of the couple's housing precarity by proposing a plan which she argues can help them all secure financial and housing stability. After the women are evicted from their bungalow, Angelou takes over the lease and allows them to continue living there, but under one condition: that they "turn tricks" three to four nights a week. She assures them that when "the trade builds up" they will have enough money to purchase a home of their own. However, this comes at a cost. Sex workers relied predominately on male intermediaries, like pimps, taxi drivers, bouncers, and bar owners, to help secure their safety, since women's mobility in public spaces had been severely curtailed due to Progressive Era antiprostitution legislation. Essentially, women could be arrested for vagrancy and prostitution if, for instance, they were found in a bar or a public street without a male proxy (some bars would not even allow women to enter), dressed provocatively, or were accused of "disturbing the peace," among other things.[40] Women were even refused housing, because the state's Red Light Abatement Act threatened owners with forfeiture of property for renting to prostitutes.[41] On top of that, the mere presence of a black woman with a white man violated local miscegenation laws.

Angelou's refusal to turn tricks with the women is also a form of hierarchy and respectability. Her choice to pimp Johnnie Mae and Beatrice, instead of tricking herself, is strategic, since this arrangement allows her to completely control the operation, reap the most profit (without doing any sex work), decrease her chance of being arrested, and more importantly allow her to maintain a degree of respectability. After she lays out her plan, Beatrice asks her, "'Where will you work?' Me, turn tricks? What did they think I was?" She tells them, "I'm going to stay on at the restaurant. Shouldn't call attention to myself, you understand" (61).

The structure of Angelou's syndicate illuminates how discreetness, hierarchy, and the inclusion of men are integral to the success of her disreputable business venture. She employs the services of an unnamed white cab driver, using the pickup line "Are there enough houses of ill repute to service the naval personnel?" She also employs Hi Hat's bouncer, Hank. The men are charged with bringing tricks to the brothel, securing the money, and making sure tricks leave in a timely manner. Angelou knows that cab drivers usually get paid $45 to solicit servicemen at Camp Pendleton, so she pays Hank $86 dollars, since interracial (black/white) sex is more harshly criminalized by authorities. The everyday routine entails Hank turning on the porch light at two-thirty in the morning, indicating a "clear coast," and then Angelou entering and paying "the workers." Each trick pays $342 to have sex with both women. However, Johnnie Mae and Beatrice together only profit

$86 dollars after Angelou pays Hank, the taxi driver, and then herself.

Angelou has other risks to consider, such as arrest. At that time, San Diego was still arresting black women for miscegenation under the guise of prostitution-related offenses. Angelou nearly escapes prosecution. She provides us with a moment of comic relief during a heated exchange with Beatrice: "You come over here every night collecting money, acting like you somebody's pimp. But you too good to turn a trick. And you keep this big rough sonofabitch watching us all the time. Well, you can kiss my black ass" (71). Johnnie Mae threatens to call the vice squad on their pimp. Soon after, Angelou makes her sudden departure from San Diego. Johnnie Mae and Beatrice understand that they are in a hierarchal labor position, with Angelou reaping economic profits without participating in sex work herself. She considers the women "ungrateful," telling them that if she had not helped them they would be on "the street, or back in some white woman's kitchen" (71).

In an unpublished short story (or chapter), "Aunt Sukie," who might have been the original "fictional" character in *Gather Together*, Angelou again deploys the *sex worker as trickster*. The story describes a scene of a sex-working black woman playing "badger games." Sukie, a black sex worker, picks up a white "sailor" who wants to have sex with her. She accompanies him to a rooming house, and takes his money before sneaking out. As LaShawn Harris points out, some women did this to protest the continued subjugation and devaluing of black women's bodies—black sex workers were always paid less than white women, so "badger games" became a way to "augment the low wages they earned from sex work."[42] Even though black women are highly desired, the construction of their undesirability, what Miller-Young calls the "myth of prohibition," becomes a way to devalue their worth as objects of consumption.[43] The following is a story in its entirety:

"Can we have a date, honey?" His words stumbled off his tongue like drunk sailors out on a spree.

"Have you got a place, honey? Can you suck it honey?"

Lust struggled on his thin lips and his pale blue eyes tried to find yes in Baby Girl's face.

"Honey, I want you. I love colored girls. Honey."

"Colored girls know how to do it, honey, don't they?" He lifted his big head and looked into the shadowed room.

"How far is it, honey? How much will it cost, honey?"

His snores crackled in her ears, and she slipped from the bed and dressed quickly. When he awakened she was laying his wallet on the dresser.

"Whore bitch, give me back my money." Without waiting he lunged from the bed and threw himself at her. She moved quickly and the door shuddered from his weight.

"Give me my money, nigger whore."

"I'm cut. My God, you've cut me." He fell away from her, trying with both hands to push the blood back into his body.

"Help! I've been cut. Help!"

In the dim hall Baby Girl heard roomers double bolting their doors. On the ground floor the manager hissed at her,

"Stupid bitch, you brought the heat?"

She looked at him, and he was disgusted with his fear.

"I paid you didn't I? Call the ambulance fool, somebody's been hurt."

And she was outside in the cool dark night.[44]

Sukie is playful, has autonomy. Flips off her intermediary. She is unapologetic about the chaos she has caused because again, Sukie is a trickster and that is her job. Sukie exposes the uneven racialized and gendered economic stratification and how the sailor economically benefits from this arrangement. Yes, the hotel operator is inconvenienced—a small price to pay for running a quasi-commercialized brothel.

However, what seems to trouble Angelou more is how an arrest would tarnish the respectable image Mrs. Cleo has of her. She is not "afraid," since pimps and madams were rarely charged with prostitution, but her concern is the Jenkinses. Mrs. Cleo, who is not very nice to Angelou in the beginning, grows to consider her a respectable young woman.

> I had a vague worry—that a sudden large bank account would put the vice squad on my trail. I wasn't afraid of the police, since I wasn't turning tricks myself, but I was terrified of how a police investigation would influence Mother Cleo. She'd toss me and my baby out of the house with much damning me to the depths of hell. There were other places to go of course, and with the money piling up in secret places I could afford anyone to tend my child, but the fact was that I cared for the Jenkinses and what they thought of me was important. Their home and their ways reminded me of the grandmother who raised me and who I idolized. I wouldn't have them offended. When my illicit business reached its peak, I joined their church, and stood in the choir singing the old songs with great feeling. (62)

Miss Cleo reminds Angelou of her grandmother, whom she called Momma—a humble beacon of Christian humility in a Jim Crow South, who makes Angelou handmade dresses.

Angelou decides to return to Arkansas after leaving San Diego; however, she soon realizes that Stamps is no longer a safe place for the new woman she is becoming. While there, she visits a department store to pick out a dress pattern. When a racist white saleswoman instructs her to stand to the side while she passes her in the aisle, Angelou becomes infuriated. Another saleswoman overhears the dispute and orders Angelou to share her name. Angelou lashes out, "And where I'm from is no concern of yours, but rather where you're going. I'll slap you into the middle of next week if you even dare to open your mouths again. Now, take that filthy pattern and stick it you-know-where" (91–93). Although Angelou feels that her response to the sales clerks was justified, Momma doesn't. "You think 'cause you've been to California these crazy people won't kill you? You think them lunatic cracker boys won't try to catch you in the road and violate you? You think because of all your all-fired principle some of the men won't feel like putting their white sheets on and riding over here to stir up trouble? You do, you're wrong. Ain't nothing to protect you and us except the good Lord and some miles. I packed you and the baby's things, and Brother Wilson is coming to drive you to Louisville" (95). Although Angelou has imagined Stamps, and the black folk in the town, as a sort of harbor of safety, she is again out of place.

She returns to Baxter's boardinghouse in San Francisco, where she again attempts to obtain formal employment, this time by applying to the US Army's Officer's Candidate School. For Angelou, joining the military would afford access to basic resources. Baxter is excited seeing her daughter in a military uniform. "Government is going to give you an education and a start in life and you're going to give class to that uniform." Angelou cheerfully submits to the required physical exam. The female recruiter informs her that a dance school she attended is listed on the "House Un-American Activities list," a federally created list of organizations deemed politically radical during the Red Scare. However, Angelou might not have fared better in the army. In *Glory in Their Spirit: How Four Black Women Took on the Army during World War II*, Sandra Bolzenius's examination of black WACs reveals how white superiors assigned black women to the most menial of tasks and denied them additional training after enlistment, which affected their ability to find jobs after discharge.[45] By comparison, the white WACs held a variety of jobs and received the training necessary for their advancement. Moreover, black women in WAC accounted for only 4 percent of the division. The WAC recruiter's dismissal of Angelou's application was likely a common technique used to prevent integration into the US Armed Forces. Angelou is back to square one—doing dancing gig work in San Francisco, looking for other work.

"Wild West Rhythm"

To start on a clean slate, Angelou moves to Stockton, California, a city in the San Joaquin Valley. She begins working as a fry cook at the restaurant of her mother's friend. Unlike San Diego, the valley was not a hotbed of police surveillance and criminalization, in part due to the different racial and class dynamics. After the creation of the Bracero Program in 1942, many Mexican and Filipino farm laborers began to reside in the area, many of whom entered California through the US-Mexico border near San Diego. Angelou gives us a thick description of the racial and economic geography: "Stockton had an unusual atmosphere. Situated in the agricultural San Joaquin Valley, it had long been a center for the itinerant workers,

Southerners drawn from depleted farms, Mexican and Filipinos from their poverty-stricken countries who had raised large families on meager incomes since the early 1900s. World War II had enriched the town's blood attracting blacks from the South to work at the local dry dock, the shipyards and defense plants in nearby Pittsburg" (141). To "add juice to [her] dry life," after her 4:00 p.m. shift ends Angelou exchanges "the sweaty uniform for a clinging one-shoulder deal and high-heeled shoes" before heading to the bar (142). It is here where she meets Big Mary, who eventually becomes Clyde's babysitter. It is also where she meets L.D. Tolbrook—a man she describes as her father's "age . . . [and] . . . color" (142). He will also be her introduction into disreputable sex economies in the rural area.

Though Angelou describes the San Joaquin Valley as less policed than San Diego, black women's sexual services with brown transnational labor had to be discreet—and were also less profitable. The fact that black women were secluded in houses along the highway instead of going directly to laborers near their camps, like some Mexican and white prostitutes, is indicative of a restrictive (racialized) geography in this rural landscape. In *Defiant Braceros: How Migrant Workers Fought for Racial, Sexual, and Political Freedom*, Mireya Loza traces how even among indigenous and mestizo workers, the color line was still heavily policed.[46] Her archival research reveals, for example, how a Pennsylvania mayor forbade workers from associating with black women: "They were less concerned with the presence of the sex worker in the camp than with her racial identity."[47] Additionally, though black women faced less criminalization in this sexual geography, they were also paid far less, having to split their earnings with madams, pimps, and the procurers who brought them to the rural area. As well, their clientele were poor farm laborers who did not have as much disposable income as white servicemen. Black women were considered less desirable and their pay also reflected that.[48]

Angelou works under the authority of Clara Minnie, who operates a brothel exclusively patronized by Bracero workers. She initially meets Clara when accompanying L.D. to pick up cash from the black madams who work for him (141). Their stops include northern inland California cities such as Fresno, Merced, Mendota, and Firebaugh. Angelou writes how they "had cabins along the road with access to the transient field workers," and how these places smell like "disinfectant and artificial flowers," which she considers "as tell-tale as a red light over the door" (148, 151). She provides a thick description of interracial (black/Mexican) prostitution via Bea, who, like other women, prefers tricking Mexican farm laborers instead of white men. She explains to Angelou, "You got it easy. I was turned out with white men. They want to talk all the time. They tell you how beautiful you are and how much they love you. And wonder what you're doing being a whore all the time they're jugging in you and paying for it. Then when they get finished they got the nerve to ask you how you liked it. And talk about your freaks! White men can really think of some nasty things to do" (168). At the working-class brothel Angelou is instructed to be transactional and not romantic with the "Mexican tricks." Bea tells her, "Remember, the men come here to trick, not to get married. Talk to them dirty but soft. And play with them." Clara instructs Angelou to not "open [her] legs wide. They are tricks, not your old man, so don't try making love to them. That's why we call them tricks" (346). Angelou's first trick is Papa Pedro. As instructed, she removes Pedro's clothes and uses the "trick pan and towels" to wash him before sex. She keeps most of her clothes on during the sex act and washes him again after he ejaculates. "I had expected the loud scream of total orgasmic release and felt terribly inadequate when the men had finished with grunts and yanked up their pants without thanks. I decided that being black, I had a different rhythm for the Latinos and all I had to do was let myself learn their tempos" (168). She is disappointed by this experience.

While she frames Beatrice, Johnnie Mae, and Aunt Sukie as cunning tricksters, she does not position herself in this way. She fails to become as popular as the other sex workers at Clara's house. The men all choose Bea. "Despite my youth and high school clothes and stilted Spanish, I wasn't popular at Clara's. The men preferred Bea. She had a swing to her hips and a knowing smile that I couldn't imitate. Then, Mexican farm workers obviously had no erotic fantasies starring black teenage girls; they came to a whorehouse for a whore, and Bea answered their needs" (172).

After a week L.D. returns and becomes upset after talking with Clara. He angrily tells Angelou, "I talked to Clara. And there wasn't hardly any money at all. I don't think you tried . . . Clara says you sit around like a judge, never saying anything to them. And that you talk to the tricks in Spanish like a goddamn schoolteacher" (174). While working in Clara's brothel, she treats the other workers similarly to how she treats Beatrice and Johnnie Mae in San Diego— with contempt. She describes the other women as delusional for thinking their "Daddys" love them.

> Their conversations were tightly choreographed measures, and since I didn't know the steps, I sat on the sidelines and watched.
>
> They were too cynical to understand that we were in love and that after I had helped him out of trouble, after he had a divorce,

we were going to be married and live in a dream house with my son and lots of flowers. I would not share my plan with hard hearted whores. (172)

She sees their men as pimps, while denying that L.D. is one himself, instead referring to him as a "gambler." Angelou thinks that her sex work will be rewarded with a husband and refuses to socialize with the other women. She sees this work as an investment in "helping [her] man." This framing of sex workers is very different from that of the women in San Diego.

Angelou chooses not to position herself in this way because, I argue, she was protecting *her* image. In interviews well after the publication of *Gather Together*, she recalls her apprehension of disclosing her sex work. "They'll hate me."[49] However, her husband at the time encouraged her to write it, telling her, "Write it. . . . [People] have tried to reach an exit and found the doors not only locked, but no doorknobs on it. And they have done many things. It's important that you write it." Before she sent the manuscript to the publisher, she called up "the family" (her mom, brother, and son) to get their approval. After reading the passage Angelou was most insecure about, her mother stood up and held out her hand: "Is it ready for the post office? I will take it myself." Obviously, the publication of *Gather Together* was a proud moment for Vivian.

Like pulp fiction narratives, Angelou frames *Gather Together* as a cautionary tale. "I wrote to tell young people, who've been told that their parents have no skeleton or in fact they have no closets, that I will admit to where I've been. And they can see that and realize that you may encounter many defeats, but you must not be defeated. It may even be necessary to encounter the defeats, so you can know you. How you can rely upon yourself, where you can pull yourself up from."[50] In the same interview, Angelou told the story of a "young street prostitute" who comes to get her autograph during a book tour in Ohio. She described her as having "false fingernails . . . lots of false hair . . . [and] a young face of 18." She tells Angelou, "You give me hope." "If no one else said anything to me [about the book], it's sufficient" Angelou recalled.

She frames herself as a victim of coercion and manipulation instead of admitting that she did it to make money. This framing is important because it brings up important questions regarding the politics of representation. As Juana María Rodríguez explains, auto/biographies by porn workers, as a genre, "tend to traffic in sad stories of teenage sexual abuse and addiction and when, and if, they survive to tell the tale themselves, generally end with the triumph of true love."[51] Unlike her original intention, to show the woman "who didn't make it," *Gather Together* ends with *Angelou* promising to leave the disreputable life. The book closes with these lines: "I had no idea what I was going to make of my life, but I had given a promise and found my innocence. I swore I'd never lose it again" (214).

Outside of her literary world, in interviews with friends and strangers, Angelou continued to be an evasive trickster, often reacting to the mention of her sex archive with comedy, ambivalence, or annoyance. Ephemera in the archive of Rosa Guy, housed at the Schomburg Center in New York City, point out that Angelou continued to revel in the fact that she was a pimp in San Diego long after the publication of *Gather Together*. In 1998, Oprah Winfrey threw a multiday cruise for Maya Angelou in celebration of her seventieth birthday. One of the many party favors was a book, "Maya Celebrates 70," that included a chronology of her most notable achievements thus far.[52] "At 18: For two months, madam of a two-woman whorehouse in San Diego" was one of the six "Significant Events: The Second Decade, 1938–1947." The others in this decade were graduating with honors from high school; receiving a dance scholarship; giving birth to her son, Guy; becoming the first black woman to work as a San Francisco streetcar conductor; and becoming a "Creole-style cook." However, what seems to be an obvious omission from "Maya Celebrates 70" is an entry about her time as a brothel worker in the San Joaquin Valley. While Angelou might have been boastful about being a "madam," during interviews she became rather coy and even defensive when asked about being an actual prostitute. "A Conversation between Rosa Guy and Maya Angelou" (1983) poses an open-ended question regarding her labor as a sex worker: "For instance, when you were a prostitute and you decided to make this break because of your son. I could understand that. What always impresses me is, how did you come to the point where you decided?" Angelou does not directly answer the question and instead shifts to discussing the one consistent love of her life: writing. In analog video, *Maya Angelou: Gather Together in My Name*, an upload by VisionaryProject in 2010 on YouTube, she recalls a moment when an interviewer inappropriately brought up the topic.

> "Maya Angelou, how does it feel to know that you are the first black woman to have a national best-seller of non-fiction and second book nominated for the Pulitzer [Prize]—and to know that at 18 you were a prostitute?"
>
> "Aw, but there are many ways to prostitute oneself. And you know a lot about that, don't you dear?"[53]

She does not seem proud at all about her time as a brothel prostitute. However, we cannot take this interpretation of her life at face value.

Though she is coy in the public eye, her other cultural forms reveal deeper moments of interiority.[54] Her poems, in particular, gesture toward a spiritual awakening through sexual freedom. The poems in *Just Give Me a Cool Drink of Water 'fore I Diiie*, written three years before *Gather Together* in 1971, represent the "blues mode in the Angelou canon."[55] They are also representative of an experimental space. The poem "They Go Home" tells the story of a woman, possibly a sex worker or a promiscuous disreputable woman, who becomes emotionally attached to the married men she dates.

> They went home and told their wives,
> that never once in all their lives,
> had they known a girl like me,
> But . . . They went home.
> They said my house was licking clean,
> no word I spoke was ever mean,
> I had an air of mystery,
> But . . . They went home.
>
> My praises were on all men's lips,
> they liked my smile, my wit, my hips,
> they'd spend one night, or two or three.
> But . . .[56]

In another poem, "Still I Rise" (1978), monetizing her corporal resources enables Angelou to "harness the subjective power of eroticism."[57]

Does my sexiness upset you? Does it come as a surprise
That I dance like I've got diamonds
At the meeting of my thighs.

Her clever maneuvering around her disreputability paid off when the Hallmark corporation approached her about a partnership in 2002. In "Why Maya Angelou Partnered with Hallmark," Dr. Ayesha Hardison explains that the partnership enabled Angelou to "take her message of compassion, understanding and transformation to a larger audience."[58] As Hardison explains, the collaboration between Hallmark and Angelou was an "ideal match"; Angelou already "talked with a Hallmark-like affect." Life Mosaic, very different from Mahogany, is a product line Hallmark created in 1991 that targeted African American audiences. The new collection appropriated Angelou's poetic brand, which had been well solidified in American culture. Hallmark used various materials, including interviews and her creative canon, for the collection. The Life Mosaic collection offered a vast range of products including cards, flower vases, and picture frames, among other things, imprinted with Angelou's words. The collection also had items such as journals, which allowed people to create their own stories and narratives. Hardison points to how the journal "foster[ed] interplay between the owner's personal history and Angelou's truisms." The partnership between Angelou and Hallmark was a huge success, amassing $45 million in the first five years.

Yet Angelou still incorporates disreputability through her Hallmark items by honoring the most unapologetically disreputable character from *Gathering Together*, Vivian "Lady" Baxter—her mother. The focus on thriving in a white heteropatriarchal world is a critical message that Angelou conveys, and one which Lady Baxter taught her most about. As I stated earlier in this chapter,

Angelou's relationship with her mother was complex. However, in her final autobiographical volume, *Mom & Me & Mom* (2013), she seems to offer closure on their relationship—"You were a terrible mother of small children, but there has never been anyone greater than you as a mother of a young adult."[59] At her mother's memorial, Angelou vowed to celebrate and honor her mother's passion for life: "I looked at my mother's lifeless form and thought about her passion and wit. I knew she deserved a daughter who loved her and had a good memory, and she got one."[60] In a Life Mosaic birthday card for mothers, Angelou encourages women to honor their mothers: "She was the most passionate and bravest person I ever knew. And funny."[61] For Angelou, the art of living is black women's unique strength and contribution to the world. In relief on a sage-green ceramic flower vase from the Life Mosaic collection is "Thriving is elegant."[62] In *Wouldn't Take Nothing for My Journey Now* (1993), Angelou remarks on her life and her perspective on the art of living: "Living well is an art that can be developed: a love of life and ability to take great pleasure from small offerings and assurance that the world owes you nothing and that every gift is exactly that, a gift."[63]

By the end Angelou is still an intermediary of literacy. Through literature, she reconstructs ideas about black womanhood and motherhood—ideas that celebrate and empower black women despite the tribulations. Her message of uplift has transcended generations. Although Angelou could not please the sophisticated literary and artistic crowd, her books still hold meaning for everyday black people. She produces her own genre of writing. Early on she was teaching bodily tactics and tools for black sexual worlds, which would later prepare her for, and inform her pedagogy within, black literary worlds.

Conclusion

By leaning into commercial and racial capitalism, Maya Angelou again offers the nation a certain kind of (black) respectability and an intermediary position between the dualism of the disreputable and the respectable—but the disreputable still haunts her narratives. Being a hallmark and a ho becomes a part of her citizenship and relationship to the nation. She was once in the life and then transitioned to national emblem. A lifelong patriot, Angelou performed service labor as a sex worker servicing the troops and Bracero farm laborers in post–World War II California and later as an inaugural poet in 1993 for President Bill Clinton (and the larger nation) in Washington, DC. Both are about creating ideas of belonging and what it means to sacrifice for the country. Angelou plays off both enterprises. She understands militarism as a set of conditions, but also as a form of resistance. By starting off her career in sex work as a pimp and brothel worker in militarized spaces, she learned that servicing the sexual and emotional needs of soldiers was also a form of patriotism, since these men were doing an important service for the nation. As a sex worker servicing non-black men, she also learned that her labor had to be somewhat hidden due to the racial, sexual, and gender regimes of whiteness and respectability and in order to preserve the nationalist (and homogenous) idea of the soldier, citizen, and worker.

Though Angelou characterizes her sex work history as part of "the episodic, erratic nature of adolescence," I argue that the sexual knowledge she obtained during that time enabled her to use disreputability as a resource, creating opportunities to advance her career as a sex worker to one of America's most celebrated cultural producers and figures.[64] Her sex work resulted not in a devaluation of the self but rather in a practice of learning to value the self. Her participation in interracial sex work enabled her to dispel antiblack discourse about black women's undesirability. By discussing Angelou's sex work, I do not mean to scandalize her but instead to show how she pushed back and maneuvered in militarized spaces to not only survive but to thrive.

In chapter 3, I begin where Angelou the migratory sex worker leaves off—the latter 1940s in San Diego. As Logan Heights and its surrounding areas became a dumping ground for what the city considered its most disreputable populations, San Diego intensified this spatial segregation with the construction of military bases and freeways—along with rezoning these areas (see map 2).[65] Simultaneously, downtown urban renewal began. I center the life narrative/story of Granville "Bubba" Hughes, a black gender-nonconforming trans woman whose life was shaped by these development processes. By detailing her life in both downtown and Logan, we get to understand how black institutions created space for black trans women in ways that gay activists did not. Unlike Angelou, Bubba was a migratory sex worker who decided to stay in San Diego—and passed during the COVID-19 pandemic. The remaining chapters also take a different methodological approach by combining critical ethnographic methodologies, including my own experience/engagement with interlocutors.[66]

3 "We Were Just Negro Queens"

Safe Space Activism and Queer Masonic Theology

Most of the blacks who didn't think they were all uppity hung out at Fifth and Market. Back then Hillcrest was like . . . we just didn't mingle. We were just Negro queens. We had the white society—they thought they were above us. They just didn't frequent our side of the tracks . . . a lot of the blacks hung right down in the heart of San Diego . . . it wasn't a gay area—it was just downtown. Everybody hung downtown.

GRANVILLE "BUBBA" OMEGA HUGHES

There were clear racial and class divisions between the downtown and Hillcrest queer communities in the late twentieth century. For Bubba, a black trans queen who migrated to San Diego in 1965, the city offered a type of cosmopolitanism that her hometown of Phoenix, Arizona, lacked. Bubba saw men "kissing and holding hands," when she came to visit her aunt a year prior in 1964—the next week, she moved to San Diego. At the same time, Bubba understood that downtown was a racially segregated place, a place where some white gays did not "frequent." Nicole Murray-Ramirez, a former street-involved Latine queen who served as the city of San Diego's human relations commissioner (HRC), revealed that there were racial and class divisions even among drag queens.

Some members of the San Diego Imperial Court, an international fundraising organization known for elaborate female impersonation/drag balls, characterized its younger incoming members (including Murray-Ramirez) as "downtown Mexican trash."[1] Bernie Michels, cofounder of the Gay Center for Social Services, explained in an interview with Michael E. Dillinger that by the 1960s and 1970s the downtown area had become "skid-rowish," and therefore "middle class lesbians and gays felt more comfortable in Hillcrest rather than downtown."[2] During this time, the San Diego Downtown Association, considered the old guard, was being replaced by San Diego Inc., a small but influential group of downtown business owners who also wanted to capitalize on a "middle- and upper-class desire for a sanitized urban experience."[3] Sex-working black queens were especially surveilled and targeted in this cleanup with Ordinance 9439 (Section 56.19), a municipal statute that criminalized cross-dressing. White gays and lesbians did not condemn the predatory policing of queens in downtown; in fact, they sought to differentiate themselves from gender-nonconforming people, especially sex workers. As Becki Ross and Rachael Sullivan argue in their research on antiprostitution gay activism in mid-1970s Vancouver, "the drive to expel prostitutes from the imagined gay community became part of the bargain made by (some) predominately white gay men to enhance their transition from lowly criminals and deviants to enterprising, morally upright citizens and community leaders."[4]

While early twentieth-century Progressive Era reformers actively participated in campaigns to obliterate prostitution, in the latter twentieth century safe space activists represented another set of reformers invested in condemning and removing sex-working people from the cityscape during major development processes—which disproportionately affected black queer women, black queens, and trans queens. While city boosters and speculative investors considered queens in downtown as a blight that needed to be removed from the cityscape, safe space activists, which included members of the local Gay Liberation Front (SDGLF), the Metropolitan Community Church of San Diego (MCCSD), and some lesbians, cynically mobilized the idea of downtown blight as a fundraising strategy to obtain a building for the Gay Center for Social Services, which was subsequently placed in Hillcrest.[5] This network would lay the groundwork for the Greater San Diego Business Association (later renamed the San Diego Equality Business Association). While early fundraising revolved around obtaining a brick-and-mortar location for the Gay Center for Social Services (now called the Center), it was one part of a larger vision by two of the most recognizable gay-rights activists in San Diego—Jess Jessop and Bernie Michels.[6] Michels was most active in the MCCSD, a local chapter of a larger homophile religious organization, while Jessop was a prominent leader in the San Diego Gay Liberation Front, also a local chapter of a national organization but more radical and confrontationist. Though the MCCSD was considered "the" gay organization at the time in San Diego, Jessop wanted to create a secular organization to support the local gay community. Both Michels and Jessop decided to work together to build a gay constituency in the city of San Diego.[7] As Jessop admitted, "we had to become bankers"; and as historian Michel Dillinger explains in his article "Hillcrest: From Haven to Home," the "investment of the gay community . . . [in] . . . Hillcrest from isolated obscurity [to] . . . premiere commercial and social scenes in San Diego [was an example of] gay-motivated positive gentrification."[8] Michels, a member of both the SDGLF and

MCCSD, claimed that downtown was "skid-rowish . . . [and that] middle class lesbians and gays felt more comfortable in Hillcrest rather than downtown."[9] This was also a time when social scientists began to express tolerance for homosexuals but not transsexuals. Jessop claimed that a large part of local gay activist discourse involved creating a distinction between "homosexuality" and "transvestism/transsexuality."[10] Cynthia Lawrence-Wallace and Peggy Heathers, a black/white interracial lesbian couple who were also cofounders of the Center for Social Services, described queens as "projecting all the things about women that we are trying to get away from . . . bitches without substance."[11] As the work of John William Gove shows, early LGBT activism in San Diego was fraught with factions, including the invisibility of race, class, and gender.[12]

I call the stakeholders involved in San Diego's gay neighborhood development *safe space activists* to capture how the idea of safety was principally a racialized and classed one. Scholars such as Samuel Delany, Martin Manalansan, and Christina Hanhardt have illuminated that these gentrification efforts mirrored larger policing strategies that targeted working-class queers, many of whom were black and brown.[13] While my work is indebted to the work of this scholarship, safe space activism is different in San Diego because it is both a US-Mexico border city and a military base. The policing of marginalized others in San Diego has been positioned as a matter of national security. Since the city's economy is wholly dependent on the military, the US military/federal government exercises a great deal of power and sway over local politics—more so than in New York City and San Francisco. As I have shown in chapter 1, eradicating prostitution, especially the "worse elements," has been a central concern for the military and city stakeholders. Gay pornography rings involving marines have been well documented, and policing has selectively targeted and arrested downtown queens and other gender-nonconforming people. Even more, the safe space activists in San Diego are very different from those in the Bay Area or New York City. Many of these activists, including some drag queens, were military veterans—which historically has been a rather conservative contingency. And as I will discuss in the final chapter, this militarized gay culture has prevented a more leftist politics from emerging in the city.

By using interviews with Granville "Bubba" Hughes, a black trans queen I met in 2013, I demonstrate how black institutions in working-class communities served as places where black trans queens and other gender-nonconforming people created alternative forms of kinship as a respite from anti-black, antitrans, and antipoor safe space activism. More importantly, what the interviews also reveal is how Bubba was still able to rely on some of these institutions as she transitioned from a sex-working queen to a church deacon. Bubba and her drag revue group, the Plutons, performed and socialized in black bars, "juke joints," restaurants, and fraternal orders from the 1960s to the 1980s in San Diego. A downtown staple was Robert Clay's Silver Sands Café, located on Fifth and Market, which opened in 1964. Despite Clay's ability to secure funds to reinvent Silver Sands, the downtown business association pushed him out in the 1990s. His café was the last remaining black business in the area. The one institution that has prevailed despite gerrymandering and the recent outflux of black people from California is black fraternal orders, like the Elks and Masons. While the black Christian church is an important social and political institution in the black freedom movement, fraternal orders have received an inadequate amount of scholarly investigation.[14] While

Bubba did drag shows at the Elks Lodge in southeast San Diego during her younger years, the Fidelity Lodge No. 10, also in the southeast, is where she worshipped as a parishioner. Given the racialized and classist forces of gentrification and safe space activism, how did it happen that some of the black institutions that Bubba depended on in her younger days survived to sustain her as a black queer elder?

As the ethnography in this chapter will show, these black institutions have, to this day, continued to serve and benefit their black community members.

"Everybody Hung Downtown"

The proliferation of gay bars and enclaves in downtown San Diego was the result of the mobilization of troops for World War II. As Allan Bérubé explains in his book, *Coming Out under Fire: The History of Gay Men and Women in World War II* (1990), the war effort thrust many gay men and lesbian women into unfamiliar cities, such as New York, Chicago, San Francisco, and San Diego, away from their established gay networks. "With only a few hours in a big city, gay male and lesbian GIs were forced to rely on commercial establishments near the heart of the city to find the gay life quickly."[15] At the start of the war there were 38,075 service people, and then 193,296 by March of 1944. By the end of the war, numbers dropped dramatically, with 176,000 in January 1946 dropping to 45,000 in April 1947.[16] The numbers of black servicemen (and women) during the World War II era in San Diego varied and are not readily available; however, around one million African American women and men served in the armed forces during World War II.[17] In June 1944, the *Chicago Defender* reported

"Negroes stationed on most [naval] bases throughout the area."[18] In the following year, April 21, 1945, the *Defender* ran another story on black recruits, "San Diego Bluejacket Signalmen Cited for Efficiency," featuring photographs of black sailors at a US Navy base.[19] Many servicemen and women decided to stay in San Diego after the war.[20] Queer institutions proliferated in port cities along the West Coast. As Nan Boyd explains in her study of queer San Francisco, California's liquor control administration (the State Board of Equalization) placed a low priority on controlling vice; instead, it was concerned with the "financial management of liquor production and distribution."[21] Similar to in San Francisco, militarized gay tourism in San Diego gradually expanded following the repeal of Prohibition.[22]

Early twentieth-century queer culture was located in and around urban theater districts, where female impersonators and other vaudeville-like acts and burlesque acts performed—places like the Orpheum Theatre at Sixth Avenue and B Street, where Brass Rail was housed from 1934 to 1957.[23] Brass Rail is regarded as the first gay bar in San Diego according to Paul Detwiler, director of the documentary *San Diego's Gay Bar History* (2018).[24] He found more than 135 gay bars operating in San Diego since the 1940s. Other notable places included the Circus Room at 1039 Fourth Avenue and the El Cortez Sky Room at 702 Ash Street.[25] The Circus Room was across the street from the racially segregated U.S. Grant Hotel. In Detwiler's film, George McGuire, a World War II veteran, reminisces on his arrival in the city in 1942 and how Circus Room was his first gay bar. The outside was later restored to resemble its original circus-themed front, with a clown's face painted on the walkway and a red circus tent/big top ornament on top of the front. The Circus Room was part of a network of institutions owned by

Nate Rosenberg and Louis H. Provost that included another cocktail lounge (the South Seas Room) and a restaurant (the Show Biz Supper Club).[26] Built in 1927, the El Cortez Hotel was the tallest building at the time. Inside of the hotel, on the fifteenth floor, was the Sky Room. In 1956, the hotel added an outdoor glass elevator that took patrons to the Sky Room.[27] Allan Bérubé describes Bradley's and Blue Jacket as popular places for the working class in the city's Tenderloin area, where "GI and gay recreational life overlapped."[28] Servicemen stationed in isolated parts of San Diego County bought Greyhound tickets to downtown, where they were dropped off at the Armed Services YMCA.[29] A variety of businesses accommodated servicepeople, including locker rooms, cheap motels, restaurants, and adult-themed entertainment.[30] Yet California's antimiscegenation laws, not abolished until 1948, meant that early historic gay bars were also racially segregated places. David Monod, in *Vaudeville and the Making of Modern Entertainment, 1890–1925*, notes that discrimination in white-led productions caused African American customers to instead support "colored vaudeville."[31] The Creole Palace in the Douglas Hotel, a black hotel and cabaret, was home to the Creole Cuties Chorus and other forms of vaudeville for black and non-white audiences.[32]

While servicepeople and civilian employees kept downtown businesses afloat during World War II, the area still experienced an economic decline due to suburbanization and the opening of retail malls in Linda Vista (1942), College Grove (1960), Mission Valley (1961), and Grossmont (1961). In 1959, a small but influential group of downtown stakeholders created San Diego Inc. with the intent to address the decline of sales. The group spearheaded the construction of the Community Concourse in 1963, which "acted as the catalyst to millions of dollars' worth of downtown construction projects" by earning the city the coveted title of "All American City" from the National Municipal League. The new Concourse, located at Broadway Street, served as an unofficial dividing line between the new central business core and the city's array of adult-themed entertainment and counterpublics.[33]

As mid-twentieth-century urban renewal processes began in downtown, municipal, state, and military authorities led an attack on gay bars and institutions.[34] Authorities began targeting downtown gay bars, followed by places near Oceanside and the Camp Pendleton Marine Base. Downtown continued to be a popular destination for servicemen, including US Marines, who were stationed thirty-eight miles away in the city of Oceanside, still within the county of San Diego. Cadets would take a bus from Oceanside that would drop them off at the Armed Forces YMCA on Broadway (see map 3). Many would immediately stop at the 7-Seas Locker Club, where they would rent civilian clothes before enjoying a night out on the town.[35] Military authorities, however, sought to curb these activities. Yet some bars fought back against military policies and jurisdiction. In 1960, the Alcoholic Beverage Control appeals board ruled unconstitutional the military mandate for owners to post "off limits" or "out-of-bounds" signs in the fronts of their buildings.[36] Arnold Payseno and Mary Satterly, the owners of Blue Jacket (750 India Street), had their liquor license suspended because they "refused to post the signs." A letter from the chair of the Armed Forces Disciplinary Control Board, Navy Captain R. C. Young, reported that military authorities asked Payseno to post the signs "because of the patronage of sex deviates at the establishment." In 1962, Payseno and Satterly had another victory when the Third District Court of Appeal in Sacramento ruled that the state cannot mandate that owners post "off limits" signs.[37] Authorities

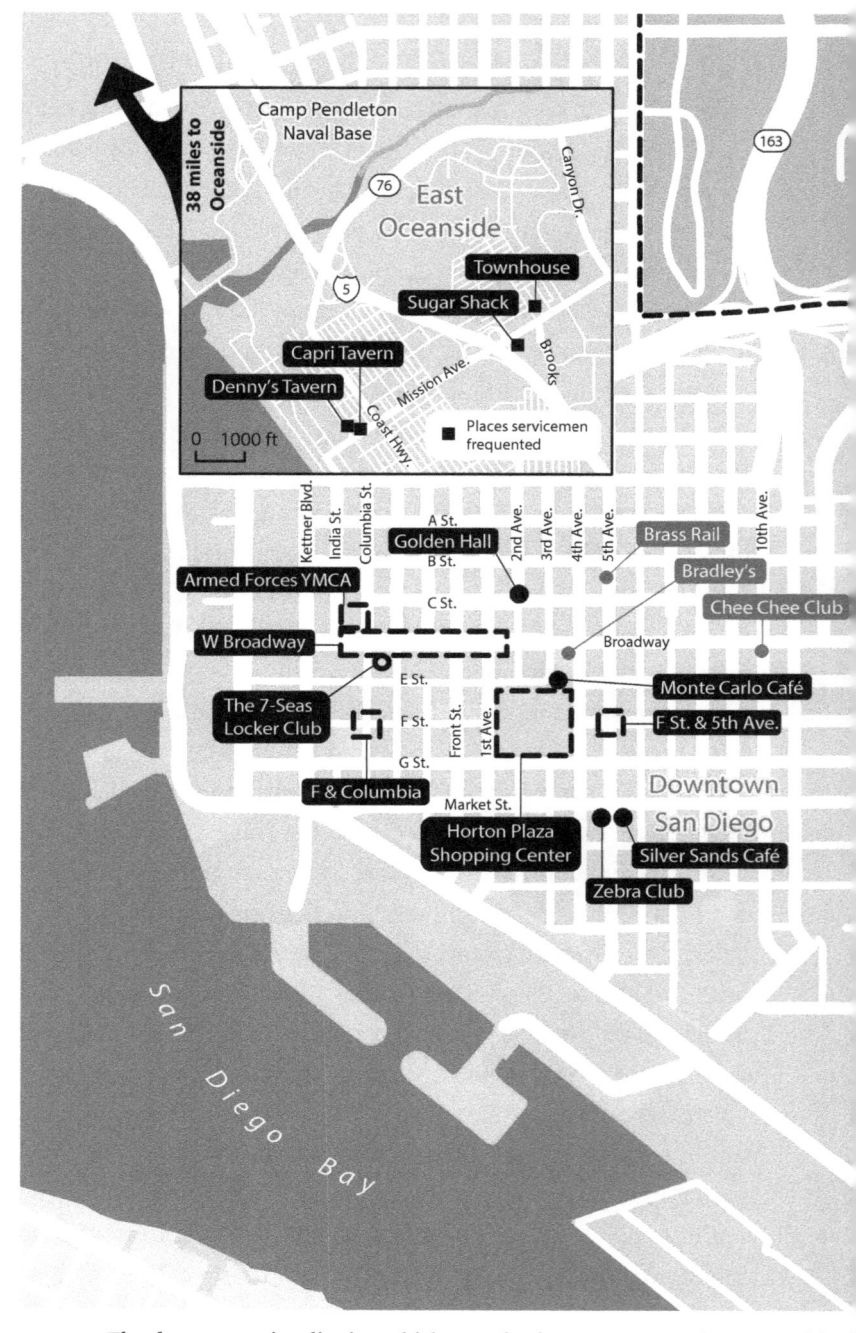

MAP 3. The downtown vice district, which was also known as a popular gay cruising zone from 1965 to the 1990s. The *Damron Guide*, a gay tourist guidebook, played a critical role in the designation of different institutions and geographical spaces as reputable or disreputable. The area was infiltrated with servicemen, who traded in their military

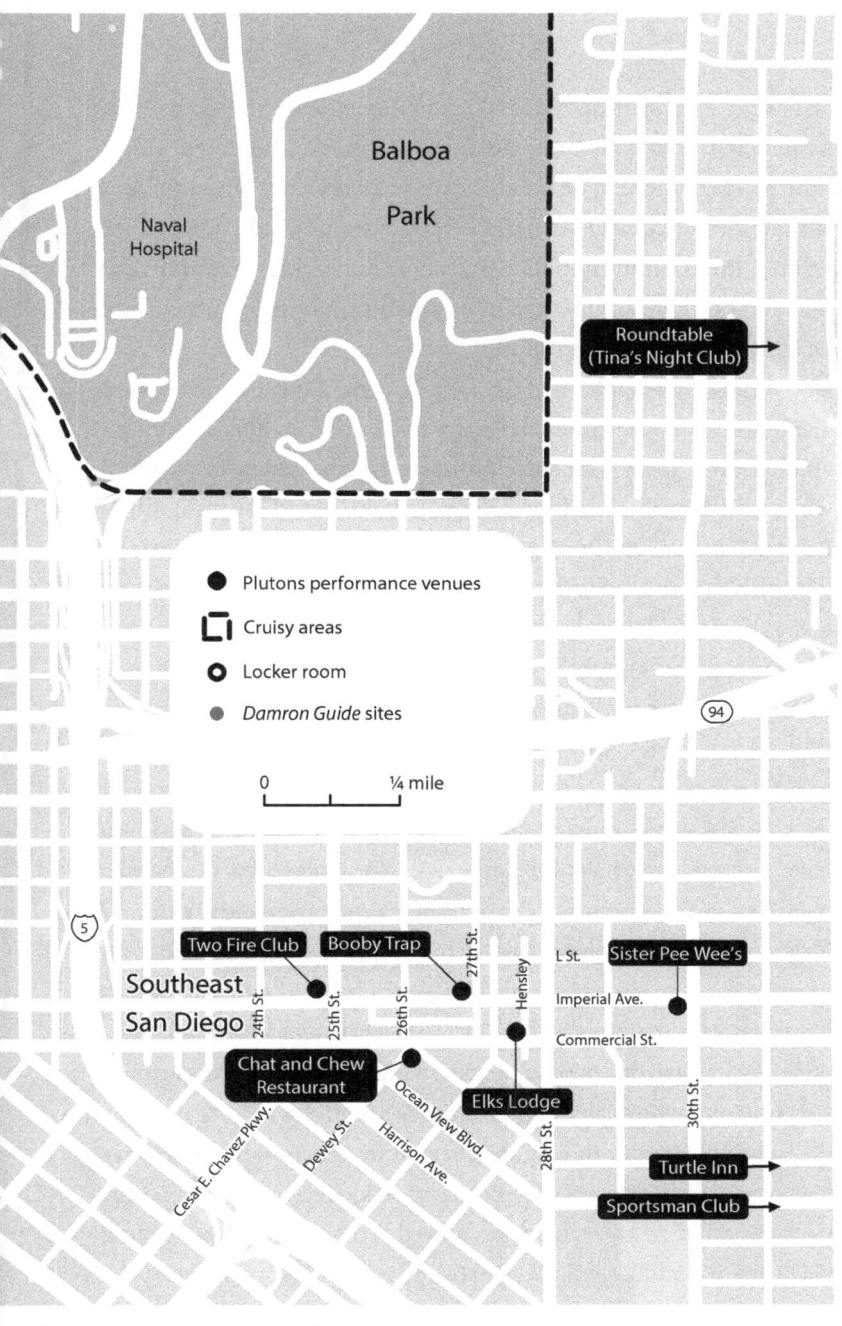

uniforms at locker rooms for civilian clothes before a night out on the town. Gay institutions were racially segregated. The main interlocutor of chapter 3 had a black drag revue, the Plutons, who mostly performed at black institutions in downtown and southeast (Logan) San Diego.

also went after peep shows, and again met pushback. In July 1965, a municipal court ruled that peep-show films confiscated during a raid on a bookstore at 862 Fourth Avenue were "not obscene" and subsequently acquitted two men.[38] Despite some judicial victories against them, military police and local authorities continued to raid and place off-limits signs at gay institutions in downtown and Oceanside well into the 1980s.[39]

Despite this crackdown on bars, in 1964 Silver Sands opened and immediately became a haven for black queens. While Bradley's and the Chee Chee Club were primarily frequented by low-capital white and Latine queens, black queens preferred Silver Sands.[40] Robert Clay, a black business owner, opened Silver Sands Café at 565 Fifth Avenue, near the corner of Fifth and Market—less than one mile from Horton Plaza. Bubba considered Clay's place a downtown "monument": "Everybody [knew] where Silver Sands was, if no other club." Bubba described the atmosphere outside of Clay's institution: "Some of the people would come—we were like a fashion show to them. We was out there! And they would park on the side of the street just to see what we were wearing—what do we have on, what our hair looks like. And we knew a lot the people [who] sat in their cars and party right there in their cars with us." The accidental shooting death of Reginald Eugene Clark on January 8, 1970, a person the *Union* described as "a [black] young man dressed in women's clothing," further reveals how black trans queens were patrons of Silver Sands.[41] Bubba would also hang with Mexican and white queens on the Plaza after Silver Sands closed.

In 1966, a year after Bubba arrived in San Diego, authorities began to selectively arrest downtown street queens using Ordinance 9439 (Section 56.19), which prohibited "in a public place, or in a place open to public view . . . apparel customarily worn by the oppo-

FIGURE 10. A Silver Sands matchbook. Source: author (from eBay).

site sex, with the intent to deceive another person for the purpose of committing an illegal act."[42] San Diego Police claimed that "men posing as women" were targeting sailors by taking them to downtown hotel rooms and robbing them.[43] Bubba and other black queens were victims of this policing while at Silver Sands.

When I moved to San Diego there were problems with the police department. We would go downtown on Fifth and Market, it used to be a club there called Clay's [Silver Sands] . . . that's where we hung out at. But the police would harass us a whole lot. They would come through—take our hair off, take our water titties out. They did all that. Take us to jail, when we went to court we had to go court with just makeup on lookin' like a hot mess. They would parade us down the street and they would chain us together. We would walk from the jail down to the courthouse. We walked right down Horton Plaza looking like a fool.

Despite the perils of being trans queens in public, straight clubs in downtown (and in other parts of the city) offered queens like Bubba opportunities for more pleasurable experiences.

Always did straight clubs. I wore drag for years, that was my life. The straight clubs, I had more attention really. The atmosphere was much different. People would openly talk to you and stuff. It wasn't like 'cause you gay in a straight club you gone be sitting there and people were going to be looking at you funny—it wasn't none of that. They were very friendly.

Though Bubba dressed every day in women's clothing in her hometown of Phoenix, Arizona, San Diego offered her a certain type of cosmopolitanism. Bubba, born in 1945, was considered the "Mother" of her hometown.

I was the first gay person, to my knowledge, that came out. We had the gay people there, but they were in the suit and tie . . . more or less undercover somewhat . . . I wasn't. When I hit the streets I had my hair did, my makeup on, my sissy clothes—that's what it was back then. They named me the "Mother of Phoenix" because I was the first black gay person in that area that was out in the public—dressed, you know, makeup, lipstick, hair, but I was always accepted. I never had a problem being accepted.

Bubba created her own all-black drag club revue, the Plutons, playing "in every little hole," including "raggedy broke-down juke joints." The Plutons performed in predominately straight clubs inside and outside the city. The downtown circuit included the Monte Carlo Club (317 E Street), the Zebra Club (560 Fifth Avenue), Golden Hall (202 C Street), the Douglas Hotel (210 Market Street), and Silver Sands Café (565 Fifth Avenue)—the Douglas Hotel and Silver Sands Café were black-owned. In the southeast, the Plutons performed at go-go bars like the Booby Trap (2674 Imperial Avenue), restaurants such as Chat and Chew Restaurant (317 Dowey Avenue) and Sister Pee-Wee (2971 Imperial Avenue) (see figure 12), fraternal orders like the Elks Lodge (6 Hensley Street) (see figure 13), and bars such as the Turtle Inn (4212 National Avenue) and the Sportsman Club (5079 Logan Avenue).

When Bubba and the Plutons were able to catch rides, they would travel to Oceanside, thirty-eight miles outside of downtown, and party at a place called Townhouse, owned and operated by Charlesetta Reece Allen.[44] According to Bubba, Townhouse was the "only club [in Oceanside] with a whole lotta black faces." Like many working drag queens, Bubba would also perform sex work after the show. In Oceanside, for example, she would "take dates" to a hotel or they would go underneath bleachers near the beach. Although Bubba and the Plutons performed throughout the city, downtown remained the central place for sex-working queens,

FIGURE 11. Arola Davis in dance outfit and boots. Davis was possibly a dancer at the racially restricted go-go clubs in southeast San Diego, such as the Booby Trap. Source: San Diego History Center.

since it was where the militarized sex tourism market was most concentrated and saturated. Straight audiences learned important lessons about gender, and many for the first time, since drag-queen performances attracted people who might not otherwise have been introduced to gay politics. Drag queens disrupted gender respect-

FIGURE 12. Sister Pee Wee's Soul Food, 2971 Imperial Avenue. Source: Yelp.

ability by switching back and forth between performing as a woman and as a man, to demonstrate the construction of a binary gender system. But as Verta Taylor and Leila J. Rupp argue in "Learning from Drag Queens," "there is more going on [in drag performances] than just mimicking traditional female beauty."[45] The places Bubba performed were for mostly non-exclusive straight bars catering to black working-class servicemen who sometimes had queer liaisons with black queens.

Bubba's unapologetic public gender performance deviated from the more respectable drag queens, often called "female impersonators." Although female impersonators were sometimes also categorized as queens, performing as the latter was usually considered unskilled and less-valued work done by low-capital people without proper tutelage. As Nan Boyd notes, female impersonators were generally regarded as respectable: "whether drag queens imitated female impersonators on the streets or female impersonators transported queer style and subjectivity to the stage, female impersonators signified public respectability for drag queens."[46] Conversely, "street drag," according to Susan Stryker, was the most disreputable: "street drag was almost universally

FIGURE 13. Clementine McDuff
Elks Lodge #598, Hensley Street.
Source: Facebook.

condemned and largely relegated to territories coextensive with prostitution, hustling, and other economically marginalized activities."[47] Bernie Michels, in his dissertation at San Diego State University, defined a female impersonator as "a male professional entertainer who attires himself, takes on the mannerism, and performs in the role of a woman; may even perform in either a nightclub or a theater. The fact of being a professional performer distinguishes a female impersonator from a drag queen." He defined a drag queen as "a man, other than a professional performer, who is dressed in women's attire."[48]

Street-involved drag queens, who wore women's clothes inside and outside clubs, were prohibited from employment as female impersonators in higher-paying gay institutions. The Show Biz Supper Club in Hillcrest, considered the first reputable drag revue in San Diego, prohibited performers from wearing feminine clothes or drag outside of the club, in order to avoid offending their straight patrons or catching the attention of vice cops.[49] Norman Braxton, a US Navy servicemember from Pasadena, moved to San Diego in 1967 and became the first black performer at Show Biz. He explained in a documentary, "We weren't allowed to go out in public as a female impersonator. You were coming as a gentleman, you'd put your makeup on, and then do your show. When the show was over, you took your wig off. We had a uniform that we wore and then we would mingle with the crowd. There was no one there in the crowd with wigs on and that type of thing because most times we had mostly a straight crowd audience and they would get confused." He continued, "We weren't allowed to have breasts or overexaggerate [playing a woman]. As long as we looked like the character we did and that we could be a male, we had the job." Though a self-proclaimed "older queen," Braxton still limited his gender transgression to the stage: "I'm an entertainer, I don't wear women's attire all the time. I only do it when I'm asked to perform."[50]

While Bubba relied on sex work and performing drag to survive, she also expressed how it nourished her in other ways: "It wasn't a whole lot of money. I think we did it for satisfaction, for ourselves." The queer kinship between straight-identified men (many of whom were working class) and queens was something that was meaningful and beneficial to Bubba. Besides the satisfaction Bubba received from sex with straight men, being in the life also enabled non-gay-identified sailors to develop a relationship with her. These chosen family members and kinship networks were based on mutual reciprocity.

A ship coming in and a ship coming out. A lot of fresh mens . . . just left home. No sense of knowledge. Some got mixed in with the wrong crowd and some didn't. All of them I didn't fool with. Some of them were my sons—they would call me "mom." If you have a party, you have a house full of sailors. Even if you would go out at night—that was our thing . . . to go find somebody. But you know, everybody didn't mess around.

It's all in how you treat people. And I treated them with respect. And I didn't try to force me on them. If you want to do it, we cool, if you don't, I'm cool with that. I can still be your friend. And a lot of them would come and talk to me. They were away from home and they want to go AWOL. Just lost . . . I talked to a lot of them. When they went overseas, they would send me all kinds of stuff back. Just me being nice to them.

They would also defend her when she faced harassment: "The guys that know me and that I click with, not on nothing sex based, just being a real tight friend. If one of their homeboys said some real negative things concerning me, I love it, because they would stop them real quick and put them in their place . . . they looked after me like family." Getting attention from straight men was part of the thrill of cruising and finding dates, but another outcome was forging black kinship.

However, the intermingling of gay-identified men with straight non-gay-identified men was seen as counterproductive by safe space activists in the early 1970s. Though cruising, in which non-gay-identified men would discreetly seek out other men for casual sex, happened in all parts of the city, sex-working queens in downtown bars and Horton Plaza were especially targeted by safe space activists.[51] Though most gay men congregated and created community through the local bar scene, both Jessop and Michels saw gay bars as detriments to gay liberation, specifically due to the culture of cruising. The new gay modernity centered on visibility and "coming out" of the closet.[52] In his master's thesis for the school of social work, Michels described how "at least half [of the city's gay scenes] involve gay men cruising men with non-gay self-identities."[53] He blamed gay men for "coaxing" men who were "sexually frustrated, and lonely," at hustler bars.[54] For Michels, cruising was dangerous and perpetuated violence against gay people, as "very often the beatings and murders are committed by those with non-gay identity and usually they take place as a result of extreme guilt feeling after the participants have engaged in sex." Similarly, for Jessop the "darkness of dingy gay bars [was a] cocoon of safety" for gay people who should otherwise be "fighting for their [gay] rights."[55] Jessop would often proclaim, "if you don't stand up for yourself, nobody else will," and try to convince people at the bar of the "benefits of coming out."[56] Michels also expressed how other gay people, including bar owners, saw him and Jessop as a "threat" because they were so "visible [and] outspoken."[57] According to Jessop, the bar crowd was afraid that homophiles and gay liberationists would "bring the wrath of society down on [them]."[58]

For assistance in differentiating between reputable and disreputable bars, white middle-class gay men used gay travel guides—usually *Bob Damron's Address Book*.[59] Like the *Negro Motorist Green Book* (1936–1966), which designated businesses that accommodated black patrons in the Jim Crow US South, the *Damron Address Book* (1965–2021) was a travel guide that located gay-friendly businesses in the US. These pocket-sized guides were deemed "the essential guide to the United States and Canada" and a resource that "no gay man preparing for a business trip or a holiday should be without."[60] The places in the guides were accompanied by a letter-based classification system indicating the demographic of the establishment. The 1965 guide had twelve "explanations of listings": Very Popular (*); Coffee (C); Dancing (D); G (Girls, but rarely exclusive); Hotel (H); Mixed, and/or tourists (M); Private (P); Pretty Elegant (PE);

Restaurant (R); RT (Rugged, often commercial); Shows (S); and, S-M (Some motorcycles).[61] Although other directories such as the *International Guild Guides* attempted to do the same thing, the *Damron Address Books* were more prominent and respected.

Yet as historians Amanda Regan and Eric Gonzaba contend, these guides were not only representative of difference but also *produced* difference. The guides are especially useful in "examin[ing] historical racial attitudes in LGBT communities."[62] For the categories, the only explicit mention of race involved places mostly frequented by black people. Yet, more physically geographic categorizations, such as RT (Rugged, often commercial), AYOR ("At Your Own Risk"), and a later redefinition of RT (raunchy types—downtown type places—often hustlers), also had racial and classed-based undertones. The category B, "black predominate" (1970) and later "blacks frequent" (1972), indicated to the mostly white male readers the racial demographic of the place—which could have been interpreted as a caution to certain readers or a way for those who fetishized black men to have an insight as to their whereabouts.[63] RT stood for "rugged, often commercial" in the inaugural guide and then was changed to "raunchy types—downtown type places—often hustlers" in 1972.[64] AYOR, which stood for "At Your Own Risk," was added in 1977.[65] These place-specific categorizations—that is, downtown—were "designations of safety concerns" in 1977.[66] The Damron Guides linked sex workers (hustlers) and "downtown types" (likely people who live in the inner city), who were some of the most marginalized queers, to places of vice, crime, and deviance. In the 1970s, since the San Diego black gay community was relatively small, the guidebooks never used "B"; however, the listings still indicated the places they likely congregated at—which were in downtown San Diego, especially Horton Plaza.

Damron's Address Book never included Silver Sands, the popular black bar, but listed other nearby disreputable bars and places in Horton Plaza, including cruising areas. While Bradley's (303 Plaza) and the Chee Chee Club (959 Broadway) were consistently categorized as RT (Raunchy Type) or PT (Sleazy), the greater Horton Plaza area was categorized as a popular cruising area throughout the mid- to late twentieth century. While Show Biz Supper Club was consistently rated as R* from its inception in 1970—indicating a popular restaurant for gays—downtown bars were mostly categorized as its antithesis. According to activist and politician Nicole Murray-Ramirez, Bradley's "was where all the hustlers went, all the sailors went."[67] Bradley's is even mentioned in Bérubé's *Coming Out under Fire*, where it is described as one of the many institutions located in the Tenderloin areas, "the sailor bar and servicemen's bars—which middle-class GIs called 'rough' bars—that catered to enlisted men of many races, gay civilians, and 'trade.'"[68] The guides listed "Broadway—from Horton Plaza to the Armed Services" as a cruisy area throughout the '70s to '90s.[69] The YMCA was also listed as a cruisy area up until the 1970s, until military authorities were able to curb some of the action. The Brass Rail, which is now considered the longest-operating gay bar in the city, was designated as a cruisy area in 1977–1979 and categorized as RT in 1968.[70] Starting in 2005, the Damron Guide stopped listing San Diego cruisy areas "because the SDPD aggressively polices these areas," which might have meant that police were also using the guides to set up stings.[71]

While other places, such as Balboa Park, were known as cruising areas, safe space activists were less sympathetic to the policing of queer culture in downtown. The editors of *The Prodigal*, a radical periodical published by the gay-affirming MCCSD, ran a column in the May 1972 issue about the policing of "plaza drag queens." The column, written by Alan Smith, begins with him discussing his role as a guest panelist for a graduate sociology class at San Diego State University. The other panelists included several San Diego vice officers. Smith specifically asked officers about Ordinance 9439, outlawing cross-dressing, and "the plaza drag queens": "These officers, speaking only for themselves and not speaking for the department (as they were very careful to point out) stated that it was not their policy to intimidate or harass person[s] dressed in clothing of the opposite sex unless they were committing a crime or appeared to be endangering themselves or others."[72]

The officers explained that they were most interested in "transvestites being 'trick rolled,'" or a trick that "might get rolled by the transvestite." Smith decided to give the vice cops the "benefit of the doubt that they were speaking candidly," even positing that "they were a more enlightened and selective cross section of the San Diego Police force than the ordinary cop" because they took time to speak to students. In the same column, Smith discussed his presence in a municipal court where a "provocative black female with a deep bass voice" was being arraigned on charges of prostitution before the honorable Douglas R. Woodworth. Smith described Woodworth as an "enlightened and compassionate jurist" for using gender-affirming pronouns when speaking to the defendant, and for having suspended her sentence—but encouraging her to "find an honest way to make a living." Smith concluded the column by advising readers to keep a copy of Section 56.19 of the ordinance so that "hopefully [gay men and women] can point out to [an officer] that [they] are not deceiving another person for the purpose of committing an unlawful act."[73]

The surveillance and arrests were heightened when Mayor Pete Wilson finally signed off on the Horton Plaza Redevelopment Plan after the Republican National Convention, which was initially scheduled to be held in San Diego, pulled out three weeks before its scheduled start date after Richard Nixon's financial contribution to the city came under fire. In an attempt to save face, Wilson named the week of August 21, 1972, the proposed week of the convention, as "'America's Finest City' Week."[74] Even though most San Diegans were against the convention, Wilson hoped it would shore up new investments in the city. The US military—the city's bread and butter—was threatening to leave town, since it was becoming more invested in research and intelligence gathering than manufacturing.[75] In 1974 the San Diego City Council hired urban planners Kevin Lynch and Donald Appleyard to make a report on the downtown area. Though Lynch and Appleyard said the area should feature a diversity of activities and representations of downtown life, they also warned the council of how the overuse of private interests would be damaging: "[The] center of the city [is a] place that people identify with, sharing reflected glory or shame, depending on their quality. People are proud of cities whose unique centers present a clear image to themselves and to visitors. . . . It will be unfortunate if the renewal program banishes the liveliness and substitutes for it an empty space ringed by bank fronts . . . thus the city becomes a collection of private islands, which ignore each other and ignore the general public."[76] The ethical concerns voiced by Lynch and Appleyard foreshadowed the urban development process in San Diego that eventually displaced long-term residents of the downtown area.

In 1975, San Diego established the Centre City Development Corporation (CCDC), a public/private partnership that would negotiate with downtown San Diego's private businesses to "implement property acquisition, relocation, clearance, public improvements, public facilities, public financing, and design review of all private improvements in the downtown's redevelopment area."[77] The CCDC argued that downtown San Diego's blight could be blamed on how its "tax base was deteriorated, its adult entertainment uses proliferated, most of its residents occupied single rooms in old hotels, its street people abounded, and its overall appearance south of Broadway was one of acute physical decline."[78] According to the CCDC this created a "major problem," and the only solution was to work with the private sector to create numerous projects to promote "major retail, restaurants, festival retail, residential, office, convention facilities, hotels, and cultural and recreational uses."[79] The four major redevelopment areas were the Columbia District for the financial center, Horton Plaza for the retail mall, the Maria for private residences, and the Gaslamp Quarter for cultural/historical/commercial.

Many downtown business owners welcomed both the development of downtown and the criminalization of certain residents. Newspapers in San Diego and Los Angeles reported on the "positive" aspects of the development. The editors of the *San Diego Union* and *Los Angeles Times* agreed with the Gaslamp Project promoters by citing how the Victorian themes would give citizens "a sense of history," in stark contrast to the "cheap hotels, X-rated movie houses and porno parlors" that were in proliferation in the current "red-light" downtown area.[80] The *San Diego Tribune* characterized the cleanup of downtown San Diego as an act of war to produce safe zones:

> Putting the Gaslamp Quarter on the map, says one very interested party, is not so much a civic improvement program as it is like the war in Vietnam. But that war took place in the steaming jungles

and rice paddies of a far-off continent, the shock troops of the Gaslamp for their fighting in the mean streets of Broadway, right in their own back yard. Here the enemy is not the Viet Cong but the decades of official neglect and inhabitants' abuse that have left what was once San Diego's heart an open sore of decay. . . .

"We're building 'safe zones' the same way they did in Vietnam," says tax lawyer and booster Jim Schneider, who owns the Keating Building at the corner of Fifth Avenue and F Street. "The Gaslamp is something like Vietnam—though I've never been there—and we have to secure areas so it is safe for the people to walk in them and shop in them. If you were in the jungles in Vietnam you'd have had to look behind you all the time in case somebody was creeping up on you. It's kind of that way still in some areas of the Gaslamp. But with every new project that's going up, we are creating more safe areas."[81]

This quote suggests that there are people who are in need of protection and others who are the perpetrators of violence. The link between war zones and communities of color is not a coincidence, but represents an ongoing tension of characterizing the border town of San Diego as a patriotic city in an attempt to distance it from the always already lawless Tijuana, Mexico. In "Reinventing Downtown San Diego: A Spatial and Cultural Analysis of the Gaslamp Quarter," Jordan Ervin details the measures the city took to remove disreputables from the downtown area. In order to ensure that properties conformed to the Victorian-themed cultural identity, the historic board restricted the size of the buildings along with regulating the colors, fonts, and lighting of signs. The design of "transient-proof" garbage cans and the removal of city benches further solidified the cityscape as a space for middle/upper-middle-class residents and tourists. Additionally, public parks were closed at night in order to prevent the homeless from sleeping there. As public transportation between the city and suburban areas was established, bus stops and benches within the Gaslamp area were removed. Furthermore, in order for police presence to not be considered a form of "heavy-handedness," police officers patrolled the area by horse and foot, sometimes blending into shopping crowds or posting on rooftops. In addition to police presence, businesses would also contract private security. Police vice squads would often raid long-established businesses and threaten customers and business owners suspected of violating zoning ordinances. The renovation also limited the type of businesses allowed in the area. Specifically, zoning ordinances disallowed businesses such as adult entertainment as well as charitable organizations that provided food and lodging for the unhoused/low income.[82]

Since gay bars were being left out of the new downtown development, several bars agreed to partner with Michels and Jessop to fundraise for a brick-and-mortar location for the Gay Center for Social Services—which was also a strategic way to stay connected with their gay clientele. Diablo's, Bee Jay's, the Barbary Coast, the Club, the Brass Rail, Mary Hang-Up, Jerry's Hole, and the Show Biz Supper Club agreed to create a show that would take place four times every year. An article in *The Prodigal* explained: "Actually it will be more than a show. Not only will there be a stage production, but evening-long dances with live music will be offered. Costumes will be encouraged and there will be prizes. There will be a raffle— even an auction of valuable products."[83] The owners "pledge[d] to give from their own tills any amount not raised by the regular events—up to an agreed-upon basic budget for the Gay Center." Their first event, a Carnivale at the Unicorn Theatre on February 1,

1973, was a success according to Michels, raising over $3,000.[84] The first location of the Center was at 2250 B Street, and it eventually moved to another location in 1980—by then Hillcrest was solidified as a gay neighborhood.

Unlike the downtown area, safe space activists were able to claim space in Hillcrest and redevelop the area, which also encouraged the redevelopment of surrounding neighborhoods. Within three decades, the demographics of Hillcrest changed significantly—from a diverse working-class and older community to a mostly white male middle-class demographic. Dillinger's "Hillcrest: From Haven to Home" details the rise of a gay constituency in the neighborhood. During the 1920s and 1930s, Hillcrest was considered a "thriving" area with a "diverse population," which consisted of reasonably priced housing for families and single persons near the downtown area. By the 1960s, it was predominately populated by seniors and was becoming a densely populated area. However, the development of the Mission Valley shopping center impacted the area's previously prosperous commercial businesses. During the 1970s, Hillcrest suffered economically, which affected quality in housing and political representation. It was known as an area of "elderly and low-income residents living in run-down housing"; however, the high percentage of seniors indicated that the area was about to "undergo a major demographic change." The major changes were race and age. Consequentially, the new gay and lesbian residents were mostly white men under the age of forty-five, according to exit-poll results in 1992 and statements by San Diego homophile group leaders during the 1970s. The "gay age bracket," ages twenty-five to forty-four, increased by 120 percent between 1970 and 1990—while the population over forty-five dropped down to 27 percent, after once accounting for 45 percent of Hillcrest's residents. The decline in the elderly population and the increase of the "gay age bracket" was seen as a "positive indicator" for gays and lesbians in Hillcrest. White males between the ages of twenty-five to forty-four in Hillcrest exceeded San Diego's average by 19 percent. Additionally, the low percentage of legally married couples indicated that the "gay age bracket" impacted the area. There was also an increase in the presence of lesbians in the area, which also ultimately surpassed San Diego's average by 1990. Additionally, Balboa Park was a popular cruising space for gay/lesbian sociality and encouraged the designation of the Hillcrest area as the central place for gays and lesbians in San Diego. The revitalization of Hillcrest, once considered a "dormant and isolated neighborhood," influenced the development of surrounding areas such as University Heights, Mission Hills, Normal Heights, and North Park.[85]

Yet Bubba still preferred black and mixed-raced working-class institutions, considered disreputable spaces by safe space activists, instead of the predominately white middle-class gay institutions that were forming in Hillcrest. She did visit some of the Hillcrest bars but felt they were not hospitable to her or her friends.

> I've been to some of the [Hillcrest gay] clubs every once in a while . . . me and my friends, we would go to the club. At the time when I went to the club, the gay clubs, they had their own little cliques. If you don't know them it's no coming "my name is so and so . . ." They don't do that . . . at that time, I don't know how they do now. If you didn't know nobody in that club, you'd just be sitting there. And sometimes I would do it just to see how open they would be to another gay person. If they didn't know you, you didn't know somebody in that clique, you'd be sitting at the bar by yourself or the table by yourself.

There was an obvious race and class division between the downtown scene and Hillcrest.

Yet the racial and class divisions were not only among middle-class gay activists but also even among other poor and housing-precarious people in downtown residential hotels. Since San Diego opposed government aid to build federal housing structures in the city, downtown's single-room occupancies (SROs) provided low-capital folks, including servicemen, with the most affordable short- and long-term housing in the city.[86] Divisions between black and white (mostly elderly) single-room occupants were vividly illustrated by anthropologist Kevin J. Eckert in *Unseen Elderly: A Study of Marginally Subsistent Hotel Dwellers* (1980). Eckert's own description of those who lived south of Broadway (the Tenderloin district) and north of Broadway (mostly white occupants) is quite telling: "outsiders—and many of the media—fail to distinguish between the aged residents and other poor people of the area and those who are hiding something."[87] He distinguishes between different SROs, including the Wells Fargo and Ballentine hotels, which housed mostly permanent residents and women; the Balboa Hotel, which was considered middle-class; and lower-rent occupancies like the General Lee.[88] These SROs provided communal support and were often an alternative to nursing homes for many of the occupants. Yet for many, the area was becoming a "less desirable place . . . [due to] prostitution, more alcoholism, and more minorities." Operators and tenants would "size up customers," admitting how "age, hair style, clothing, and race are immediate factors of importance."[89] The preferred demographic was "white military men." Though some black men and women resided in predominately white residential hotels, Eckert's interlocutors characterized most black people as undesirables in the urban sex trade: "younger black men are usually pimps who rent rooms for themselves and their wives." While most tenants, including low-capital non-English-speaking Mexican residents, were offered rooms at reduced rates, black guests were routinely charged full price, along with an extra fee for guests.[90] Some occupants even refused to patronize certain businesses: "some of the older tenants of the Ballentine are reluctant to use one of the Chinese restaurants because it borders on the 'black' area of the downtown."[91] The residents' attempts to distance themselves from their black disreputable neighbors were futile—by the 1980s most of their housing was eventually slated for demolition, leaving many unhoused.

Despite the closure of residential hotels, public restrooms, missionaries, and the main downtown bus stop from Horton Plaza, along with the removal of park benches, most of downtown's disreputable communities continued to defiantly remain.[92] As Ervin concludes in "Reinventing Downtown San Diego: A Spatial and Cultural Analysis of the Gaslamp Quarter," "The social problems that plagued the project area merely shifted to other areas of the city. Developers did not wish to genuinely address these issues, but rather sought to change the image of downtown by removing their visibility from the project areas. As a result, visitors could ignore negative elements of reality as they experienced a new downtown that appeared to lack any problems."[93] Even with the construction of Horton Plaza Shopping Center in 1985, the area continued to be a popular place for queer sex-working people. In the 1990 edition of the Damron guide, the Horton Plaza Shopping Center continued to be labeled as a "cruisy area," with the additional descriptor "Queens for Days!"[94] Sex work and other forms of disreputability continued to be visible—certainly a form of resistance against speculative investors, suburban tourists, and new business owners.

Yet Bubba, then a 40-year-old queen, was no longer interested in the Horton Plaza stroll. When she came back to San Diego in the late 1980s, after an extended trip back to her hometown of Phoenix, the glory days of her downtown stomping grounds were over. "The downtown area kinda faded away . . . they tore everything down and built it all the way up new. What they did to the black owners—they raised the rent so high that they had no other choice but to move out. Clay's—it killed him when they did him like that—he had been down there so many years." After twenty-seven years on Fifth and Market, now part of the Gaslamp Quarter redevelopment, Clay was forced to close his business in 1992. The Gaslamp Quarter Merchants Association failed to support his negotiation for a three-year lease to keep his rent consistent. The *Union* described Clay, the only black restaurant-bar owner left in downtown, as a "stubborn dinosaur."[95] Desegregation led to the closure of many bars and clubs in southeast San Diego. Bubba mentioned how Tina's nightclub (formerly Roundtable) was the last popular black bar left in Southeast (see figure 14). As the only remaining black bar, it was often overcrowded and led to many noise complaints, which eventually led to its closure.[96] Bubba was also disappointed in the new visibility politics and new spatial ordering of gay life and culture in the city. For her, gay life was no longer "mysterious," it was "so mainstream now"—"everything [gay] has gone to Hillcrest." While she said that it was good that gays were "getting rights," "gay was no longer on its own shelf."

By the 1990s, Hillcrest had a sizable gay constituency—however, Michels and Jessop were no longer active in local politics.

FIGURE 14. Tina's Night Club, 1956 Fifty-Fourth Street. Source: Yelp.

Both men found it difficult to work with each other. Michels described Jessop as "difficult." "[He] was lonely, so this [political organizing] was his life . . . when things didn't go his way, he would get terribly frustrated . . . he'd pull away." "There was a rivalry between the two of us." After a very successful fundraiser in 1973, Michels resigned, saying that he was "burned out" along with having disagreements with the lesbian cofounders of the Center. Jessop would often come to the defense of those who felt marginalized at the Center. His untimely death in 1990, due to complications from AIDS, heavily impacted leftist gay politics in the city. As I will examine further in chapter 4, issues around gender, race, and class continued to plague the Center, with black feminists leading the charge against racism there in the late 1980s.[97]

The four-decade urban redevelopment processes in downtown worked in tandem with processes of dispossession in other parts of the city, mainly through racial covenants, which impacted both black and Latine residents in San Diego.[98] The city was displacing black residents not only in downtown but also in areas where many black people attempted to resettle. It was as if the state was trying to push out black people altogether. Though racially restrictive covenants were federally outlawed in 1948, the practice was still widely used by white owners. Additionally, the consequences of these covenants were already cemented into the geography—with neighborhoods that were already racially segregated and white homeowners who were committed to maintaining the color line. By the 1960s, state authorities and real estate agents were fighting to uphold discriminatory housing practices in San Diego. In 1964, Dr. Martin Luther King Jr. visited San Diego to mobilize voters against the passage of Prop 14, a housing initiative that sought to overturn the 1963 Rumford Housing Act.[99] The Rumford Housing Act prohibited owners, landlords, or agents from discriminating against ethnic and racial minorities, a pervasive practice prior to 1963. It was at the El Cortez Sky Room, a gay bar, where California Real Estate Association representatives convened to decide whether they would sponsor Proposition 14.[100]

As a result of racial covenants, Logan Heights was one of the few places where black and Latine residents were able to own property.[101] The greater Logan area had undergone many changes since its incorporation and subsequent annexation to the city of San Diego. After World War II, white property owners left the area in favor of other nearby neighborhoods, such as Mission Hills, Kensington, and East San Diego. Due to racist land-use and zoning policies, such as redlining and gerrymandering, along with federal disinvestment, working-class communities had an overabundance of vacant commercial storefront spaces. Business owners, including religious leaders, seized on this opportunity to use these spaces for a variety of business endeavors and projects. In the next section, I will demonstrate how black people pushed back against these disinvestments by creatively making place for marginalized community members. The use of Bubba's life history is again integral to the story—as she transitioned from a sex worker in the Tenderloin to a more conservative black religious life. What is most critical is that regardless of her gender or gender performance, black people (including cisgender male leaders) made room for her in the community—something safe space activists were vehemently opposed to doing.

Black Queer Storefront Masonic Theology

Some of the remaining brick-and-mortar black institutions that have survived processes of development in San Diego are black fraternal orders. Since these organizations are exempt from federal income tax and operate under a lodge system, they can save a substantial amount of money that can then be redirected toward their members, along with lower operational costs needed for their facilities. These racially segregated secret societies parallel other white civic societies like the Elks, Masons, Odd Fellows, and Knights of Pythias, and other "independent orders." As Joe W. Trotter explains, "The growth of black fraternal associations is closely intertwined with the larger history of voluntary associations in American society," beginning in the 1800s.[102] In "Duty to the Race: African American Fraternal Orders and the Legal Defense of the Right to Organize," Ariane Liazos and Marshall Ganz contend that "after the loss of voting rights and the subsequent disintegration of the Republican Party in the South, fraternal orders and churches remained as the only large-scale, translocal organizations available to most black people."[103] Yet their existence was threatened by white civic societies. In their examination of early twentieth-century legal cases, Liazos and Ganz demonstrate how white fraternal orders "challenged the legal status of black parallel orders through both civil and criminal means."[104] The NAACP took up many of these cases, leaving a judicial archive of resistance. Yet not only have US black fraternal orders been understudied, but prominent intellectuals within (and outside) the field of black studies have also claimed that they are not a worthy object of scholarly attention—which Trotter argues has "had profound implications for the study of black fraternal orders."[105]

The queerness of these institutions, particularly their pageantry and rituals, came under attack by E. Franklin Frazier and Gunnar Myrdal, for example. Trotter argues that "until, recently, historians shared certain stereotypes of fraternal orders as unrealistic ventures into fantasy due to their exotic rituals and regalia."[106] In their analysis of fraternal culture, Bayliss J. Camp and Orit Kent state that the "excitement, drama, and 'meaningfulness' of an order's rituals were important parts of what attracted potential recruits."[107] Fraternal initiations are akin to theatrical productions "complete with spoken lines, costumes, set and prop suggestions, and directions for movement." More importantly, Camp and Kent note how "the explicitness of the moral messages contained in the initiation lectures and dramas also made the content analysis relatively straightforward," which allowed the practice to be accessible to working-class men.[108] These rituals enabled men to form a sense of brotherhood, which some note was at the expense of black women—who were excluded from these ceremonies. Women's orders like the Daughter Elks, which served as "auxiliaries" to the mens' orders, did not inherently "attempt to inculcate strong bonds between female members." However, as Camp and Kent's research reveals, some black female auxiliaries exercised "more active, autonomous, protofeminist models."[109] Though the fraternal rituals were represented by prominent intellectuals as deviant and even embarrassing, they still adhered to hierarchy and gender—these conditions still enabled a former sex-working black queen to be included in a ritualized performance—a Sunday Baptist church service—when the space converted to a storefront church.

My concept of black queer storefront masonic theology derives from the synergy I experienced at Greater Johnson's current home at Fidelity Lodge No. 10.[110] The more expansive mutual-benefit spatial practices that the space enabled are what I discovered was the most urgent and immediate usage it offered during my two brief visits to Fidelity Lodge No. 10 on two separate weekends in April of 2014 and 2017. While Fidelity is technically not a storefront church, I argue that the space is transformed into one on Sundays. When Bubba joined Greater Johnson in 1991, it was a storefront church at 2646 Imperial Avenue in Logan. In 2007, it was home to Rose of Sharon Missionary Baptist Church. As of 2022, it continues to be a storefront church, now Iglesia Cristiana Camino al Cielo. The emergence of storefront churches began during the Great Migration, as black southerners began to travel to the North and to a lesser extent the US West for a better life and economic opportunities. Southern migrants were unlikely to join established churches and instead created spaces to sustain their own Southern style of religious congregation. Usually between 500 and 1,000 square feet, these places cultivated a more intimate experience for churchgoers.[111] On the other hand, the lodge was constituted on July 21, 1903, making it the city's first and oldest operating black fraternal order.[112] The lodge bought its current building in 1956 and has since regularly held organizational meetings there on the first and third

FIGURE 15. African American men seated at tables in a Masonic hall in about 1900. Possibly a meeting of Prince Hall Lodge Fidelity #10. Source: San Diego History Center.

Friday of each month. The space operates as a rentable commercial space from 1:00 p.m. to midnight seven days a week, except 5:00 to 11:00 p.m. each second Wednesday. The organization also offers tables and chairs, a full-time attendant, a prep kitchen, a "lighted antique bar," a fully equipped DJ booth and PA system, and a disco lighting system. Event rental was $600 and required online booking. On Sundays, however, the space was converted to a sacred place. Reverend Anderson, Bubba's pastor, had rented out the space every Sunday for church services since 2010.

Bubba had been urging me, and my partner at that time, to visit her church. As a non-religious agnostic person, I was not particularly excited about visiting a church. Very problematically, I

FIGURE 16. Members of Fidelity Lodge 10, 3007 Logan Avenue. Source: Facebook.

thought that Bubba's religious life was less important juxtaposed to being a young defiant sex worker. How could this bold, outspoken and defiant queen want to simmer down for the Lord?, I thought. I mistakenly and inaccurately assumed a certain a type of feminist politics, that I often critiqued in the classrooms where I taught. Why did I assume that being religious was antithetical to a feminist ethics? Why did I assume that just because Bubba was now religious, she had become placated and passive? Only through an actual engagement with these spaces was I able to understand my own biases. This space was the most important part of Bubba's life story because her gender performance queered the space in the most exhilarating ways.

On a Saturday night in April of 2014, I attended the birthday party of a friend, Donisha Hughes, at Fidelity. I was unaware that it was being held at a fraternal order; I assumed it would be at a club or a house. I was only given an address. Since I did not initially see this as a potential field site, the archiving of this event on YouTube fills in information that I could not remember. For the birthday celebration, about sixty to eighty people were in attendance throughout the night. I met Hughes's cousins, mother, and close friends. There was an assortment of differently aged folk there, from teenagers to elders. Some guests were dressed in their "Sunday best" while others were more casual—with some coming directly from work. When guests entered, they took pictures in front of a poster reading "Celebrate Donisha—'Living Life Like It's Golden.'" Folks got up and did the two-step shuffle and the cha-cha slide while attaching dollar bills to Hughes's blouse. In one area, a buffet table had food such as chicken wings, spaghetti, and macaroni and cheese—African American cuisine staples. Hughes hired a DJ who played R&B tunes all night. Some people stayed the entire time, and some just came to make an appearance and congratulate her, maybe have a drink, and then take a plate to go.[113]

Almost exactly three years later, in 2017, I visited the Fidelity again, but not for a party—for church. I had come to San Diego after accepting a tenure-track position at the University of Missouri. The day I was scheduled to fly out, I reluctantly woke up so I could follow through on the promise I had made Bubba to attend her church. Just like for Hughes's party, I had no idea where I was going—I only had an address. I hurried up, put on what I considered church-appropriate clothing—a skirt and blouse—put the address into whatever app we were using for GPS back in 2017, and was on my way. When I pulled up to the address, I was confused and immediately had déjà vu. "Was this not the same place I went to last time I was in San Diego?" I thought. I got out of the car and stood outside the building bewildered, thinking I had mixed up the address. I texted Bubba to confirm that this was the correct location. To my relief, I heard her voice—"You at the right place!" She smiled and waved at me from the entrance door. She had the biggest smile on her face—I finally came to her church. She was absolutely delighted. We embraced and I felt comfortable now that I was with Bubba.

However, Bubba looked different: she was dressed in a traditional men's suit (and tie) with her hair tied back. I was immediately taken aback. In my many prior interactions with her, she did not wear all feminine clothes, but I did not read her gender performance as masculine either. To me, she straddled what some might consider a spectrum. I never saw Bubba in a skirt, except in some of the pictures she had on her wall, but she routinely rocked acrylic nails, her hair was always curled, lip gloss was glistening, and usually she had on some strong floral-smelling perfume. Even her bathroom reminded me of my own—scattered with Bath & Body Works products and women's makeup. A couple of times, I ran into her boyfriends, including one who was always accompanied by a large and intimidating Rottweiler. To me, Bubba was "one of the girls," but seeing her that day at her church made me uncomfortable. As cringy as it sounds, I thought, "Why is Bubba looking like a Bob? Do they know she is gay? That at one point she was a sex worker? That she wears high heels and red-tinted lip gloss? That she and her lovers have professional photos and that these portraits are proudly hung on her walls?" I was furious. I thought, "*This* church made *my* Bubba wear male drag." I immediately projected all the resentment I had from my own experience as a youth in the Church of Christ onto my experience at Greater Johnson. I was determined to queer the space, or so I thought. As a first-timer at the church, I was asked to introduce myself to the congregation.

"Christina Carney Anderson." "Anderson is a strong name," Pastor D. R. Anderson replied after I stated my name. "Where did you get that strong name from?" Obviously, he was making a joke, since he also had the same surname. I replied, "My wife!" There was awkward laughter among the congregation. Bubba also chuckled. The pastor thanked me for coming and told me that he hoped that I would be back—and to next time bring my wife.

After some deep reflection, several years later, I realized that I had made an error during this unexpected visit to Bubba's church—*I* was the one failing to understand the nuance. And despite my initial impressions from my only visit to Greater Johnson, the church made space for her gender fluidity. I soon realized the reason for her appearance, an appearance that might have been normal for her church members and pastor but not the Bubba I knew. Only men could participate in formal church services, like communion and the reading of scriptures. Bubba was wearing a suit and tie so she could fully participate in church services. Bubba held other leadership roles, including president of the culinary ministry, which is now named Bubba's Kitchen in her honor. She explained, "They know that I'm gay—we have a good time at church. Me and the ladies, we chop it up. I'm the culinary cook for the church, I'm at choir, devotion, so—I'm pretty active in the church." In a sense, Bubba got to perform and partake in many differently gendered forms of labor in the church, from communion to cooking. I mistakenly thought that *I* was a queering the space—"my wife!"—but I missed the point entirely. Despite it being a discipling space, Bubba's performance of male drag and her presence were already doing the work. The space was already doing the work. The *people* were already doing the work. The initial encounter between Bubba and Dr. Anderson began as a flirtatious exchange. They first saw each other briefly while Bubba and her friend Chuck were doing laundry at a black-owned laundromat. Anderson came inside to speak to the owners, Ivy and Johnny Williams, who were already parishioners at Greater Johnson. After Anderson left, Bubba asked Ivy, "Where that cute preacher at?" When Johnson told Anderson what Bubba had said, Anderson told her to tell Bubba, "If they want to see the cute preacher, they gotta come to the church!" Both Bubba and Chuck visited the church the next Sunday. Bubba described Anderson as the "coolest person" she knew. She was also protective of his wife, Mrs. Anderson, describing them as "one big happy family" and a family that has "never refused [her] of anything." This means something, and is far from a form of false consciousness.

This was not the first time I got things wrong. During one of our initial interviews, I called Bubba "queer." She immediately became upset and told me that calling her queer was disrespectful. Instead of kicking me out her house altogether, she decided to compassionately school me

> It's like me calling you a bitch or a hoe back then. Now, I don't know how they interpret it. Back then if you call somebody queer, freak, to one of us back then that was just putting us to the ground. . . . We took that out of the equation because we were neither of those. We're human like everyone else.

Initially, just like my experience in her church, I thought Bubba had got it wrong, that she needed to be "educated" on the new terminology—terminology that I thought was invested in helping her express herself. Yet I was in for another lesson.

Unlike queer theory, E. Patrick Johnson's genealogical concept of quare studies is useful because it "acknowledges the different 'standpoints' found among lesbian, bisexual, gay, and transgendered people of color—differences that are conditioned by class and gender."[114] Bubba's sense of quareness was first learned through her family and the larger black community of Phoenix. Despite the early realization that she was "different," her family in Phoenix, especially her mother, made room for her quareness. She explains,

> I found out at a very young age that something wasn't quite right with my demeanor . . . I always wanted to be the momma. I ain't want to be the daddy—I never wanted to be the daddy when we [sisters and brothers] were playing house. As I grew, I seen that I leaned toward boys more than girls. At that time we were kids . . . I didn't know what was going on. But as I got older I started to really like mens and boys. I didn't know how to handle that because I thought a man was suppose to be a man. At that time, I would put on my mother's dresses when she was gone. Like I said, I was always momma around the house when she was gone. Eventually, I came to grips with myself. Something was different from the rest of the boys in the family. So I kept it under wraps. I would have little girlfriends for a cover—no more than that. I started putting on the makeup around 13. Going out at a very young age . . . into the world. And I was dressing up, making my face up, always kept my hair did. My mother . . . I guess she knew . . . she called me to her side one time. She said, "I know what's going on with you. Don't be shamed, you're my child no matter what, I will always love you." As my mother told me that, I just bust all the way out. I felt this way at the time . . . I didn't care what society was thinking, my mother was my sole provider. If she could accept me, I didn't care what nobody else thought. And that was my outlet. Then I let it all hang out. From there, I just went out.

Her mother's acceptance, along with the reverence (and fear) the community had for her stepfather, enabled Bubba to live her life as a woman, something she had always felt internally.

> I use to go to the beauty shop every week. And then I put that makeup on. That nigga wouldn't know if I was a real bitch or not. And some of them would just be puzzled. I could feel it and I could see them. It ain't too many niggas in my hometown that I throwed my eyes on that I couldn't get sooner or later. I know how to work that shit. And I worked it too, baby.

Bubba's life story is exceptional, but one that troubles the "trapped in the closet" ideology that still dominates LGBTQIA+ activism and politics. Jeffrey McCune, author of *Sexual Discretion: Black Masculinity and the Politics of Passing* (2014), provides a different epistemology, "the DL," in which those who practice it reject a sexual liberation rooted in an articulated sexual identity.[115]

Quare studies was also useful as I pondered how to discuss and represent the misgendering of Bubba by some of her closest friends and family members. I hesitated to not see this as inherently transphobic or homophobic, unlike the other aforementioned instances, but instead a complex negotiation of power, inherently connected to race. After her death from cancer on April 3, 2021, during the height of the COVID-19 epidemic, one of her "children" wrote a tribute on her Facebook wall and called her "Uncle Bubba," while a video from her eulogy by Pastor Anderson also referred to her in the male pronouns: "I just hear Bubba sing again . . . Bubba couldn't sing . . . I don't care if he can't sing, I wanna hear him sing again." During one of our interview sessions, Bubba's biological sister called her "he" on many occasions—but Bubba did not appear bothered at all. Interestingly, she made a point to clarify that she wanted me to refer to her as "her," not "him." After one of our first interviews, she expressed that she "finally felt free," that "a weight had been lifted." Bubba wanted to share her life story with the world, and I was her vessel. In this moment, I felt that with her telling of her life story to me, the world would finally "get her." Yet after reading through her online tributes on Facebook, it was apparent that her family got her too, despite misgendering—which Bubba might have accepted as forgivable limitations in her over-whelmingly loving family.

> I love you sooooo much Granvally [Hughes] I swear this is the only no judgmental realest person I've ever met. The great time we have shared are burned in my memory forever. Uncle Bubba was the issssshhh nothing will every compare.—Dule Hollingsworth

> I am so sad to see you go Granvally Hughes a.k.a "Bubba." My mama loved you and you loved her the most. You really looked out for each other. You never judged anyone but always made me laugh. I promised I would look after you, and I always did showing up with plates and bags of things just like my mama did. . . . You shared some really personal things with me throughout the years and my sons love you. You said you would never forget the time my two oldest sons were driving, saw you walking, backed the car all the way up and made you get in to take you home . . . Love you Bubba—Farris Dwayne Davidson

> Dear Bubba, I wanna thank you from the bottom of my heart for realizing when my mommy wasn't 100% & steppin in for me and my brothers the love & support you gave us was way more than we could ask for. We owe a lot of our success to you. Thank You again

for doing nothing shy of what you did for us for my baby You loved Jay with everything in you and was teaching him all the right things like you taught us (how I wish he had more time with you) . . . We Gone be Lost Without You Bubba. Watch Over Us. I Love You My Rock. Get Your Rest Now. You Deserve It—Tierra King

My mother loved you, my kids loved you and you know I loved you. I am going to miss our talks. You looked out for my mother like no other. You loved each other. You said when you came to town down the street, my mother took care of you, and when you ended up in the same complex, you took care of each other. When she passed, I stepped up. I took care of you too because you were a blessing to my soul. I'm going to miss our talks. We are going to miss you. No more pain Bubba. Love you—Rhonda McKinney Poston.[116]

Though San Diego nightlife was an exciting part of her life, what Bubba was most proud of was being "a home-giver." As Rhonda and Tierra explained, their "uncle Bubba" nurtured them when their parents were unable, and Bubba also babysat their children, leaving a profound influence on her grandchildren. She told me how she served as "a counselor for different mothers whose kids were acting out"; she would "sit down and talk" to them using herself "as an example." "I don't have a school education—I have a street education and that has brought me a long way."

In addition to the online tributes, her official send-off was held at the California Cremation and Burial in National City and was attended by approximately one hundred people—a relatively large gathering during the pandemic. The repast was held at El Toyon Park at 2:00 p.m. and was more like a party. In honor of her memory, attendees took alcohol shots and smoked marijuana blunts—some of her favorite pastimes, which I was lucky enough to indulge in with her. The party lasted well into the wee hours of the next morning. Her extended family members had T-shirts made with pictures of Bubba on them, while others wore shirts that read "Bubbalicious" in bright colors.[117]

Her church community at Greater Johnson, along with her family network in Logan Heights, were more viable means of community than the LGBT community in Hillcrest. The black fraternal order not only created space for Bubba when she was a sex-working queen (on the stage singing, getting tips) but also made space for her in her older years as a black trans elder. The fraternal hall was a stable black institution that she could depend on in a way she could not with white club owners in downtown or the safe space activists in Hillcrest. It's quite remarkable that their brick-and-mortar structures are still remaining—despite redlining, processes of gentrification, and the mass exodus of black people out of the city (and state) altogether.

Conclusion

The communal and intergenerational economic structure of black fraternal orders in San Diego has enabled these spaces to provide over 100 years of service to their communities. As of 2024, Fidelity Lodge No. 10 continues to house Greater Johnson Missionary Baptist Church. The church has forged relationships with educators. For instance, it hosted a soul food dinner that featured guest speaker Mychal Odom, an Africana-studies professor at San Diego Mesa College and San Diego State University. "African Attire" was encouraged, with the theme being "African American Heritage."[118] Fidelity has also hosted a variety of other events, including a fashion pop-up event and a breakfast fundraiser, and has advertised for other businesses.

The Elks—another black fraternal order, at 6 Hensley Street in southeast San Diego—has also found creative ways to sustain and make use of space. It also has a queer history. Bubba and her drag revue, the Plutons, played there, as did other queer actors who were part of black vaudeville. According to an interview with a black resident, the traveling black vaudeville, also known as the "chitlin circuit," performed at the Elks Lodge in the early twentieth century.[119] In 2019, its Facebook page advertised "Reggae Saturdays" every Saturday, including a twerking contest for a $100 prize. The promoter listing on the advertisement was "Lady Princess." Other events hosted there have been comedy shows and themed live-music evening events.

Bubba's storefront church and black fraternal orders in southeast San Diego house a certain sexual economy that is a direct response to urban development. The displacement of working-class black queens and the ghettoization of black people has forged different forms of community and kinship—in ways that escape certain frameworks of legibility. Yet these institutions are in it for the long haul.

4 *The Gathering*

Black Lesbian Separatists and Parties for "Women Who Love Women"

In this final chapter, the book ends where it started—as I labored as a promoter for LGBTQ+ nighttime club events in Hillcrest, the state-sanctioned gay neighborhood. As a co-owner and the primary financier of Cabaret Passage (later renamed Passage Playground Productions), I was a black woman business owner—respectable and legal, but still selling sex by monetizing black women's bodies so that *I* could profit from the larger militarized sex tourism industry of San Diego. The monetization of black women's bodies is not only what I did but also what other disreputable women did throughout the twentieth century as they tried to make a profit from the city's militarized sex tourism industry. Though burnout from activism or competition hinders an ability to forge a more collective black queer community or generate enough profit to sustain for-profit or non-profit-oriented events, I argue that the gathering of black women in spaces is essential for building community in a city that likes to imagine that black people do not exist. The organization of these spaces takes hard work. As Kemi Adeyemi points out in her ethnographic study on how black queer nightlife promoters and their patrons make space in gentrified Chicago neighborhoods, promoting is a hard job that is often underpaid and undervalued: "What feels like fun, release, play, and possibility for partygoers is made possible by the hard, draining and often thankless labor of organizers when things go wrong or when their expectations aren't met."[1] The little profit that organizers make, from either bars or door sales, is not enough to compensate for this labor, often leading to burnout. Yet this labor is not futile.

The racial stratification of the city's sex economy, dating back to the early 20th century, has informed current sex economies, including those of Passage, SoulKiss, and others who sold sex by advertising parties "for women by women" to servicewomen and others who sought other women for casual sex and long-term dating.[2] The logic of miscegenation, racially segregated places, still operates in twenty-first-century queer spatial practices. During my early initial conversations with SoulKiss, they talked about how their club events were not necessarily all black, but that people racialized them as such because their flyers featured pictures of black women and not white women. Other events were labeled as raceless simply because they used white women on their flyers. In other words, SoulKiss found it problematic that the presence of a black person on marketing implied black exclusivity, while a white person's image signaled inclusivity. Naturally, as a black woman-led business, Passage also experienced the same issues. Passage was also cast as "the black party"—so for some events we created advertisements without a black person on the flyer. However, when non-black patrons discovered that the owners were black and the crowd was black, we would rarely see them again. Even more, through my own business practices I realized that creating space for black women in commercialized places was not about creating community—in fact, it undermined it. As new business owners, we often had to compete with fellow black promoters for the "black crowd." Club owners would ask us to target this demographic for nights where they had a hard time bringing in a crowd. In many cases, we had to team up with other black promoters to draw a bigger crowd to reach our minimum capacity so we would not breach our contract—which was good for our patrons but sometimes unprofitable for our business. Additionally, by making our flyers racially ambiguous we created enemies of white lesbian promoters who felt that we acted out of our place by promoting to a non-black audience. Sex work is an economy, like others, that is embedded with racist logic—with white bodies and lighter skin constructed as more desirable and thus valuable. These racial politics affected me and other black promoters because LGBT social spaces are still segregated along the lines of race, gender, and class—making these differences seem natural and commonsense—but it also has more insidious effects, including a racially stratified economy.[3]

Sustaining antiracist political activism and activities in the city has also proven difficult for black lesbians and queers. On February 11, 1991, members of Lesbians and Gays of African Descent United (LAGADU) debuted their play *The Gathering*, written by M. Corinne Mackey and directed and choreographed by Roxanna Young, at the Lyceum Theatre in Horton Plaza. The play was in response to both anti-black racism in the larger (white) gay/lesbian community and homophobia and sexism in the black community. Interviews with lesbian activists, including black lesbians, revealed how gay male leaders of the Lesbian and Gay Center for Social Services (formerly the Gay Center for Social Services) often ignored racial and gender issues, seeing them as divisive. In a 1992 interview, Bernie Michels called black lesbians and gays "separatists," in a way that seemed to underline racial tensions that were brewing during the 1990s.[4]

Vertez Burks, a cofounder of LAGADU, saw this separatism as a necessity, explaining that there was a "comfort zone to being around black gay people—even straight black people. We have a similar history . . . and there is no need to explain anything or [unintentionally] hurt someone's feelings."[5] The social scene of Hillcrest was not a welcoming place to black lesbians. Bars and clubs in Hillcrest openly discriminated against black people and other disreputables—with bouncers using the practice of "extra carding" to discourage and prohibit the entrance of certain racialized bodies.[6] The local black political scene was also contentious. Angela Davis, who organized in San Diego between 1967 and 1969—while a master's student at the University of California, San Diego—revealed how male members of the US organization, a black nationalist group locally led by Ron Karenga, became threatened by her outspokenness and accused her of doing "a man's job."[7] For them, women were supposed to "inspire" a black man so that "he might more effectively contribute his talents to the struggle for Black Liberation"—yet most of the organizing labor fell on Davis and other women within the organization.[8] It was under these conditions that black lesbians (and gays) in San Diego during the latter decades of the twentieth century decided to not only form their own black gay and lesbian communities but also use cultural production to educate and represent their intersectional perspectives and politics to a wide audience.

Just like the black lesbian separatists of the latter twentieth century, my space-making was shaped by the racism of local safe space activism—primarily the 2011 local redistricting process, where safe space activists blamed the black and Latine community, particularly the neighborhood of City Heights, for the overturning of gay marriage in California. The neighborhood I loved and lived in was drawn out of a district we shared with Hillcrest, consequentially affecting the material conditions of the marginalized residents, many of whom were refugees and undocumented. For many black people who came to our nighttime events, the dance floor become a place of resistance. We made space in a place where some wished we were not. The interconnectedness of these racial histories and spatial practices was solidified with the formation of the Mackey-Cua Project (formerly known as Queer Progressive People of Color), a queer antiracist collective, whose namesake is a tribute to local activist M. Corinne "Marti" Mackey and Jim Cua, who often worked together on projects. When one group folds, another one emerges, proving that these spaces are critical to black lesbians' survival in the city.

Separatists

Separatist Cynthia Lawrence-Wallace, as one of two black people (and one of four lesbians) on the fifteen-person original planning committee of the Gay Center for Social Services, was both invisible and hypervisible. She moved to San Diego in 1960 and was a cofounder of the Gay Center for Social Services. Her intersectional identity as a black person *and* a woman was ignored, yet her white colleagues often tasked her with educating white people about racial issues. "They were committed to having a gay center and wanted to include women . . . [but] not all the men on that committee were as committed compared to Jess. . . . Gay men seemed really good at forgetting that women existed in the world." Her partner Peggy Heathers echoed similar concerns about men at the center. "Most of the men really wanted a lot of togetherness and they didn't understand why we had a women's night. . . . Men planned groups all the time that excluded women." Lawrence-Wallace was also tokenized, which resulted in a heavier workload. "And so I feel that I'm constantly being put in the position to educate the gay community. In fact, I was just asked to speak to the Democratic Club . . . but my response is, 'I'm tired of educating white people. You talk about identifying racism. . . . Do it yourself! . . . You don't want me to tell you anyway.'" When she would bring up the lack of diversity on certain committees, instead of actually seeking out other black people they would ask her to join, creating even more work for her.[9]

Lawrence-Wallace was sympathetic and understood the need for "lesbian separatism," but she also expressed the need for black women to have their own separate sphere, apart from white women. "There was separatism in the women's community because women were also finding their womanism. That needed to be a separate situation. You just need some time alone and with other women, and you needed to be separate in order to be strong and then go back into the community if that's your choice. Men misunderstood the purpose of that separatism, as I think people do. I think people misunderstand Black Nationalism. Some of the men misunderstood that and even some women."[10] Womanism, originally coined by Alice Walker in 1983, was a popular alternative to or rearticulation of a politics centered on black women, who were often hesitant to align themselves with second-wave feminists.[11] Lawrence-Wallace was in an interracial relationship with Peggy Heathers, a white woman, who was sometimes omitted from certain gatherings. "Living with a white woman limits my social interactions . . . kinda stifles things."[12] When Lawrence-Wallace attended a black lesbian conference, Heathers was not allowed to go. Womanism also saw black women's struggles as interconnected with the struggle and plight of black men. While many white separatists would often leave the room when a male entered, black lesbians understood that black men were also exploited by white men.

Lawrence-Wallace and Thom Carey, Bernie Michels's partner—who had similar experiences, being black partners of white gay and lesbian activists—often discussed creating a social group for black gays and lesbians. Though they did an equal amount of work as their partners, or even more, they were subjected to blatant racism, and their identity was always attached to their white partners. Lawrence-Wallace pointed to a time when she and Heathers were told to come late to a friend's party so that the white neighbors would hopefully not notice that there was a black person coming to the house.

> There were two gay men who invited Peggy and I . . . they invited us over for a gathering. And we got there, it was an evening gathering, we got there and found out that people had been there earlier. It started as a barbecue in the afternoon and we said something about it . . . "Well, why did we come so late?" And they said, "Well, we didn't want to offend our neighbors. . . . We thought our neighbors might be offended by having blacks in the area during the daytime . . . and thought they wouldn't see you at night."[13]

This was a shock to Heathers. "Yes, I really became aware. I was not aware. I had never experienced it before, of course. But being with Cynthia, I began to experience it and it was incredible." Carey, a Navy veteran, faced similar battles. He also worked at the Gay Information Center and was an active member of the Metropolitan Community Church of San Diego. His safe space activism was shaped by his nonviolent activism in Goldsboro, North Carolina, where he participated in sit-ins. Michels admitted how Carey felt lonely and that people would always associate Carey with him, instead of acknowledging him as an individual gay activist. Though "closeted," Carey's labor was critical to the development of the Gay Center for Social Services.[14]

While gay liberation struggles were taken up by mostly white gay men, Lawrence-Wallace and another black queer woman in San Diego at this time, Angela Davis, were preoccupied with fighting against racism in the larger metropolitan area.[15] When asked by the interviewer if she knew of any other gay and lesbian activism happening in the city besides the Center project, Lawrence-Wallace responded that she was unaware because racial issues were front and center for her: "If so, it was overshadowed for me because of everything that was going on for black, Chicanos, Native Americans, and things like that at UCSD . . . that was my focus. And because of civil rights and all the things going on in the late '60s, early '70s and the war thing starting . . . I was much more into blackness than I was into gayness." According to Lawrence-Wallace, there was "political turmoil" on the campus, with Angela Davis leading political efforts. Davis arrived in San Diego in 1967 to work with Professor Herbert Marcuse and later earned a master's in philosophy in 1969. While a student, she was a founding member of the UCSD Black Student Union and a part of the UCSD Lumumba-Zapata Coalition and Movement. As a UCSD student leader, she also created ties with the Black Student Council at San Diego State University. Even with her active college campus activism, she wanted to build community.

Though there were some Black Panther Party members in San Diego, Davis saw the city as US territory. The US organization was founded in 1965 in Los Angeles, after the Compton Riots, which occurred in San Diego as well. A group of cultural nationalists—the Circle of Seven, who met regularly at Aquarian Bookstore in Los Angeles—were the creators; Hakim Jamal and Maulana Karenga became its most prominent leaders. They studied the work of African socialists and were deeply committed to the activism of Malcolm X and Marcus Garvey. Karenga was a cultural nationalist who advocated for a blend of West, South, and East African languages, names and clothing; he named this philosophy for black cultural revolution Kawaida, a Kiswahili term for "custom." Karenga's focus on cultural transformation put him at odds with Jamal. While Jamal advocated for the centralization of Malcolm X's ideological philosophies, Karenga was more concerned with influencing US blacks to appropriate African culture. Jamal argued how African culture had no relevance to the everyday lives of US blacks, leading to his exit from the US organization. Davis worked alongside the US organization to release Edward Lynn, a black sailor at the Balboa naval hospital who was court martialed for highlighting racism at the Balboa Naval Base. He started a petition accusing military officials of subjecting black and Mexican men to discrimination in housing, jobs, and uneven discipline among troops. Davis began to work closely with Lynn and his legal team. She also created a permanent tabling campaign on college campuses to support his defense.[16]

Davis's active role in the San Diego Black Conference made San Diego's US members uncomfortable. In her autobiography, she discusses the rampant sexism she experienced during her activist days in the military town. More importantly, she points out the contradictions in their critique. She explains how she took up the role of organizing, since male leaders either refused to do the work she was doing or were ineffective at it: "The irony of their complaint was that much of what I was doing had fallen to me by default. The arrangements for the publicity of the rally, for instance, had been in a man's hands, but because his work left much to be desired, I began to do it simply to make sure that it got done. It was ironical that precisely those who criticized me most did the least to ensure the success of the rally." Very early on, Davis understood how black male leaders failed to understand the harmful impact of gender ideology on the movement. "These men view Black women as a threat to their attainment of manhood—especially those Black women who take initiative and work to become leaders in their own right. The constant harangue by the US men was that I needed to redirect my energies and use them to give my man strength and inspiration so that he might more effectively contribute his talents to the struggle for Black liberation." Not too soon afterward, she left San Diego for Los Angeles, where she began to work more closely with the Black Panther Party (BPP).[17]

Though the BPP did not have a heavy presence in San Diego, their newsletter, the *Black Panther Community News Service* (later called the *Black Panther Intercommunal News Service*—BPINS), featured stories about anti-black police violence, serving as an important archive about the local racial and political climate at the time. As Elaine Brown, the first woman to lead the BPP (1974-77), explained, it "gave voice to the masses . . . and dedicated itself to reporting news and information in words the People could understand." BPINS "published the Party's various political positions, providing historical documentation of its ideology and philosophy, its stances on contemporaneous issues, its internal and external activities."[18] "Pigs Amuck in San Diego" reported on SDPD's routine surveillance and harassment of black people gathering in Mountain View Park every Sunday. On July 13, 1969, as retaliation for parking cars "in a particular area" on the grass, the police "soaked the grass down [so] naturally the car brakes wouldn't hold." They then stopped a person by the name of Steve Harris for a "jive traffic violation" before handcuffing and brutally beating him. Two hundred police were called for backup. Soon after, police were accused of firing tear gas grenades at the crowd in the park after partygoers refused to leave. One of the grenades exploded in an eight-year-old girl's face. Other partygoers were shot by police—including Bruce Lewis (a former BPP party member), who was shot three times, and a ten-year-old boy who was later declared dead at the hospital. One SDPD officer was killed during the police-provoked attack. It was also reported that the owner of a local grocery store, "Caps," shot a black man and "watched the brother bleed to death." After the onslaught at the park, police set up roadblocks throughout the area and sported "combat helmets and pack[ed] carbines and submachine guns." "Sporadic fires were burning in various areas of the community, but there was more shotgun fire than looting, dig it."[19]

The local BPP headquarters in downtown San Diego was also a target of the SDPD. In the same issue as "Pigs Amuck in San Diego," it was reported that on May 14, 1969, the police "had the entire block around the office blocked off, and they broke into the San Diego Branch of the Black Panther Party headquarters looking for a machine gun which they never found." The police "destroyed and stole [their] literature, equipment . . . medical supplies, the Party's film 'Off the Pig.'" They also "tore up cameras and exposed undeveloped film and generally checked the office." The following day, May 15, a woman was arrested on the way to Christ the King church, where the BPP had implemented their Breakfast Program. She was arrested for allegedly not telling police the year of her birth. Angela Davis was also subjected to harassment and detention by SDPD, which she documented in her autobiography.[20] The attacks on antiracist leftist community organizers continued throughout the 1970s.

On February 8, 1970, BPINS reported that the office of the Movement for a Democratic Military (MDM), at 429 J Street, had been raided by both SDPD and the Shore Patrol (military police).[21] This local MDM chapter was formed by sailors at the Naval Station San Diego and Marines from Camp Pendleton Marine Base in Oceanside; the larger national organization was inspired by antiwar activism of the Vietnam War, the Black Panther Party, and other militant groups of the day.[22] San Diego municipal and military police blockaded the downtown street blocks near J Street between Fourth and Fifth Avenues, where the MDM headquarters was located. Without a search warrant or permission, authorities broke down the locked doors and arrested Milton Ira Green, a rogue serviceman member of the MDM, for "unauthorized absence" (UA)—his second arrest for the same thing. MDM's downtown headquarters had been broken into on two previous occasions, and between December of 1969 and 1970, twenty-three local members were arrested on charges such as blocking the sidewalk, non-regulation haircut, and improper civilian attire.

This came nine months after the People's Armed Forces Day rally in Oceanside on May 16, 1969, when Angela Davis returned to San Diego County as a speaker for the event. Her involvement with the MDM and her critique of Nixon made her a target of California state authorities, resulting in her being fired from her teaching position at UCLA and later charged with murder in 1972. *Attitude Check*, "a serviceman's newspaper" published by the MDM, detailed the event.[23] Nearly one thousand people attended. Speeches were given by active and nonactive servicemen and women—Davis was the only nonmilitary speaker for the event. As she approached the podium to speak, she was accompanied by fifteen men for protection, since it was rumored that she was marked for assassination. She opened her speech with, "All power to the people. I'm going to say what these G.I.'s can't because of military laws—our non president Richard M. Nixon is a genocidal, hypocritical, murdering pig." According to *Attitude Check*, her opening "brought the largest and loudest applause of the day." During her speech, she also discussed the murder of BPP leader Fred Hampton, the 300-officer police raid on BPP headquarters in Los Angeles, and a "nationwide plot to annihilate the Black Panther Party"— what we now know to be COINTELPRO. The event was for the most part peaceful; however, dismantling the MDM then became a priority for the US military, with the San Diego office coming under attack from local and national authorities.

While antiwar activism was annihilated in the ranks, the Department of Defense permitted the Ku Klux Klan and other white supremacist organizations to organize on San Diego bases. The prosecution of the Pendleton 14, a group of black Marines who attacked what they thought was a KKK meeting at Camp Pendleton in Oceanside, shone a national and international spotlight on these groups. On November 13, 1976, fourteen black Marines forced their way into a room where they thought the white-supremacist Marine group of KKK members was; however, it was later discovered that they entered the wrong room. Several white Marines were seriously injured. The black men were tipped off by a flyer advertising the meeting on the base. Thirteen of them were jailed and charged with crimes including attempted murder, while the KKK members were taken into protective custody and subsequently relocated to other bases. The American Civil Liberties Union (ACLU) represented the KKK members, along with some of the black defendants, in court.

The San Diego Urban League was the first to speak openly about not only the prosecution of the Pendleton 14 but also events preceding the 1976 incident. In addition to individual acts of violence, the Urban League highlighted the systematic mistreatment of black servicemen at Camp Pendleton. In 1976 there were fifty incidents that resulted in serious injuries; in 1974 there were sixty-two cases of racial violence, with fifty-three of them considered brawls. Commanders allowed the KKK group to wear KKK insignias and carry large knives which they called "nigger stickers," and flyers advertised the group as "the white man's NAACP." One month before the 1976 incident, there was a cross-burning that took place in Oceanside; the Klan claimed credit for the incident. Then three weeks later, the Oceanside branch of the Urban League was firebombed and a van owned by a black man was shot at. The November 13 incident was the spark that ignited the flame. On April 2, 1977, the Camp Pendleton Defense Fund organized a rally in Oceanside, eight years after the People's Armed Forces Day, with a poster printed in English and Spanish.[24]

A central way the US military quelled racial unrest following the implementation of the all-volunteer force in 1973 was through a strategic marketing campaign in which the ideal figure of the white male soldier was replaced with the figure of the "good black soldier."[25] The military crafted a new brand of black masculinity that was politically and culturally legible and demonstrated the institution's newfound commitment to inclusion and equality. The military was forced to reconceptualize the figure to meet their personnel needs. This discourse ushered in "narratives of professionalization, upward mobility, and racial equality in recruiting advertisements," along with functioning to "assuage anxieties held by black recruits, communities, and the broader public."[26] The US military of the 1980s saw substantial pay increases for junior enlisted personnel and specialists, additional ROTC scholarships, greatly expanded recruitment programs (especially in the inner city), better retention of a career force, and a strengthening of reserve forces.

Lawrence-Wallace and Davis were two of many black women who sought to address the racial climate in San Diego, but their experiences, in both gay and black-led activist spaces, are representative of those of many black women during this era.[27] Their labor as leaders was integral to their groups at the same time that they were disciplined and sometimes ostracized for challenging male authority. Michels's characterization of lesbian and/or black groups as "separatist" was meant to be read as divisive, but some black lesbians embraced the term and its necessity as a community-building project. Yet the lesbian separatists' spaces were also constructed along the lines of race. Black cofounders of the Center who were also in interracial (black/white) relationships often felt like outcasts despite their invaluable contributions. Black activists' spaces were also ripe with tensions, especially over the roles that men and women should play in the movement. The discrimination against black servicemembers at military bases was the primary focus of the city's black leaders, including Davis; however, gender politics often caused tension in the ranks. Though there was much solidarity between lesbians and gay men during the HIV/AIDS epidemic of the 1980s, these networks were inaccessible to black men. In the next section, I discuss how some black gays and lesbians decided to officially form separatist groups in places inside and outside Hillcrest.

The Gathering

Welcome to our Theatre LAGADU: "The Gathering." Tonight, in honor of Black History Month, we come together to talk about ourselves as a people whose past and history has almost been the death of us, whose present has been wrought with difficulties and obstacles, and whose future—formed from dreams—has for so long been perilous to imagine. We have survived. We have survived precisely through gatherings such as this one tonight with the sharing of our hopes, fears, pains and the expression of the joy that has sustained us always.

—M. CORINNE MACKEY

Even though racial and gender turmoil continued to plague the LGBT community, many lesbians, including black lesbians like Lawrence-Wallace, assisted their gay brothers during the HIV/AIDS crisis in the 1980s. In 1981, a group of San Diego lesbians formed the Blood Sisters program as a form of solidarity with gay men who were dying of AIDS; Lawrence-Wallace was an active member. This was significant since many blood banks in California outright rejected blood donated not only by gay men but also by lesbians. The San Diego Blood Sisters operated during the entire 1980s, inspiring similar initiatives in other parts of the country. Lawrence-Wallace and Heathers were heavily involved in the local program. Beth Hutchinson revealed how other organizations made sure their efforts were a success. For instance, Albert Bell, a member of the San Diego Democratic Club, enlisted gay men to support the women by creating the Little Brothers of the Blood Sisters, which provided lesbians transportation to and from the blood bank. Yet some lesbians were critical of these nationwide blood drives organized by women. As Hutchinson notes, since most gay men ignored women's and lesbian issues, the blood drive was just another example of the invisible labor that was being undertaken by lesbians on behalf of the larger mostly white gay male community.[28]

By the late 1980s, some black lesbians and gays also felt sidelined by the larger white gay community and subsequently formed the group Lesbians and Gays of African Descent United, which centered black political concerns. The cofounders included M. "Marti" Corinne Mackey, Phyllis Jackson, Cynthia Lawrence-Wallace, Vertez Burks, Larry Lawrence, and John Guinn. The organization was committed to a "Black agenda," which included "bridging the gap between the black gay and lesbian community and the overall black community"; "to create and maintain a safe environment for lesbians and gays of African descent in order to share our experiences, strengths, and hopes; to provide direction for our futures; to sustain visibility, and to give voice to our long held silence. In keeping with that stated purpose, LAGADU will direct itself towards such specific work like maintaining a men's and a women's caucus, and sponsoring various social, cultural and educational events."[29] LAGADU had several committees, including public relations, cultural/social, fundraising, newsletter, educational, archival, membership/outreach, health and social concerns, and political action. Since many black women did not feel comfortable in Hillcrest or were not out, LAGADU general meetings were held at the Urban League in southeast San Diego, which Burks describes as a "midpoint" meeting place, since "Hillcrest was very white, [blacks] didn't feel comfortable there."[30] Though Burks frequently participated in social groups that were predominately white, she also found community in groups that focused on race and class.

Many people had a hand in organizing LAGADU, but most people considered Mackey the central organizing leader. She was inducted into San Diego's LGBT Community Wall of Honor in 2004, its inaugural year; the awarding committee included Nicole Murray-Ramirez, who was the creator of this memorial. In 2011, I attended the actual placement of a bronze plaque acknowledging Mackey at its current location at 909 Centre Street. Others included on the committee were Jeri Dilno and George Murphy—the Center's chief executive officer, director of public affairs, and director of major gifts. Other inductees soon followed, including Cynthia Lawrence-Wallace, Vertez Burks, and Peggy Heathers. Before her death in 1992 from cancer, Mackey served on the board of the Center and the San Diego Police Department Shooting Review Board as a member of the Human Dignity Ordinance Task Force and as a volunteer instructor for the San Diego Police Academy.[31]

Mackey is remembered most for her full-length play *The Gathering*, which premiered during Black History Month on February 11, 1991, at the Lyceum Theatre in Horton Plaza. Many LAGADU members participated in the production, which was supported by the Centre City Development Corporation and with "generous contributions" from "LAGADU Friends and Supporters." According to the playbill, *The Gathering* was a homage to black people's survival in America: "We have survived precisely through gatherings such as this one tonight with the sharing of hopes, fears, pains and the expression of the joy that has sustained us always. Black people have black art and artists in particular to thank for their survival. Part of the reason why and how we have survived has been because of our art and our artists who have told us again and again who we were and how we are so deserving of a life. Our artists have shown us love—in words, in pictures, in song and have kept us going." The play was also a call to acknowledge the intersectional experiences of black gays and lesbians. "We are especially honoring Black gays and lesbians who for too long have been left out of celebration of Black survival and history. Left out if we insisted on the revelation of ourselves.

We must learn that no single individual's or particular group's seeking of liberty and freedom can mean very much unless justice is everyone's right. Intolerance of differences and the denial of equality and freedom to some is the blight that works against us." Although the audio of the VHS copy of this performance is inaudible, the playbill still offers rich commentary on the intentions of the playwright.[32]

Yet there is one recording of a performance, "The Nigger God," that has allowed us to get a more intimate glimpse into Mackey's radical politics and the politics of the time. What is clear of this community theater show is that the black women actors are not only questioning the legitimacy of a God but more importantly illuminating how Christianity is a tool of racial subjugation. In this three-person skit, God, played by LAGADU member Phyllis Jackson, is portrayed as a very uncompassionate, ambivalent god with the humor and rawness of the iconic comedian Richard Pryor. "The Nigger God" is the third performance out of four—some others include a comedy sketch and monologue. Vertez Burks is the MC for the night, and jokingly describes how she and Mackey first met, and how Mackey is a "true lesbian" because she loves cats and meditating. She then introduces Mackey's skit: "So this group is going to do a piece called 'The Nigger God' and it's going to be their search for their spiritual inspiration. They are a non-acting, non-performing performing group."[33]

This community-based performance is representative of the everyday realities of black life, in ways that more highbrow productions might miss. As anthropologist Jan Cohen-Cruz notes, community-based performances are "characterized by deep interaction between artists and constituents grounded in a shared aspect of identity or circumstances. . . . That is, community

FIGURE 17. Front of the playbill for *The Gathering*, a play written and directed by Corinne "Marti" Mackey, at the Lyceum Theatre. Source: Lambda Archives of San Diego.

based performance is hyphenated not just grammatically but also a practice. Community based art is situated between entertainment and efficacy, art for pleasure and art the concretely *does* something."[34]

Mackey is forcing her audience, some of whom might be congregants at MCCSD, a supposedly gay-friendly church, to question the "seduction" of religion. She ponders what it would look like if instead, black women's voices and experiences were the guiding theology on the long road to a radical black liberation. Mackey sets the stage—she is sitting on a barstool, dressed in all black with an Afrocentric hat of the 1990s while reading from her notebook. Some music plays in the background. There is a black woman in front but to the side of her, donning ladies' fashion hats and waving a fan as if she is ridiculously hot. She stays silent during the first half of the skit. Mackey reads, "This is a tale about God's seduction and how we often believe at the expense of our own revolutionary salvation. It's also about the appearance of the Nigger God revealed to two seekers, seeker X and seeker W. The meaning of God's seduction is that we take her inside ourselves and become our own mini-gods and fight the revolution." Mackey's message seems to be in a line of thought that religion or religiosity, Christianity in particular, has been a central tool in the state's subjection of black life in the United States.[35] On one hand, Christianity has been used to justify the trafficking of black bodies; but then there is also a theology of hope for black people. She then transitions and starts describing the black women elder congregants in the church:

> Sisters in the front-row pew called "The Mothers of the Church"
> ... smelled of lavender and lilac and often walked with canes who
> wore thick support hose ... with heavy black shoes, and who would

land down the aisles on Sunday morning leaning onto the shoulders of white-gloved ushers. Sisters who would with a glance would strike terror into a small child's heart. Dressed in blacks and browns and grays... Their longevity, that they wore like a bandage that stretched the length of the pew gave us some inspiration, gave to others and not so unconsciously, the desire to move forward in this life. Testifying, spoke about their journeys—how long, how they survived, who assisted, what miracles has been gotten. . . . What this had been about and what has life been for. Questions that inspired their stature . . . questions unanswerable and more than that, questions not Christian-like to ask.

The revered sisters of the church are not only the backbone of the institution but also potentially disreputable women whose stories might be too disreputable to share during church-service hours.

At the 1:12:56 mark in the video, the Nigger God appears. "One God they were told to believe in—after death their death their life would give them life. The other god, the nigger god, no one said to believe in but she believed in him anyway," Mackey reads. She continues while the woman sitting in the pew gets up and passes out pieces of paper to the audience before she hangs a sign around Mackey's neck that reads "Nigger." "Nigga . . . nigga . . . nigga, does that word trouble you?" Mackey asks the audience. Soon after, traditional black church music plays. She playfully encourages the audience to keep clapping. Then suddenly Mackey and the church lady start angrily questioning God's commitment to their own happiness, orgasms included. "Have you been waiting on me by any chance?" Finally, *she* appears. Jackson, the Nigger God, struts in, hands on hips, in heels, sporting a red blouse with part of her breasts exposed. The audience cheers and whistles. Jackson is tickled; she laughs as well. "I don't know why you want to place all your burdens on me, and place them under my feet," she says. The church lady replies, "Didn't you say you'd be there for me always? That I can take my burdens to you and leave it there?" "Nah! I ain't said nothing like that." Mackey poses another similar question. God, played by Jackson, responds "SSHHHIIITTT," while in the church. The audience belts out a loud roar. Cursing, as a form of speech, was one of the trademarks of comedian Richard Pryor, who rose to stardom in the 1970s. His bold and provocative banter paved the way for other black comedians, including Eddie Murphy. As Kate Brown argues in her examination of Pryor, his cursing "suspends and even reverses the violent misidentification and disparities imposed by race relations during the period of his career."[36]

Unlike the white God, the Nigger God is there to tell the truth, unapologetically, using mostly cursing to dispel the myths about an all-knowing and supreme being, God—a God that only seems to be protecting white lives, at the expense of others. Again, Mackey asks God a follow-up question. "You better not fuck with me!" God warns her. At this point, Mackey cannot hold it in, she starts laughing, joining the audience. Jackson's character, the Nigger God, is the star of the show. The church lady suddenly jolts up from the church pew and sarcastically starts to mock God. "Got problems can't cope, try this new miracle drug—God. God will take care of you. Only $19.95." She tries to convince the audience to buy the special powder. The Nigger God follows up after the advertisement, "Sing your fucking songs, pray your prayers, preach your sermon, but leave me the fuck alone!"

The play is an eclectic mix of drama and comedy, sensuality and raunchiness, using black vernacular culture. "Don't confuse me with that other God. . . . They call this god Sweet Thang," God says as she gyrates and then begins caressing Mackey. "I like your big big hands on me. . . . Now that's why people call your name sometimes," Mackey suggests coyly. The Nigger God is seducing her, hugging and caressing as church music plays in the background. Mackey does not fear God anymore, she wants to fuck God.

Tragically, "The Nigger God" was the last production of Mackey's. In 1992, she died at the age of forty-two, leaving behind her longtime partner Phyllis Jackson. Jackson donated some of Mackey's articles and ephemera to the Lesbian and Gay Historical Society of San Diego. Vertez did as well, since she had her own business as a videographer and would routinely record gay and lesbian events.[37]

LAGADU disbanded in 1994; however, other groups were formed to fill in the gaps. A year after Mackey's passing, another group centering black lesbians emerged—the Afrikan American Gay Women Association (AAGWA). The group was formed in 1993 by Joy Mattison, Jimmy Lovett, Denise C., and Cheryl Bradford, and was active up until 2000. Lovett, who had been a member of LAGADU, agreed that there was a need for a group for black women only:

> After LAGADU ended, we wanted to start another group for gays and lesbians. Joy and myself worked together on the plans and, eventually, we were joined by the other two members, and during many group conversations and a neighborhood club community survey we decided that an all-gay women's group was much more needed.

At first I was hurt because we had worked on some good ideas for the group, but then I started to see the bigger picture and I, too, agreed it would [be] better to address these Afro-American gay women issues.[38]

Though men were not allowed in the group, AAGWA was part of a black business network called the Collective Voice of San Diego: An African American Coalition for Progressive Change, which included Chimpanzee Productions, Friends Unlimited, Karibu, World Beats Center, Spectrum, Shades of Color, Project Unity, Imani Worship Center, and Jay and AC Production Inc. Starting in 1996, AAGWA, the Lesbian and Gay Historical Society of San Diego (today the Lambda Archives of San Diego), and Karibu organized the first Marlon Riggs Film Festival at Diversionary Playhouse. In 1989, Marlon Riggs's film *Tongues Untied* was released. The film used Riggs's own personal narrative of the black gay male experience to offer a provocative rejection of white gayness and interracial relationships while promoting an "autonomous black gay culture."[39] Organizers for the San Diego Marlon Riggs Film Festival screened *Black Is . . . Black Ain't* (1994) and *Anthem* (1991) and featured special exhibits at the San Diego Historical Society. AAGWA went on to organize its first Women's History Month film festival in 1997 and two in the following year.

In 1995, John Guinn, a native San Diegan, established Karibu, which means "welcome" or "enter" in Kiswahili, to improve black African American men's access to HIV/AIDS care in San Diego. It has been noted by scholars, such as Cathy Cohen in *The Boundaries of Blackness: AIDS and the Breakdown of Black Politics* (1999), how the HIV/AIDS epidemic of the 1980 and 1990s was sidelined by traditional black Christian churches.[40] Karibu is one of many localized groups in the United States that created support groups and resources for black men in the 1990s. A big part of its mission was "making more African-American men aware of the dangers and preventative actions surrounding HIV and AIDS and making treatment more accessible." The group held support meetings every Wednesday. The Urban League of San Diego was its first sponsor, followed by the Center. In fact, a current twenty-unit permanent housing program for LGBT youth, sponsored by the Center, is named after Guinn's support group.[41] Guinn's local grassroots activism on behalf of black men living with HIV/AIDS was preceded by his involvement with LAGADU in the late 1980s.

The group was pivotal in directing black lesbians to resources in the community through its newsletter, which listed black spaces hospitable to black gay women (see figure 18). This mapping was an alternative to popular gay guide books. Some of the places "Where Sistahs Hang" sometimes overlapped with places recognized in the Damron guide book, for example, like David's Place (3766 Fifth Avenue), Obelisk the Bookstore (1029 University Avenue), and Rich's (1051 University Avenue), while others overlapped with places that were locally recognized as lesbian institutions, like the Flame. Even more, some places "Where Sistahs Hang" were not marked in Damron or were relatively lesser-known places, like Java De Paradigm (see map 4). I frequented some of these places while in San Diego, from 2008 until 2016, and a few are still operating today.

LAGADU was a trailblazer in that it was the first group to support black lesbians and gays in San Diego. Part of that care included meeting at black-dominated spaces because of racism at the Center. Mackey was a cofounder and leader of LAGADU but was

Zami Says...

Where do Sistahs hang?
The Flame   Club Bombay   Obelisk
Rich's I   David's Place   Java De Paradigm
Cafe Euphoria   World Beat Center   The Blue Door
Where do Sistah's Eat?
City Deli   The Juice Club   Thai-Phoon
Pick up Stix   The Big Kitchen   Sally D's
Hamburger Mary's
Where do Sistahs do their Hair?
Savvy
Where do Sistah's shop for Clothes?
Apparel Zone   International Male   The Gap
Any Thrift Shops
Where do they get their Spiritual Touch?
Metropolitan Community Church
Where do they work and Live?
EVERYWHERE
Where do Sistah s Get their Herb?
Longevity
where AAGWA Sistahs get a free consultation...
Where do we Entertain Ourselves?
Diversionary Playhouse
Hillcrest Landmark Theatre
Where do they get their Erotica?
The Crypt   Unmentionables   Condoms Plus
&The AAGWA Erotic Splash
Where do they Get their Music?
The Wherehouse

Off the Record
91X Reggae Makossa
Z90
What do the Sistahs Read?
Zami   Gay and Lesbian Times   Melanin Sistahs
Update   Lesbian News   Dyke News
Where do the Sistahs Go for Vacations?
San Francisco   Los Angeles   New York City
Provincetown
How do the Sistahs Dress?
Femme, Butch, and Everything in Between
How do the Sistahs Walk?
With Conviction
Talk?
With Action
Love?
With All Their Hearts
What's the last thing sistahs have to say?
COME HERE!!!   COME OUT!!!   WE RECRUIT!!!

ZAMI

FIGURE 18. From an Afrikan American Gay Women Association (AAGWA) guide. Source: Lambda Archives of San Diego.

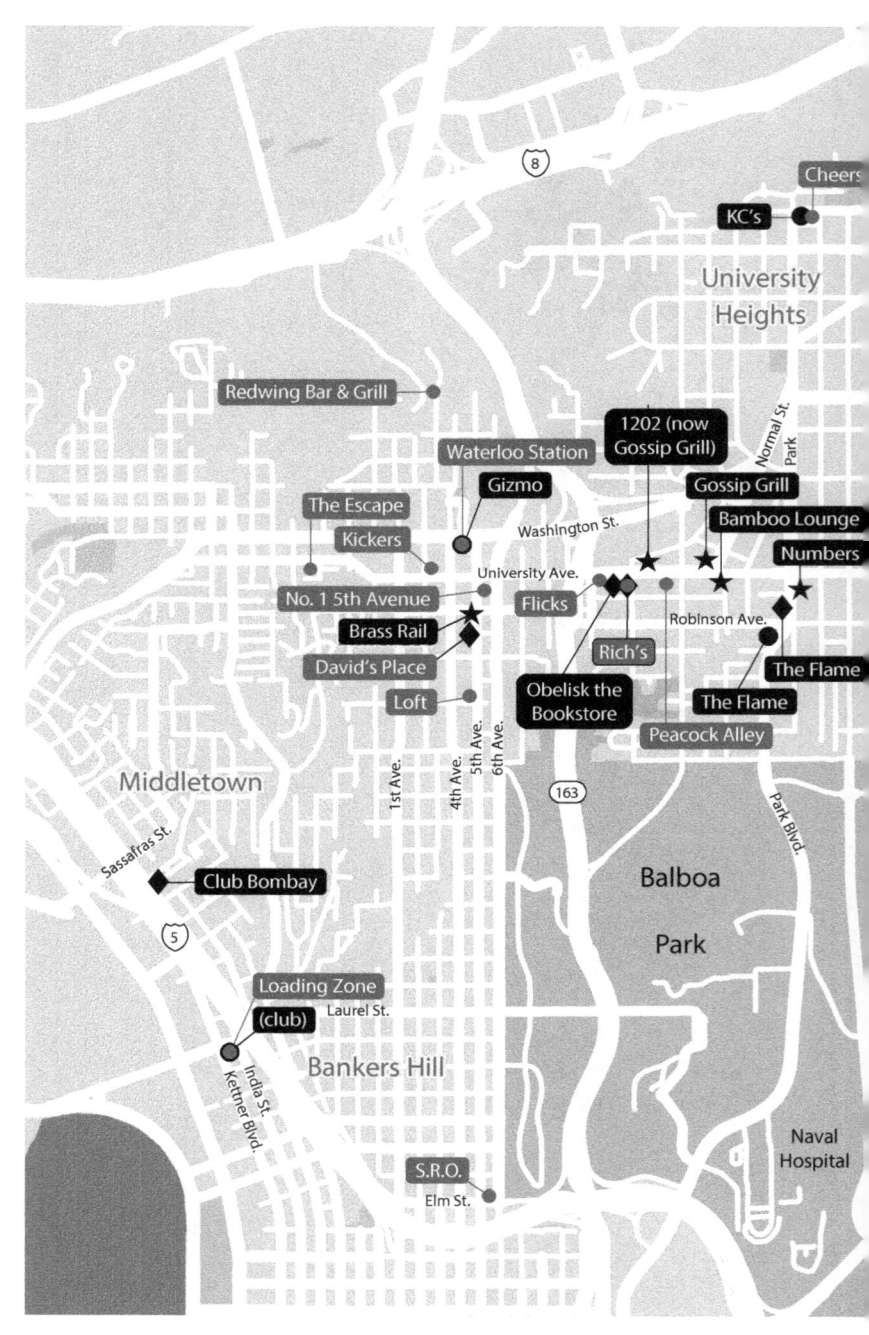

MAP 4. A map spotlighting the overlapping of commercialized public spaces that local lesbian and queer women frequented throughout the 1980s to 2011 in San Diego. The Afrikan American Gay Women Association (AAGWA) indicated where "Sistahs Hang" in a 1995 newsletter publication. The bars marked by the the *Damron Guide*, a gay tour-

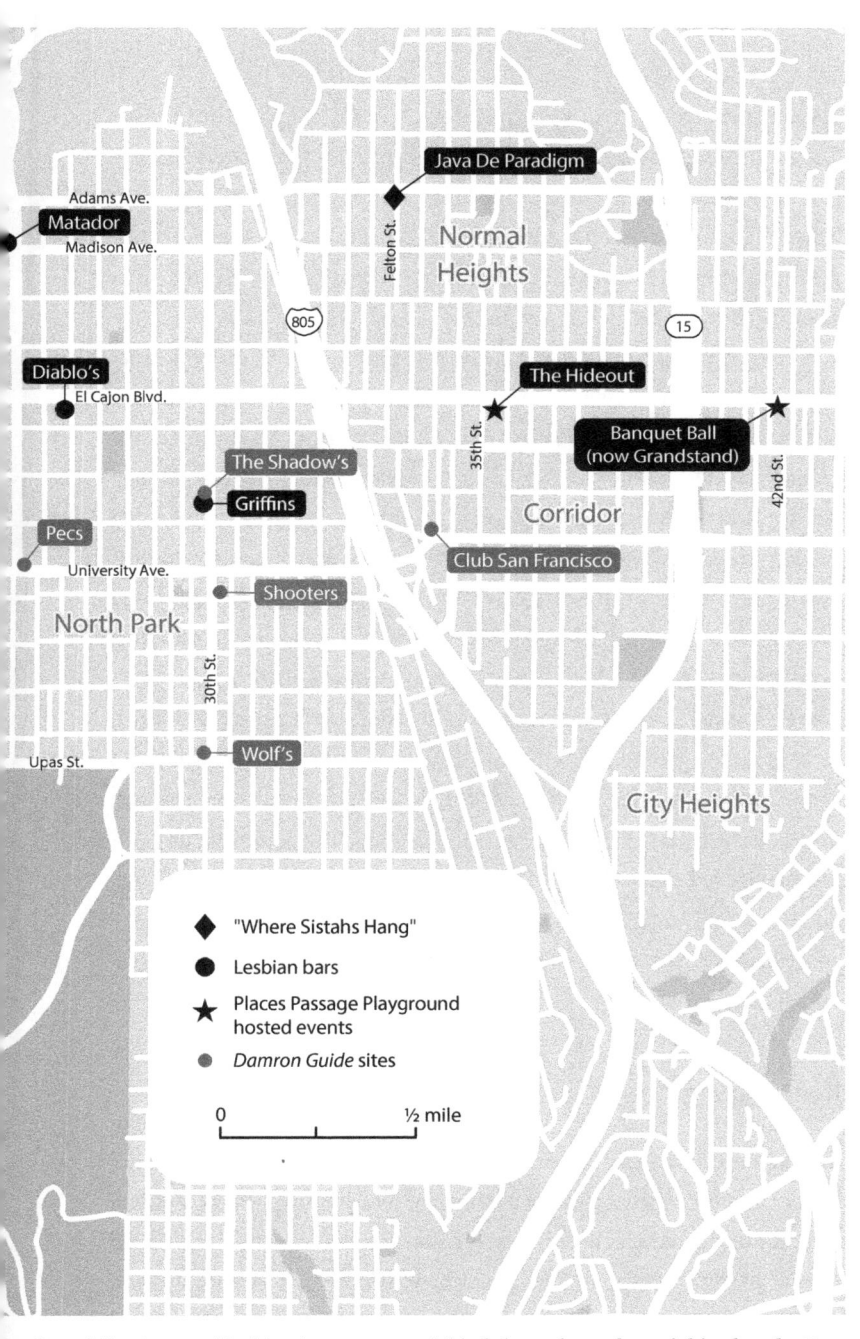

ist publication, and lesbian bars were sprinkled throughout the neighborhoods. Passage Playground, a black women-led nightlife events planning company, hosted events in Hillcrest and some near the Corridor and City Heights neighborhoods.

also known for *The Gathering*. The archive of her plays at the San Diego Lambda Archives includes the objects that most vividly capture her radical black feminist politics and poetics. Her plays were reflective of the current local dynamics in the larger gay community. They also challenged the status quo, like the role of religion in creating divisions among people.

The political power of San Diego's gay and lesbian residents skyrocketed as the twenty-first century approached. In 1991, the city's police force held a Coming Out Day rally at department headquarters, supporting openly gay and lesbian officers; and for the first time ever, gay and lesbian police marched in the local Pride parade. In 1992, Cynthia Lawrence-Wallace was appointed to the County Human Relations Commission. By 1993, San Diego became one of the battlegrounds for "don't ask, don't tell" and political pressure to lift bans on gays/lesbians in the military.[42] The following year the Lesbian and Gay Men's Community Center, formerly the Center for Social Services, officially opened its new facility at 3916 Normal Street.[43] Council members and the mayor worked to get $700,000 in public money. Openly gay people began to hold prominent roles in the municipal government, with the San Diego Democratic Club endorsing gay or gay-friendly candidates.[44] Yet racial issues continued to loom over the LGBT community.

Redistricting

By the time I arrived in San Diego, the racial climate of Hillcrest had not improved. Tensions had instead been amplified. In 2011, the city underwent the decennial redistricting process—the same year Cabaret Passage had its first party. While we were imagining ourselves being included in the very fabric of Hillcrest, safe space activists were attempting to expunge black, brown, and immigrant people from their city council district. Like safe space activists of the mid- to late twentieth century, Hillcrest stakeholders were using racialized metaphors about safety to profit—choosing instead the annexation of Balboa Park, a huge tourist attraction within the city limits, over what they saw as City Heights, which had race-related issues and thus was not profitable.

Since the 2001 redistricting cycle, gay activists had been insisting that Hillcrest should be a protected neighborhood.[45] Safe space activists of the Hillcrest town council argued that gays and lesbians were a "special interest" group that needed protection since they were not a protected class in federal civil-rights legislation. During the preliminary city council meetings, representatives of the Hillcrest town council used data from the San Diego registrar to map Proposition 8 voting trends—claiming that the bordering neighborhood of City Heights was to blame for the passage of Proposition 8. Prop 8 was a 2008 ballot measure that banned same-sex marriage in the state, and many white gays and lesbians blamed black communities for its passage. Safe space activists largely blamed residents of City Heights, a predominately black, Latine, and immigrant neighborhood. Yet political-science research about Prop 8 in California concluded that the proposition would have likely passed regardless, even if Latine and black communities had turned out in lower numbers—thereby concluding that black and Latine voters were not to blame for the passage of Prop 8.[46] As Ta-Nehisi Coates noted in his article "Prop 8 and Blaming the Blacks" (2009) for *The Atlantic*, inaccurate exit poll results as well as racism were to blame for these accusations. However, Coates also questioned the assumption that black people "owe" white people, especially white gay people, their vote: "But frankly, I have no use for people—gay, straight, white, red, rich, poor—who feel like black people 'owe them.' I have no use for people who like to trot out their history of supporting 'black causes.' I have no use for people who want to compare gay racism with black homophobia."[47] Prior to Obama, Bill Clinton, a Democrat who was very popular among black voters, signed the Defense of Marriage Act in 1996, allowing individual states to refuse to recognize same-sex marriages.[48] Regardless of the accuracy of these claims, black people (and people of color more generally) were regarded by safe space activists as an impediment to their political aims.

At the city-sponsored "town halls" on the matter, safe space activists relied on "exit poll data" that allegedly provided proof that residents in City Heights overwhelmingly voted against Proposition 8, and therefore were homophobic. Yet what seemed to be at stake was the inclusion of Balboa Park, which would then make the district a tourism powerhouse. Prior to the 2011 redistricting process, the city was split into eight council districts. The creation of a new, ninth district was suggested by the Hillcrest town council, among others. The council further argued that City Heights needed its own district to further working-class and immigrant-based politics for Latino and East African residents, while advancing LGBT political interests. According to their data collection, 70 percent of blacks voted in favor of Proposition 8. They also used the locations of gay businesses, domestic partnerships, and membership in the Greater San Diego Business Association (GSDBA) as indicators of where LGBT communities resided in the city.[49]

Realtor Linda Perine, a member of the LGBT Redistricting Task Force and GSDBA, was the most vocal about removing City

Heights from District 3. During a pre-map hearing on May 2, 2011, Perine presented her data and argument in support of removing City Heights from District 3:

> In 2008 a general election was held and a proposition was placed on the ballot. The purpose of that proposition was to deny the fundamental right to marry gay and lesbian citizens. That proposition, proposition 8, passed in San Diego County with a 52 to 48 percentage vote. However, in some neighborhoods, that unprecedented assault on the Civil Rights of a group of citizens was resoundedly rejected. In percentages ranging from 60 percent to 83 percent, these neighborhoods stood strong for the Civil Rights of the LGBT community. It is our premise that these neighborhoods should form the core of the LGBT community of interests. If we look at the numbers, in the neighborhoods, [directs attention to slide presentation on screen] we will see the support for marriage equality by neighborhood; Hillcrest, Bowling Gain*, University Heights, South Park—this is District 3. But if you look further down, Park West, you see Little Italy, Harbor View, you see downtown, you see Mission Hills, downtown, Park West, and Old Town. It is our premise that if you are going to create the strongest pro-gay, pro-LGBT district possible it should be comprised of the neighborhoods for the strongest support for the fundamental civil rights for LGBT folks. The average support of these selected neighborhoods was 74-percent. That is 33 percent more than the city of San Diego and City Heights.[50]

Gay activists such as Perine cited data from the San Diego registrar regarding Proposition 8 as a rubric for determining which neighborhoods should be included in a "pro-gay, pro-LGBT" district. Perine proclaimed that the proposed district (which, of course, did not include City Heights) defeated Proposition 8 with 60 to 80 percent of the vote, while City Heights opposed Proposition 8 by only 49.7 percent. She concluded that City Heights was a homophobic area because the majority of residents voted for Prop 8.

Perine held meetings at the LGBT Center in San Diego as well as at gay bars in Hillcrest. Chris Shaw and Doug Snyder, owners of Mo's Universe—Hillcrest's "bar-and-restaurant empire," including Mo's Bar & Grill, Gossip Grill, Baja Betty's, Inside Out, and Hillcrest Brewing Company—are considered founding members of the gayborhood. Both white gay men, they have strived to create "hetero-friendly gay restaurants."[51] They served on San Diego Pride and Hillcrest's business associations beginning in the 1990s. Mo's Universe posted about Perine's meetings on its website: "The LGBT Redistricting Task Force is asking folks to show up to support the LGBT community district. Having a district which is friendly to LGBT concerns and able to elect LGBT candidates is VERY important. Just showing up to support District 3 is a BIG HELP. It will take less than an hour and it will make a BIG difference."[52]

Dave McCullough, chairman of the Hillcrest town council, supported Perine by presenting a similar map that would ultimately exclude City Heights from District 3. Rather than citing the voting patterns for Proposition 8, as Perine did, he instead argued how the neighborhoods in the proposed District 3 already "naturally flow[ed]" together:

We would like district 3 to move further west. . . . It would include areas such as Mission Hills, Park West, Midtown, Little Italy, Golden Hill, Cortez Hill, and Old Town. These are areas with huge tie-ins to many areas of the current western portions of today's District 3. These areas are all very historic areas that naturally flow.

These are areas, places when walking from neighborhood to neighborhood are in many ways indistinguishable from each other and are the quintessential 'sign' neighborhoods—the neighborhoods with the neon signs. These also border or closely border San Diego's finest asset and one of my favorite things in San Diego—Balboa Park in District 3. And by the way, let's keep Balboa Park in District 3![53]

McCullough went on to elaborate that when he "strolls" between "Mission Hills, Park West, Midtown, Little Italy, Golden Hill, Cortez Hill, and Old Town," "it is as if [he] never left the neighborhood [Hillcrest]." And because of this "flow," he claimed that people who share this visual/economic spatial imaginary "deserve" to have their communities intact and their interests protected. During the town hall he explained that Hillcrest and western neighborhoods naturally belonged together, but eastward neighborhoods such as City Heights did not. In response, an online community magazine, *Zenger's Newsmagazine*, profiled the May 3 pre-map hearing, arguing that the removal of City Heights from District 3 was racially motivated.

The article, "San Diego Queers Split Over City Redistricting," insisted that the map was classist and racist. When the reporter from *Zenger's* asked McCullough if his map could be interpreted as classist and racist, he responded: "To me, the underlying issue is not race or ethnicity . . . it's fair and equal representation. But putting City Heights in its own council district, you're better representing it."[54] Indeed, there were possible material benefits of collapsing City Heights into a single district. Rather than expecting Hillcrest residents to address economic disparities, City Heights could represent itself and potentially become a site for the articulation of class consciousness. However, this potential was undermined by white property owners in the new district gaining increased political leverage.

The creation of a new ninth council district was intended to "unite" City Heights along the class interests of its low-income residents; however, it ended up reinforcing the political clout of the district's wealthier white neighbors. Mateo Camarillo, chairman of the Latino Redistricting Committee, was displeased that the SDSU College Area and the neighborhood of Kensington-Talmadge, both considered white and wealthier than the neighborhood of City Heights, were incorporated into the new District 9. The largely white residents of these wealthier neighborhoods accounted for a large percentage of the district's voting power: 45 percent. As Camarillo asked, "What do these communities have in common with the multicultural, multilingual (80 languages spoken), diverse immigrant communities of City Heights?"[55]

When Camarillo decided to run for the council seat in 2012, he was defeated by Marti Emerald, a white homeowner in the Kensington-Talmadge neighborhood. Residents of Kensington-Talmadge moved to gentrify the neighborhood by bringing in mainstream commercial chains, such as Trader Joe's and Henry's. Both grocery stores cater to white middle- to upper-class shoppers. Residents in City Heights expressed that this move would raise property values and gradually displace poor residents who would no longer be able to afford the higher rents. However, Catholic Charities, an organization that provides social services to the neighborhood's residents, thwarted that plan by purchasing the land and financing the development of a YMCA. Catholic Charities hoped that "the facility would integrate City Heights and Kensington-Talmadge residents, who don't often interact across the boulevard."[56]

In the end, the Hillcrest Redistricting Task Force and the Latino Redistricting Committee aided in the reorganizing of District 3 and the creation of a new District 9, which resulted in displacing over 67,000 City Heights residents from District 3 (about 50 percent of the district's original population). The new District 3 is now 70 percent white, while the new District 9 is 50 percent Hispanic, 23.2 percent white, 11.2 percent African American, and 13.4 percent Asian. While the new district ushered in a possibility of Latino/black voting strength, many of City Heights' residents are refugees and not able to vote. Similarly, while the creation of a majority-minority district was represented as a victory for minoritized populations in San Diego, it reinforced the idea that poverty, race, and immigration rights were not relevant topics to LGBT political discourse. At the same time, the Latino Redistricting Committee did not advocate for LGBT issues in the new District 9. The dichotomization between race/class and sexuality/sexual orientation alienates LGBT people who live in poverty and whose political interests intersect at different scales.[57]

What the following section takes up is how black women take their activism to the dance floor, especially when local LGBT safe space activists are actively pushing them out.

Passage Cabaret

At the time, I was naively unaware of this larger racial dynamic regarding the redistricting, but I did know that I hated going to clubs in both Hillcrest and the Gaslamp District downtown. Gay and lesbian bars intentionally played techno and Top 40, but never solely hip-hop, R&B, or soul—a way to prevent a certain "demographic." The crowd was always white and I did not always feel welcomed on Latino nights at the Brass Rail, mostly because it was majority men. The downtown black club scene, mostly straight, was also a disciplinary space—often enforcing "dress codes," meaning patrons were not allowed to wear sportwear, hats, or any other dress that did not fall into the category of business casual. They were trying to attract more reputable-looking black people, preferably college-educated and aged. This, however, also created an opportunity to tap into a certain market.

By the 2000s, LGBT communities across the US were having their own Ebony Prides and Black Prides, separate events that intentionally were celebrated on a weekend different from the official Pride date.[58] In Marlon Bailey's ethnographic study of ballroom culture in Detroit, Black Pride events are where many of his interlocutors gathered to access health care services, make money, create friendships, and find lovers.[59] Many of the initial Black/Ebony Prides were part of the National Confederation of Black Prides, which no longer exists.[60] San Diego was a city that also had these separate events. In a video in the San Diego Lambda Archives, there is an eight-minute clip from Mr. and Miss Black Gay San Diego, an "annual charity pageant" from 1999.[61] In 2015, the San Diego Black Coalition was created, along with a yearly conference they sponsor. In 2024, the organization changed its name to San Diego Black Pride.[62]

The first lesbian parties I attended when I moved to San Diego were parties curated by SoulKiss—known for the tagline "for women who love women"—and predominantly featured black women, often embracing and kissing, on their advertisements.[63] SoulKiss operated from 2007 to 2015. Although the Flame officially closed in 2004, it hosted the night I first went in March 2010. SoulKiss had other events outside Hillcrest, in City Heights, usually at dive bars. What kept me coming back was the gathering of black women, go-go dancers, hip-hop/rap music, and the dancing, always the dancing. The curation of a vibe takes work. First, you must find a bar that is OK with the clientele being mostly young black folks (twenty-one to thirty-two) and playing predominately hip-hop/rap. You don't want to host a party for free, so you must negotiate with managers or owners about establishing a door price or receiving a cut of the bar. You also must deal with meeting partygoers' expectations and become a professional in conflict avoidance as a matter of safety for staff and patrons. A central way we publicized was through a visual economy of black queer joy on social media platforms. Whether there were two people or two hundred, we made sure to take pictures of partiers, always smiling, holding drinks, looking happy, and feeling good. Later we edited them and decided which ones to post and whom to tag. For most promoters, this gig was a side hustle that they managed along with one or more jobs—as servers at pancake houses, administrative assistants, mostly in other service-related industries. Some used it as a platform to showcase their independently released music or other businesses. Yet they made the time to produce these events, oftentimes with little capital or luck. Burnout is common.[64] SoulKiss lasted eight years, Passage more or less five. Global Male, whose black gay promoter has consistently advertised to hip-hop and Latine communities, longer than SoulKiss, is still hosting parties at the Brass Rail.[65] Some of the successful nights for Passage were when we partnered with other black promoters; however, that did not guarantee that we would make a profit (see figure 19).

While many people told us that they were glad to see "more options," I saw the experience as divisive and disruptive to a more long-standing black queer woman-led business that no longer made those places as enjoyable for me. As Kemi Adeyemi concludes in her ethnography of queer parties curated for black women

FIGURE 19. Promotional flyer for a joint collaboration between Passage Playground and SoulKiss.

in Chicago, since "growth can lead to competition" we were often promoting parties on the same nights, which might have forced black partygoers to choose between the two promoters. Adeyemi's interlocutor explained how "somewhat related parties undermine black queer people's abilities to effectively face issues as a community."[66] As I discussed in the previous chapter, what made Silver Sands a black queer space was that it was the *only* black bar in downtown—meaning there were more opportunities for social experimentation and contact within and between differently gendered black people in one place.

Yet what led to the closure of Silver Sands was the lack of building ownership, which comes with the power to change the atmosphere, from advertisements to the hiring of staff and security.[67] A

FIGURE 20. Promotional flyer for Cabaret Passage's first event. Source: author and Facebook.

problem would always arise, especially between homophobic male security and queer black patrons, especially those who were masculine-presenting. We often had no recourse, especially for those events located in Hillcrest. By curating our first two events at a rentable event hall in City Heights instead of a club in Hillcrest, we maintained more control over the operation, but we spent well over what we made in profit (see figures 20 and 21). Early on, most people were deeply suspicious of us, either because our events were seen as a threat to more long-standing parties attended by black women or because most people had not heard of us, since we were not in the official LGBT tourism district. The labor of getting ready to go out is real—taking time off from work, coordinating childcare, managing safety at night (including parking or ride-sharing), putting on clothes, etc.[68] How did they know they were going to have a good experience at our event? Was it worth it? Since

FIGURE 21. Promotional flyer for Cabaret Passage's second event, a New Year's Eve party. Source: author.

we did not make a profit from our first event, we decided to publicize in Hillcrest and on the UCSD campus for the second event. Though the first event put our name in the scene, we did not make any profit. We understood that we needed to integrate ourselves into the Hillcrest community. We first promoted at UCSD, where I was a graduate student. The LGBT Center in Hillcrest also provided space for us where we screened an episode of a black woman-directed web series along with a Q&A. Gossip Grill, the lesbian bar, let us host a themed night called Tittle Tattle Tuesday, where we hosted karaoke and gave away tokens for free drinks. Even more importantly, we encouraged people to follow us on DowneLink, Facebook, Twitter, and Instagram. Our tasks shifted from trying to turn a quick profit to generating buzz through events that did not initially make a profit but did expose us to a wider audience. Passage would later go on to create non-club events, like the more family-friendly roller-skating and bowling nights and a singles-only wine-tasting event.

Yet expanding events to become more palatable to a wider, whiter, non-black audience also had consequences—these spaces became no longer pleasurable for their original audience. The case of the Las Hermanas coffee shop provides an example. It was opened by Dolores Valenzuela (a.k.a. "Mal Flora"), Carlotta Hernandez, and Teresa Oyos on 4003 Wabash Avenue during the explosion of lesbian woman-owned coffeeshops and bookstores in the 1970s. Las Hermanas operated from 1974 to 1980 and was a space that was initially used to provide housing for Latine domestic-abuse survivors. However, it gradually became overtaken by white women who chose profit over a more communal economic structure. As Alex D. Ketchum explains, "white feminists who began to attend the coffeehouse usurped power and changed its dynamics, making the environment less friendly and inviting to the community that had formed it originally."[69] A letter, "Coffeehouse Controversy," published in the *Lesbian Connection* on June 1, 1978, describes an incident where a performance by S'irano Avendis (Sally Piano) was canceled by staff at Las Hermanas because the performer allegedly "put down straight wimmin."[70] The anonymous writer of the letter saw this as an act of "censorship of wimmin by wimmin in a wimmin-only space."

> How can coffeehouse workers censor performers; on what basis; for what reasons? As one of the La Hermanas workers later admitted, her decision had been totally based on her personal feelings because she is the mother of two sons. S'irani was censored from the coffeehouse because she was considered "politically incorrect."' If one woman was censored from the coffeehouse, who's to say who will be censored next? Las Hermanas is a wimmin's community space—or is it?

They continued, "We feel La[s] Hermanas is being patronizing to straight wimmin by trying to 'protect them' from 'being offended.'" The anonymous writer of the letter obviously seemed troubled that the space was being whitewashed to please the influx of straight white woman patrons. By making the space accessible to a wider, whiter audience, Las Hermanas' original radical posture was diluted.

By year two, I already felt the impact of burnout, and I also felt aged out of nighttime club culture. It was not bringing in a livable wage, and it caused economic strain and trust issues between business partners. I decided to take a backseat on laboring as a promoter but continued to support my partner by doing what I could to maintain a stable household for us while she continued to labor for the meager wages the LGBTQ scene offered. Still, I do not regret my decision. I invested in a business because I wanted to curate spaces that were more hospitable to black women in San Diego, and especially the neighborhood of Hillcrest. These black-led LGBTQ spaces were not exclusive to San Diego, but a national trend due to similar racial dynamics in other locales, nationally and internationally. More longstanding groups, like SoulKiss, created a model for other business owners like myself, who wanted to also tap into the local niche black LGBTQ economy. Yet the curation of more spaces was not beneficial to black women patrons or business owners, since it created competition and division among black business owners. The inability to own property was a major obstacle that prevented black women business owners from making spaces more accommodating to their black women patrons. Even more, opening the space to patrons beyond the niche market also created problems, such as making the space less comfortable for its initial community members. Disillusioned with commercialized spaces, I became interested in more activist spaces, such as the Mackey-Cua Project (formerly known as Queer Progressive People of Color). Though I was not heavily involved in its activities, it offered a respite and a different perspective from the politics of commercialized space-making.

Mackey-Cua

The legacies of Marti Mackey and Jim Cua were the inspiration behind the founding of the Mackey-Cua Project: Queer Progressive People of Color, which sought to create a multiracial and multigenerational space to challenge the problematic race and class politics of mainstream LGBT discourse. Cua was a cofounder of the Gay/ Lesbian Asian-Pacific Islander Social Support group, founded a year prior to LAGADU in 1988.[71] He was also instrumental in the creation of LAGADU, thereby highlighting the interracial dynamic of these groups.[72] Fofie Bashir, a cofounder of the Mackey-Cua

Project, believed that a gay/queer organization must also be political and address how queer people of color were fighting not only for marriage but also for other basic human rights such as job security and access to education and health care.[73] Bashir's experiences working alongside conservative peers in the nonprofit sector compelled her to start an organization that worked to combat asymmetries resulting from race, class, and sexuality. Though she had extensive experience and success organizing around queer/lesbian of color issues in other cities, such as Los Angeles, New York, the District of Columbia, and the San Francisco Bay area, she confessed that doing this in San Diego had been a difficult task. She discussed how the LGBT movement needed a more visible "multidimensional" approach, which would advocate for the needs of poor LGBT people and LGBT people of color.

Bashir's desire to create an LGBT group was engendered by the fact that she could not find an LGBT group in the area with a political agenda. I first met Bashir in early 2011 at an event that catered to queer people of color organized by my former business partner. Later, Bashir contacted me about participating in a group she and others initially called Queer Progressive People of Color. Though I did not necessarily consider myself a member of the group, I went to several meetings and was put on the mailing list. In the first official meeting, which consisted of twelve people, we introduced ourselves and talked about what important issues the group would address. Initially, I hesitated to join the group, after my experience with another women-of-color LGBT group that insisted on *not* being political. Bashir had experienced the same resistance to political organizing from queer people/women of color in San Diego. She found that grassroots organizing differed in San Diego due to a generational gap: The "older group seemed disinterested," and she had "to take the extra steps to explain why we even need to do [political organizing along with social events]." In other cities that she had lived in, political organizing was a "given" and "easier to coalesce."

Creating the Mackey-Cua organization was important to Bashir because of the "intersections" in her experience: she was shaped not only by being lesbian and black but also by her father's experience as an immigrant. Her mother is African American, while her father immigrated from Ghana in the mid-twentieth century. Bashir recounts that African was the "worst thing you [could] call somebody" growing up. However, her father's experience of being a non-American black gave her a "much broader perspective" in relation to "both the lines where we need to fight in terms of racism [and] lines where we don't need to perform black victimhood." Though she experienced intense forms of misogyny within the LGBT community, she was expected to "compartmentalize and prioritize" certain identities over others within the black community. According to Bashir, black politics is always about how "we going to stand by our black men," and when black women attempt to center their experiences within black politics, it is "seen as dogging the black men."

While centering intersectionality within black organizations is an ongoing battle, Bashir expressed that proclaiming herself as a black lesbian has not been an issue within her family or larger community. She said she was "very blessed" and "didn't have a coming-out story, [but] just assumed that everybody was going to know." Her sister is also queer. Her grandmother had known since her late teens. Bashir grew up in Detroit, left for Los Angeles at nineteen, lived briefly in the Bay Area, and then migrated to the East Coast (New York City and DC), where she lived for eight years. Her time working in production in New York was her most memorable. She recalled it as an "empowering experience" and described herself and her black lesbian coworkers as a group of "fierce-ass black lesbians."

Bashir stressed the importance of discussing how the black community negotiates queerness. During our interview, I asked for her thoughts on Prop 8 and how gay communities in San Diego used it to label the black community as inherently homophobic. She called this the "worst scapegoating" and looked forward to other critiques of this representation. She disagreed with the view that blacks live fearfully in the closet. As an example, she explained that there had always been queens and flamboyant gay men in the black church and "nobody cared." She expressed that narratives about black homophobia need to be reframed to bring complexity to these experiences, instead of being evaluated on "other people's terms" that "look at things in these certain boxes."

Bashir explained how the Mackey-Cua Project's identification as queer purposely "make[s] the assumption that we are all included." For her, queer is an "understanding" without the acronyms. She further explained: "there doesn't have to be a very specific boundary or binary code of who identifies as what." At the same time, she admitted that she is still invested in spaces specifically for black queers and black women: "There are specific issues . . . that's not about comparing and contrasting. Anti-blackness is exported all over the world. Black women need their space to deal with that." She described Mackey-Cua as a space that cannot be claimed, but rather is "willing to be teachful."

Based on its Facebook business account page, the Project is still quite active, often promoting local events, including cultural ones, in San Diego.[74] As an interracial collective, its formation was due in part to activism by people of color in the late '80s and early '90s who faced similar racial and gender dynamics of safe space activists. Bashir's desire to create space was based on the fact that there were no leftist-radical groups in San Diego. The intersections of her own identity, being a black lesbian as well as a child of an immigrant, impacted her view of the world. Though black LGBTQ folks often battle homophobia within their communities, she did not face condemnation from her family—one of many instances that disrupt the idea of black people being inherently homophobic. For Bashir, what is most important is how black people make room for queer people in communities in ways that often are precluded in white-dominated, anti-black spaces.

Conclusion

Race and sex discrimination in both black and gay/lesbian spaces led to the creation of "separatist" groups during the late 1980s and early 1990s in San Diego. LAGADU, founded by black and non-black people of color, was a popular group that challenged the politics of local safe space activists. One of its most notable cofounders was Marti Mackey, whose plays served as a cultural critique of the times. However, safe space activism only became stronger in the twenty-first century, as black communities in San Diego, particularly City Heights, became scapegoats for the statewide gay marriage ban in 2008. As a co-owner of Cabaret Passage, I undertook my own business and space-making practices in response to these racial tensions. The activism of color of the twentieth and twenty-first centuries came full circle with the creation of the Mackey-Cua Project, emphasizing the interconnectedness of struggle and perseverance in the city.

Epilogue

On February 23, 2022, the California Coalition to Decriminalize Sex Work (DSW), composed of sex workers, organizers, and allies, celebrated the passage of SB 357, also known as the Safer Streets for All Act (SSAA).[1] The new measure struck down California Penal Code Section 653.22, "Loitering for the Purpose of Engaging in a Prostitution Offense," which allowed law enforcement to use discretion in policing and to arrest people based on how they looked, where they were standing, and whether they had condoms on them. An analysis of the penal code's enforcement in San Diego found that black adults, while making up only 3.4 percent of the city's total population, accounted for 56.1 percent of those charged. "SB 357 repeals a Jim Crow law that criminalized Black and trans people in public spaces," argued Fatima Shabazz of the DSW Coalition.

However, by repealing that specific section of the penal code, SSAA did not decriminalize sex work, it only eliminated one tactic authorities use to detain sex workers and their clients. The sustained effort by DSW to pass SSAA was eclipsed by new laws that subjected other street-involved people in sex economies to police harassment and incarceration. Under these new laws, authorities could still arrest sex workers caught with clients in public and private spaces.

While in their custody, police then pressured sex workers to incriminate their clients or accomplices with the promise of release without sex-crime charges. The new laws enabled continued targeting of communities of color and "ethnic gangs"—the masterminds of sex-trafficking rings, according to authorities.[2] As Beth Richie contends, "reform efforts are not designed to significantly change relationships of power between the ruling class and those who serve and support it through low-paid wages, traditional gender relationships, and so forth."[3] While SSAA successfully lobbied to end the criminalization of trans sex workers, it created a way for antitrafficking advocacy groups and authorities to shift their policing efforts to another group—marginalized men (and women) who undertake differently situated roles in street-based sex work economies.

Decriminalization is the focus of many sex-work activists, and antiwork scholars point to how even these radical political ideologies reinforce sex work as a moral crisis to be remedied by state intervention. L. H. Stallings succinctly elaborates on this dilemma in *Funk the Erotic: Transaesthetics and Black Sexual Cultures*:

> The current domestic and international sex workers' movement must resist dominant classifications of its efforts as strictly a labor movement or a limited human rights issue about the human trafficking of women and children. In each case, both are connected to moral panics around sexuality and problematic discourse of rights. Thus, national and international policies meant to contain sex in general also explicitly end up policing racialized bodies in non-Western nations. Positioned solely as a sexual morality issue, none of these panics and policies ever fully confronts how the ethics of work society systematically organized around capitalism creates various industries, sexual or not, that factor into the problem of

human trafficking. Current knowledge production and politics centered on sex work and sex workers means that some scholars and activists are contributing to the production of more machines. Capitalism may finally do what morality, stigma, and criminalization could not do.[4]

Sex-work scholar Melinda Chateauvert similarly cautions against state intervention, like legalization. As she notes in *Sex Workers Unite: A History of the Movement from Stonewall to Slutwalk*, "based on the experiences of sex workers in other countries, US activists are skeptical that government regulation of the industry will enhance their rights as workers or as citizens."[5] An ethnographic examination of marginalized sex workers revealed how legalization would make them vulnerable to state surveillance, which could affect their access to food stamps and other state benefits; about half of those interviewees also had a history of injection drug use, which would make them more suspicious of the state.

While arguments for and against pro-sex-work legal reforms remain debatable, many sex-work scholars instead center the anti-sex-work politics and revolutionary understanding of disreputability. As a local case study, San Diego offers an example of how black women found creative ways—in a continuously anti-black world— to sometimes thrive and always imagine different methods of approaching space and making place.

Notes

Introduction

Epigraph: Granville "Bubba" O. Hughes (San Diego resident), interview by the author, March 2014.

1. "Ordinance No. 9439 (New Series)," *San Diego Union and Daily Bee*, June 5, 1966, sec. I.

2. Redburn, "Before Equal Protection"; Ferris, *Crossing the Stage*; also see Boyd, *Wide-Open Town*, 183.

3. Faderman, "LGBT in San Diego."

4. "Claims Disorderly House Suppressed," *Evening Tribune* (San Diego, CA), September 3, 1914, 14.

5. Mumford, *Interzones*; Guevarra, "'Skid Row'"; see also Espiritu, *Home Bound*.

6. "Rids Streets of Vagrant Women," *San Diego Union*, March 3, 1910, 8.

7. Bailey and Shabazz, "Gender and Sexual Geographies of Blackness."

8. "Women Must Move Says Chief Wilson: Police Head Issues Orders to Rooming House Keepers Outside District," *San Diego Union*, March 17, 1910.

9. Pliley, "Prostitution in America,"; Fischer, *Streets Belong to Us*, 10, 29, 44, 73.

10. See McKittrick and Peake, "What Difference Does Difference Make to Geography?"

11. Fischer, *Streets Belong to Us*, 8, 77.

12. See M. Davis et al., *Under the Perfect Sun*.

13. Halberstam, *Female Masculinity*.

14. McKittrick and Peake, "What Difference Does Difference Make to Geography?"

15. McKittrick, *Demonic Grounds*, xix.

16. Hartman, *Wayward Lives*.

17. Hartman, 4.

18. Adeyemi, *Feels Right*, 50.

19. Goluboff and Sorensen, "United States Vagrancy Laws"; Goluboff, *Vagrant Nation*.

20. Chateauvert, *Sex Workers Unite*.

21. Berg, *Porn Work*, 21.

22. Stallings, *Funk the Erotic*, 20.

23. Miller-Young, *A Taste for Brown Sugar*, 18.

24. Berg, *Porn Work*.

25. Mario Koran, "There's Virtually No Such Thing as Voluntary Sex Work, Says DA," *Voice of San Diego*, April 12, 2018, https://voiceofsandiego.org/2018/04/12/theres-virtually-no-such-thing-as-voluntary-sex-work-says-da/.

26. Hua, "Telling Stories of Trafficking"; Chuang, "Exploitation Creep and the Unmaking of Human Trafficking Law." For a global perspective see Blanchette and Da Silva, "On Bullshit and the Trafficking of Women"; Mitchell, *Panics without Borders*.

27. Hua and Nigorizawa, "US Sex Trafficking."

28. Chuang, "Exploitation Creep," 611.

29. Brooks, "Innocent White Victims and Fallen Black Girls," 513.

30. Pliley, "The Sex Wars"; see Hanhardt, *Safe Space*.

31. Although Kelly Lytle Hernández's *City of Inmates* is very useful in examining the caging of people of color and marginalized white men in California, it does not document histories of Black imprisonment until the 1960s. For a study on the mid-twentieth-century prison industrial complex in California, see Gilmore, *Golden Gulag*.

32. Sarah Haley, *No Mercy Here*, 4–5.

33. Haley, *No Mercy Here*, 82, 101, 119, 288; Feimster, *Southern Horrors*; Hicks, *Talk with You Like a Woman*.

34. Feimster, *Southern Horrors*, 65.

35. Freedman, *Their Sisters' Keepers*.

36. Beth Richie, *Arrested Justice*; McCorkel, *Breaking Women*.

37. Shabazz, *Spatializing Blackness*, 2.

38. Fischer, *Streets Belong to Us*.

39. Ciani, "A 'Growing Evil' or 'Inventive Genius'"; McEvoy, "In Places Men Reject"; Guevarra, "'Skid Row'"; Espiritu, *Home Bound*.

40. Ross and Sullivan, "Tracing Lines of Horizontal Hostility," 611.

41. Mulroy et al., *Seeking El Dorado*; Wheeler, *Black California*; Lapp, *Blacks in Gold Rush California*.

42. S. Moore, *To Place Our Deeds*.

43. Madyun and Malone, "Black Pioneers in San Diego."

44. Shragge and Walshok, *Invention and Reinvention*; Abremski and Roben, "UC San Diego, the Military." Also see Hennessey, "San Diego, the U.S. Navy, and Urban Development."

45. Gonzalez and Lipman, "Introduction: Tours of Duty and Tours of Leisure."

46. Teresia Teaiwa's concept of "militourism" is useful in framing how the military plays a central role in creating tourism for servicemen and personnel, including brothels and other adult industries. Teaiwa, "bikinis and other s/pacific n/oceans."

Chapter 1

1. Complaint, Irene Shepard vs. James Byers; in another publication, I spelled the last name Shepard as Shepherd because it was the most consistent name across federal and municipal publications—i.e., the US census and the city directory.

2. Complaint, Irene Shepard vs. James Byers.

3. See Hennigan, "Property War."

4. For information about the facility, see Dietzler, "Individual Histories of Detention Houses," 97–99.

5. Application of Shepard for Habeas Corpus.

6. "United States of America, Bureau of the Census, Fifteenth Census of the United States, 1930."

7. Shragge, "'New Federal City,'" 334. Originally in Nash, *American West Transformed*, vii, 17, 56–59.

8. Shragge and Walshok, *Invention and Reinvention*, 37.

9. Macphail, "Shady Ladies," 12–14.

10. Macphail.

11. Bellon, "House Wreckers," 1, 8.

12. Bellon, 1–2.

13. Bellon, 2, 6; also see Dunlap, "Reform of Rape Law."

14. "Reformers Want Stingaree Closed: Members of the Committee Encouraged to Believe Police Will Act," *San Diego Union*, October 2, 1912.

15. "Startling Disclosures: What A Council Committee Has Discovered; Leveling Blackmail of Prostitutes," *San Diego Union*, February 19, 1888.

16. *Evening Tribune*, October 12, 1919, 5; Kneeland, "Modern Boston Tea Party"; Cimino, "Safeguarding the Innocent."

17. "Reformers Want Stingaree Closed."

18. "Open Discussion of Social Evil Bring Many Letters from Union Readers," *San Diego Union*, October 16, 1913.

19. McKanna, "Prostitutes, Progressives and Police," 61.

20. "Claims Disorderly Houses Suppressed," *Evening Tribune*, September 3, 1914.

21. "City Council Votes for Suppression of All Redlight Saloon Resorts," *San Diego Union*, February 11, 1910.

22. "Legal Advertisements: Ordinance No. 3985," *San Diego Union*, February 15, 1910.

23. "Two Hell Holes Closed: Casino Theatre and Weeping Willow Saloon Are No More," *San Diego Weekly Union*, February 14, 1895.

24. "Flaunting Vice: Disgraceful Scenes in San Diego's Slums," *San Diego Union*, February 18, 1888.

25. "At midnight last night the police raided the two resorts in Stingaree, known as the 'parlor houses' in distinction from the crib houses." "Raids Made in Stingaree," *San Diego Weekly Union*, June 16, 1904; "Successful Police Raid: Seven Red-Light Women Arrested Last Night—'Parlor Houses,'" *Evening Tribune*, June 11, 1904. For a discussion of cribs and parlor houses, see Rosen, *Lost Sisterhood*, 87, 92, 94; for a discussion of cribs, see Butler, *Daughters of Joy*, 50, 60, 86.

26. Bellon, "Walter Bellon Manuscript."

27. "They Left City Very Suddenly," *San Diego Union*, March 24, 1902; Carlton, "Blacks in San Diego County" (1977), 165–66.

28. "California, U.S., Prison and Correctional Records, 1851–1950." Ancestry.com.

29. "Rids Street of Vagrant Women: Chief Wilson Lays Down Law with Warning of Undesirable Class," *San Diego Union*, March 5, 1910; "Clamps Lid on Stingaree Next Monday Morning: New Ordinance Closing So-Called Temperance Joints Then Becomes Effective," *Evening Tribune*, March 11, 1910; Nagel, "San Diego's Chinatown and Stingaree District," 18.

30. "Rids Street."

31. "Clamps Lid," 5.

32. Groth, *Living Downtown*, 5.

33. Cimino, "Safeguarding the Innocent"; C. Wilson, "Why The Y?"

34. Groth, *Living Downtown*, 93–94.

35. Groth, 93.

36. Groth, 104–5.

37. "Women Fight with Stones on Street," *San Diego Union*, February 24, 1910.

38. "Makes Bluff at Killing Herself: Negro Woman Shoots Hole through Shoulder Because She Was 'Blue,'" *San Diego Union and Daily Bee*, March 30, 1909.

39. "Double Row of Prisoners Face Police Justice," *Evening Tribune*, August 11, 1910.

40. "San Diego Ward 5, San Diego, California. (Washington DC: Census, 1910)." Ancestry.com.

41. "San Diego Ward 5."

42. Ancestry.com search for race (Black) and Ward Five.

43. "'Knocked Me Down and Jumped on Me': Colored Women Tell Judge of Trouble Which One Was Worsted," *San Diego Union and Daily Bee*, April 23, 1910.

44. "Negro Women Have Trouble on H Street," *Evening Tribune*, February 8, 1910.

45. "U.S., City Directories, 1822–1995." Ancestry.com.

46. "Negro Women Have Trouble."

47. "San Diego Ward 5, San Diego, California (Roll: T624_95, Page: 10B, Enumeration District: 0153, 1910: U.S. Census Bureau)." Ancestry.com.

48. "San Diego Ward 5, San Diego, California (Roll: T624_95; Page: 2a; Enumeration District: 0153; FHL microfilm: 1374108, 1910)." Ancestry.com.

49. "San Diego Ward 5, San Diego, California (Roll: T624_95; Page: 2a; Enumeration District: 0153; FHL microfilm: 1374108, 1910). Thirteenth Census of

the United States, 1910 (NARA microfilm publication T624, 1,178 rolls). Records of the Bureau of the Census, Record Group 29. National Archives, Washington, DC." Ancestry.com. "San Diego Ward 5, San Diego, California (Roll: T624_95; Page: 2a; Enumeration District: 0153; FHL microfilm: 1374108, 1910)." Ancestry. com. "San Diego Ward 5, San Diego, California (Roll: T624_95; Page: 2a; Enumeration District: 0153; FHL microfilm: 1374108, 1910)." Ancestry.com.

50. Blair, *I've Got to Make My Livin'*, 141.

51. "Rids Street of Vagrant Women," 8.

52. *San Diego Union and Daily Bee*, March 14, 1909, 15.

53. Chen, *Chinese San Francisco*, 76; Pascoe, *Relations of Rescue*, 13–14. White reformers described "yellow slavery" as organized transnational sex-trafficking rings run by Chinese immigrant men who smuggled Chinese women to work as sexual slaves in US Chinatowns.

54. See Donovan, *White Slave Crusades*, ch. 6; and Donaldina Cameron's "San Francisco Mission" of Donovan's *White Slave Crusades*, 110–28.

55. Hirata, "Free, Indentured, Enslaved."

56. Almaguer, *Racial Fault Lines*; Pascoe, "Miscegenation Law, Court Cases, and Ideologies of 'Race.'"

57. Coleman, "African American Women and Community Development."

58. "San Diego Ward 3, San Diego, California (Roll: T624_94; Page: 17a; Enumeration District: 0149; FHL microfilm: 1374107, n.d.)." Ancestry.com.

59. "Suspected Negro Woman Arrested," *San Diego Union*, March 28, 1910.

60. "Suspected Negro Woman Arrested."

61. "Had 'Grip' Packed for Trip to San Quentin: Is Jailed," *San Diego Union*, May 1, 1910.

62. K. Hernández, *City of Inmates*; Chateauvert, *Sex Workers Unite*; Fair, "Surveilling Social Difference."

63. "Savannah Georgia Court Records. Research Library and Municipal Archives, City of Savannah, Georgia, Criminal Minute Books, 1932–1934." Ancestry.com. "State vs. Anna Barnett, Case #3390, Savannah, Georgia. August 10, 1933." Ancestry.com.

64. The People of the State of California vs. Anna Barnett.

65. Ella Gates vs. John A. Gates, No. 16871, Superior Court of the Country of San Diego (California); Complaint: Ella J. Gates vs. John Gates.

66. "Girl Pleads for Another Trial," *Evening Tribune*, January 29, 1907; "Girl Must Spend 25 Days in Jail," *San Diego Union and Daily Bee*, June 27, 1907.

67. "U.S., City Directories, 1822–1995." Ancestry.com.

68. "Get 4 Month in County Jail," *Evening Tribune*, February 25, 1916.

69. "Puts Up $50 Bail," *San Diego Union and Daily Bee*, November 8, 1910.

70. "Barnett Woman Given 90 Days in the County Jail," *Evening Tribune*, April 3, 1911.

71. "Suspended Sentence for Woman Arrested," *San Diego Union and Daily Bee*, April 14, 1910; "Fighting Negress Fined Heavily for Resisting Police," *Evening Tribune*, August 11, 1910; "Smuggles Opium; Caught at Line: Negress Who Bit Officer on Leg Obtains the Drug across the Border," *San Diego Union and Daily Bee*, May 15, 1911; "Negress Fights 4 Policemen," *Evening Tribune*, July 15, 1912.

72. "Police Catch 9 Alleged 'Vags,'" *Evening Tribune*, July 5, 1911.

73. "Resident Petition for the Removal of Women: Claim That Mother and Daughter Have Bad Influence on the Neighborhood," *Evening Tribune*, May 20, 1908.

74. "San Diego Ward 9, San Diego, California (Roll: 100; Page: 7; Enumeration District: 0202, 1900)." Ancestry.com. "Lawyers Dispute over Executrix," *San Diego Union*, June 21, 1910; *Estate of Munroe* (1911), No. 2874, 161 Cal. 10th, 118, 242.

75. *Estate of Newman*, 124 Cal. 693, A5 L.R.A. 78, 57 Pac. 686; *Estate of Gordon* (1904), 142 Cal. 125, 75 Pac. 672; *In re Bauquier's Estate* (1891), 88 Cal. 302, 307, 26 Pac. 178.

76. *Estate of Munroe*; Probate Records, 1880–1920 (n.d.).

77. *Estate of Gordon*; Probate Records, 1880–1920 (n.d.).

78. *Estate of Newman*.

79. *In re Bauquier's Estate*; *Estate of Munroe*. San Diego Judge Lewis sided with the local officials who characterized Gates as unfit to be named executor; Gates sought redress through the state supreme court.

80. *Estate of Munroe*.

81. Probate Records, 1880–1920 (n.d.).

82. Probate Records, 1880–1920 (n.d.).

83. See Stern, *Trials of Nina McCall*; Rousseau, "Morons, Mental Defectives, Prostitutes, and Dope Fiends."

84. *Estate of Munroe*; Probate Records, 1880–1920 (n.d.).

85. "'I Always Walk with Willie' Sings Negress; Sure Enough She Did," *San Diego Union*, May 5, 1912.

86. Fair, "Surveilling Social Difference," 657; Gross, *Colored Amazons*, 137–38.

87. Bennett, *Africans in Colonial Mexico*. Before the annexation of the Mexican national territory to the United States, most people of African descent in Mexico did not imagine themselves as part of a larger black community. Instead, the African presence in colonial Mexico displayed a growing fluidity about race and interethnic relationality. Although Spanish colonial law still enforced a *systema de castas*, in which colonial populations were racialized, many black (enslaved) laborers were given special rights or allowed to work for a set duration until a predetermined release. Intermarriage between persons of African descent and indigenous or mestizo persons was also common. Although unevenly applied throughout New Spain/colonial Mexico and solely dependent on a (white) owner's continued approval, this system enabled a possible transition from slavery. However, the annexation of Spanish territories through the Treaty of Guadalupe Hidalgo (1848) ushered in a new set of US juridical and social relations in which racial categorizations become more essentialized and rigid. The transition from a tripartite system under colonial Mexico to an American biracial system consequently resulted in an era of heightened violence, political instability, and new manifestations of anti-blackness. Hochschild and Powell, "Racial Reorganization and the United States Census." Also see Hobbs, *A Chosen Exile*.

88. Haley, *No Mercy Here*; Snorton, *Black on Both Sides*.

89. LaShawn Harris, *Sex Workers, Psychics, and Numbers Runners*.

90. Snow, "December Bulletin," 91.

91. Rosen, *Lost Sisterhood*, 28–29.

92. "Police Enforce Abatement Law," *Evening Tribune*, June 18, 1915; "Thirteen Women in Toil of Law," *San Diego Union*, June 19, 1915.

93. Hennigan, "Property War," 129.

94. Hennigan, 128.

95. Hennigan, 185.

96. Bellon, "House Wreckers," 19.

97. "70 Buildings under Tenement House Law," *Evening Tribune*, November 1, 1913.

98. "Police Enforce Abatement Law"; "Thirteen Women in Toil of Law."

99. "Police Enforce Abatement Law."

100. "Police Arrest 13 in Vice Raid; Bail Denied," *San Diego Union*, July 31, 1915, sec. 2; MacPhail, "Shady Ladies," 2–28.

101. "22 Negro Women Driven Out of City By Police," *San Diego Union*, December 7, 1915.

102. Christensen, "Mujeres Públicas."

103. "A State Health Department."

104. B. Johnson, "Eliminating Vice," 64.

105. Chamberlain-Kahn Act, Army Appropriations Act, § Vol. 40 (1918).

106. In H. Moore, "Four Million Dollars."

107. *Social Hygiene*, vol. 5, no. 1, January 1919.

108. Luker, "Sex, Social Hygiene," 616.

109. Stern, *Trials of Nina McCall*, 62.

110. Flores-Villalobos, *Silver Women*, 65.

111. Blatchford, "Venereal Disease in the Canal Zone," 259.

112. Blatchford, 261–62.

113. "A History and a Forecast," 556.

114. Eliot and Snow, "1900–1915 Progress"; Donovan, *White Slave Crusades*, 137.

115. Bristow, *Making Men Moral*, 159.

116. Thompson and Kingery, "Syphilis in the Negro," 385.

117. Thompson and Kingery, "Syphilis in the Negro," 387.

118. Bristow, *Making Men Moral*, xviii.

119. Bristow, 163.

120. Bristow, 98, 160.

121. "Women Found in Room with Soldiers," *San Diego Union*, November 8, 1917.

122. "Three Taken in Raid on Disorderly Houses," *San Diego Union*, December 18, 1917.

123. Dietzler, "Individual Histories," 97–98.

124. Stern, *Trials of Nina McCall*, 98; Clement, *Love for Sale*, 85; Hallgren, "Mothers Raise the Army," 140; Bristow, *Making Men Moral*, 161–62.

125. Montelongo, "Illicit Inhabitants," 77–84.

126. Dietzler, "Individual Histories," 99.

127. Luker, "Sex, Social Hygiene," 622–24; Storey, "Evaluation of Governmental Aid," 3; Dietzler, "Individual Histories," 3, 9.

128. B. Johnson, "What Some Communities of the West," 498; Shragge, "New Federal City."

129. B. Johnson, 13–14.

130. In the *Trials of Nina McCall*, Scott Stern discusses a memo, "Venereal Disease among Colored Troops and Colored Civilian Population" (1918), where Johnson revealed how military camps were ignoring miscegenation rules, especially those between white soldiers and black women. Stern, *Trials of Nina McCall*, 98.

131. Saito, "African Americans and Historic Preservation in San Diego"; Toombs, "Harlem Renaissance in San Diego"; Carrico and Jordon, "Centre City Development Corporation."

132. "Attempt to Close Cafes Fails," *San Diego Union and Daily Bee*, August 7, 1917; "Say Cafe Dancing Must Go," *Evening Tribune*, August 6, 1917.

133. "Say Cafe Dancing Must Go"; "Attempt to Close Cafes Fails."

134. Stern, *Trials of Nina McCall*; Parascandola, "Presidential Address"; Storm, "Controlling Venereal Disease."

135. Carrico and Jordon, "Centre City Development Corporation"; Saito, "African Americans and Historic Preservation in San Diego"; Toombs, "Harlem Renaissance in San Diego."

136. Salmon, *Women and the Law of Property.*

137. Carrico and Jordon, "Centre City Development Corporation."

138. Saito, "African Americans and Historic Preservation in San Diego."

139. Pastras, *Dead Man Blues*, 111–12. Rowe was able to get Morton a job at the U.S. Grant Hotel.

140. Hobbs, *A Chosen Exile.*

141. Year: 1920, Census Place: San Diego, San Diego, California, Roll: T625_131, Page: 2A, Enumeration District: 319. Ancestry.com.

142. Mabel Ramsey lived in a suite at the Douglas Hotel and operated several brothels independent of the hotel. Carrico and Jordon, "Centre City Development Corporation."

143. Their address in the city directory matched the address that the census taker listed as corresponding to both Mabel Tyler and Robert Rowe four years earlier, in 1920. US City Directories, 1822–1995, San Diego. Ancestry.com.

144. 1926 San Diego Negro Directory, 60 and 62.

145. US City Directories, 1822–1995, San Diego. Ancestry.com.

146. "Five Shots Fired in 'Insult' Tilt," *San Diego Union*, January 14, 1926, 6.

147. "Ramsey Is 'Romeo' Wife's Suit Charges," *Tribune-Sun* (San Diego), January 11, 1940, 4.

148. "Police Raid Stories Clash in O'Haver Case," *San Diego Union and Daily Bee*, November 18, 1938.

149. Huff and Flanigan, *Joe Robison's Place*; Huff, *Rebuttal to the Moomjian Reply*.

150. www.sdhc.org/uploadedFiles/Resources/Affordable%20Housing%20Resources_11.14.12(1).pdf; https://sdhc.org/housing-opportunities/single-room-occupancy-units/.

151. Saito, "African Americans and Historic Preservation in San Diego."

152. Carrico and Jordon, "Centre City Development Corporation."

153. Meyerowitz, *Women Adrift*.

154. "'Zoot-Suit' Fracas Hits San Diego: Charge Whites Attack All Men Not Dressed in Conservative Suits," *Chicago Defender*, June 19, 1943, 20.

155. Alvarez, *The Power of the Zoot*.

156. "'Zoot-Suit' Fracas."

157. C. Wilson, "Why the Y?," 303–22; Travers, "Norman Baynard Photograph Collection"; Norris, "Logan Heights."

Chapter 2

Epigraph: Maya Angelou, *Gather Together in My Name* (New York: Random House, 2009), 70. Further citations to this source are given parenthetically in the text.

1. "Maya Angelou, Sex Worker and Hero"; "Maya Angelou: Sex Worker Is Part of Her Esteemed Legacy"; J. King, "Yes, Maya Angelou Was a Sex Worker"; Love, "My Journey"; Young, "From Prostitute to Professor."

2. Wood, "Almost 'No Negro Veteran'"; Onkst, "'First a Negro . . . Incidentally a Veteran.'"

3. Rosen, *Lost Sisterhood*, 33.

4. Rosen; Pliley, "Prostitution in America."

5. "Again, it is not so much if these events took place, but how she framed them in relation to her own social development"; Cudjoe, "Maya Angelou and the Autobiographical Statement," 18.

6. Cudjoe, 19.

7. Cooper, *Beyond Respectability*; Perry, *Looking for Lorraine*.

8. DeGout, "Poetry of Maya Angelou"; Maya Angelou Papers: 1927–2009 [Bulk 1961–2009], Maya Angelou Papers, New York Public Library.

9. Angelou, *Conversations with Maya Angelou*, 14.

10. Angelou, 14.

11. Angelou, 14.

12. Angelou, 15.

13. Blassingame, "Black Autobiographies as History and Literature"; Cogeanu, "Maya Angelou: A Trickster's Tale"; Cudjoe, "Maya Angelou and the Autobiographical Statement"; Lionnet, "Con Artists and Storytellers."

14. Cudjoe, "Maya Angelou and the Autobiographical Statement," 10.

15. Blassingame, "Black Autobiographies as History and Literature," 2.

16. Lionnet, "Con Artists and Storytellers," 130.

17. Lionnet, 140.

18. Rosa Guy Papers, Sc MG 903, New York Public Library.

19. Stallings, *Funk the Erotic*, 12.

20. Lionnet, "Con Artists and Storytellers," 144.

21. McPherson, *Order Out of Chaos*, 119–30.

22. Nishikawa, "Reading the Street," 4–5.

23. Nishikawa, 4.

24. Angelou, *I Know Why the Caged Bird Sings*, 69.

25. "Sad Stories"; Nealon, "Invert-History, 749.

26. "In her memoirs, Angelou never attains the level of self-knowledge that made [Billie] Holiday the artist she was. She was too careful, despite the mistakes she had made in her youth, and too much in need of approval. Could Billie Holiday have sung the way she did if she had accepted the limits of convention? Angelou did accept them. She aspired only to the traditional female roles (mother, wife), and she was determined to do whatever it took to fulfill her dream of the white picket fence." Als, "Maya in the Mirror."

27. Angelou, *Collected Autobiographies*, 163.

28. Kun, "Tijuana and the Borders of Race."

29. Froebel Brigham (San Diego resident), interview by Robert N. Geib, San Diego, CA, November 5, 1991; Robert M. Oaks (San Diego resident), interview by Robert N. Geib, San Diego, CA, October 24, 1991.

30. Angelou, *I Know Why the Caged Bird Sings*, 254.

31. Leroy Harris, "Other Side of the Freeway."

32. Norris, "Logan Heights."

33. Parker and Gay, *Official California Negro Directory*, 70.

34. Sylura Richardson Barron (San Diego resident), San Diego, CA, December 1993 (via San Diego History Center). Mr. Fitch was the first black person

elected to the Republican Central Committee, while Mrs. Fitch organized San Diego's first Republican club for black women in the 1930s. In 1936, she switched parties and became a founding president of the Logan Heights Democratic Club and a member of the Democratic State Central Committee of California. She also became the first black woman to run for the San Diego City Council. She also helped other businesses get their liquor licenses.

35. "Special Crime Study Commission on Organized Crime in California, 1945–1954," Bancroft Library, MSS 80/43C, Carton 1, Bookmaking, San Diego County (1–3).

36. "County Liquor License Chief Indicted," *San Diego Union and Daily Bee*, June 3, 1954, 1.

37. "George Ramsey Host to Many Celebrities in San Diego, Cal.," *Chicago Defender*, February 27, 1937, 20.

38. See Williamson, *Scandalize My Name*, chap. 5; Beam, *In the Life*.

39. In 1942, the first service branches for women in the military were created—the Women's Auxiliary Army Corps (WAAC); its naval equivalent, the Women Accepted for Volunteer Emergency Service (WAVES); and the airborne section, the Women's Auxiliary Ferrying Squadron (WAFS). See Bolzenius, *Glory in Their Spirit*.

40. Fischer, *Streets Belong to Us*; Mumford, *Interzones*; Stern, *Trials of Nina McCall*; Luker, "Sex, Social Hygiene, and the State," 601–34.

41. Hennigan, "Property War," 123–98.

42. Harris, *Sex Workers, Psychics, and Numbers Runners*, 157.

43. Miller-Young, *A Taste for Brown Sugar*.

44. "Aunt Sukie," b. 181 f. 10, Maya Angelou Papers, Sc MG 830, New York Public Library.

45. Bolzenius, *Glory in Their Spirit*.

46. Loza, *Defiant Braceros*.

47. Loza, 85.

48. "He described the women as diverse, remembering in particular the African American women who charged five dollars"; Loza, 86.

49. VisionaryProject, "Maya Angelou: Gather Together in My Name."

50. VisionaryProject, "Maya Angelou: Gather Together in My Name."

51. Rodríguez, "Pornographic Encounters," 315–35.

52. Rosa Guy Papers (personal), Box 1, Folder 11, Schomburg Center for Research in Black Culture.

53. VisionaryProject, "Maya Angelou: Gather Together in My Name."

54. DeGout, "Poetry of Maya Angelou, 36–47.

55. DeGout, 42.

56. Angelou, *Just Give Me a Cool Drink of Water 'fore I Diiie.*

57. Angelou, *And Still I Rise*; Miller-Young, "Putting Hypersexuality to Work."

58. Hardison, "Why Maya Angelou Partnered with Hallmark."

59. Angelou, *Mom & Me*, 97.

60. Angelou, 97.

61. See https://www.pinterest.com/pin/9570217932227240/.

62. See https://www.worthpoint.com/worthopedia/maya-angelou-thriving -elegant-vase-220703378.

63. Angelou, *Wouldn't Take Nothing for My Journey Now.*

64. Wayne Warga, "Maya Angelou: One Woman Creativity Cult," *Los Angeles Times*, California sec., January 9, 1972.

65. Norris, "Logan Heights"; K. Delgado, "A Turning Point."

66. Madison, *Critical Ethnography.*

Chapter 3

Epigraph: Granville O. Hughes, interview by Christina Carney, digital recorder, March 1, 2014. All quotations from Hughes in this chapter come from this interview.

1. Nicole Murray-Ramirez, interview by Frank Nobiletti, Mp4, moving image, May 8, 2008, https://archive.org/details/casdla_000212. Lambda Archives of San Diego.

2. Dillinger, "Hillcrest."

3. Ervin, "San Diego's Urban Trophy," 422; see also Hannigan, *Fantasy City*, 7; Hof, "San Diegans, Inc."

4. Ross and Sullivan, "Tracing Lines of Horizontal Hostility," 611.

5. See Ervin, "Reinventing Downtown San Diego"; Jess Jessop, interview by Frank Nobiletti, audio cassette, February 1990, Lambda Archives of San Diego, https://archive.org/details/casdla_000029; Bernie Michels, interview by Frank Nobiletti, audio cassette, June 21, 1992, Lambda Archives of San Diego, https://archive.org/details/casdla_000037; Cynthia Lawrence-Wallace and Peggy Heathers, interview by Frank Nobiletti, audio cassette, February 19,

1990, https://archive.org/details/casdla_000024, Lambda Archives of San Diego.

6. Michels, born in Montana in 1932, worked in finance and organized with the GLF in Los Angeles. In 1971, he moved to San Diego to pursue a master's degree in sociology at SDSU. Jessop, born in Baltimore, Maryland, in 1939, was a Navy veteran of the Vietnam War (1961–67). He also came to San Diego to attend SDSU, just two years prior to Michels in 1969.

7. Dillinger, "Hillcrest."

8. Dillinger; Jessop interview.

9. Dillinger.

10. Jessop interview.

11. Lawrence-Wallace and Heathers interview.

12. See Gove, "From the Campus to the Community."

13. Delany chronicles his own experiences in New York's porn-theater area and the logics surrounding the "cleanup" of that area that was spearheaded by Mayor Rudolph Giuliani in an attempt to reclaim spaces for gentrification beginning in the early 1990s. Though the discourse was to clean up Times Square of pornography and men, seen as culturally/morally deviant and thus *unsafe*, the space was far from this characterization. Delany demonstrates how the public sex culture was not dominated by "hustlers" but by men who frequented the area to socialize with other queer men. It is important to note that even though this area was not designated as an official gay space, the practices within it emphasized its political nature, which was embodied by bodies resisting the logics of private/public access to space. Delany, *Times Square Red*.

Manalansan demonstrates how spaces are being controlled for the interests of neoliberalism, in particular New York City's Greenwich Village, and how that informs the surveillance and policing of queer/gay/immigrant men post-9/11. The performance of a type of LGBT identity through consumption and rights to privacy serves the mainstream political goal. However, what is erased is queer of color's materiality and negotiations of space, because of the intersections of race/class. "The market is constructed to be the filter of gay freedom and progress so much that dominant discourses in the gay community disregard how this kind of freedom is predicated on the abjection of other groups of people who are not free to consume and do not have access to these symbolic and material forms of capital." This means that queer of color, people of color, undocumented people, or immigrants do not have the same privileges as others who have different relations to the state. Manalansan, "Race, Violence," 143.

Hanhardt is most critical to my work because of her analysis of *gay-led* gentrification efforts in both New York City and San Francisco—thus creating links between two bicoastal cities and showing how "social minorities" are now appropriating the language of "risks" and "liabilities" and how that has led to the "discursive construction of antigay violence as part of the history of real estate speculation fueling gentrification and gay enclave formation." Hanhardt, *Safe Space*, 62, 64.

14. Trotter, "African American Fraternal Associations," 355–66.

15. Bérubé, *Coming Out under Fire*, 113.

16. Shragge, "New Federal City," 343.

17. Pleasant, "Honoring Black History."

18. Herman Smith, "Finds Negroes Help Run Naval Base at San Diego," *Chicago Defender*, June 17, 1944.

19. "San Diego Bluejacket Signalmen Cited for Efficiency," *Chicago Defender*, April 21, 1945.

20. Shragge, "New Federal City"; Bérubé, *Coming Out under Fire*.

21. Boyd, *Wide-Open Town*, 11.

22. Detwiler, *San Diego's Gay Bar History*; Faderman, "LGBT in San Diego"; Detwiler, "San Diego's Gay Bar History." The *Bob Damron's Address Books* also document the steady increase of gay institutions, but publications do not begin until 1965.

23. "Will Impersonate Charming Woman: Young Y.M.C.A. Member to Be Feature of Coming 'Show' at Spreckels," *San Diego Union and Daily Bee*, June 26, 1913, sec. 2.; see chapter 1 of Boyd, *Wide-Open Town*.

24. Detwiler, *San Diego's Gay Bar History*; Faderman, "LGBT in San Diego; Detwiler, "San Diego's Gay Bar History."

25. Detwiler, "San Diego's Gay Bar History."

26. Lindsay, "Chi-Chi Club."

27. "Column: El Cortez Sign Is Re-Lit; Balboa Park Wins Acclaim," *San Diego Union-Tribune*, March 5, 2022, sec. Columns, www.sandiegouniontribune.com/columnists/story/2022-03-05/el-cortez-sign-re-lit-balboa-park-wins-global-acclaim.

28. Bérubé, *Coming Out under Fire*, 116.

29. "Mayor Hopes 'Y' Will Be Razed," *San Diego Union and Daily Bee*, September 5, 1975, sec. B.

30. Ervin, "Reinventing Downtown San Diego."

31. Monod, *Vaudeville and the Making of Modern Entertainment*, 38. See also Miller Hagstrom, *Segregating Sound*.

32. Furlonger, "San Diego's Bygone Burlesque."

33. Hof, "San Diegans, Inc."

34. In chapter 3 of *Wide-Open Town*, Boyd discusses the attack on San Francisco bar owners. For the attack on gays and lesbians in the military, see Canaday, *Straight State*.

35. Bérubé, *Coming Out under Fire*, 109.

36. Arthur Ribbel, "'Off-Limits' Bar Signs Held Invalid," *San Diego Union*, January 26, 1960.

37. "Off-Limit Sign Rule Voided," *San Diego Union and Daily Bee*, June 19, 1962.

38. "Peep Film Seized in Raid Held Not Obscene," *San Diego Union and Daily Bee*, July 25, 1976.

39. Roger Showley, "Councilman Notes Surprise at Action," *San Diego Union and Daily Bee*, August 16, 1975; "3 Oceanside Bars Ruled Off Limits," *San Diego Union and Daily Bee*, August 19, 1975; "4th Tavern Off Limits to Military," *San Diego Union and Daily Bee*, August 4, 1975; "Testimony Heard on Bar Action: Reasons for Placing 4 Oceanside Taverns Off Limits Given," *San Diego Union and Daily Bee*, September 11, 1975; "Owners of Off Limits Bars Ask Probation," *San Diego Union and Daily Bee*, September 26, 1975; "Navy Upholds Off-Limits Restrictions against Two Oceanside Bars," *San Diego Union and Daily Bee*, October 8, 1975; "Bar Owner Sues Marine General," *San Diego Union and Daily Bee*, February 12, 1976, sec. B.

40. Hughes interview.

41. "Suspect Held in Slaying of San Diegan," *San Diego Union and Daily Bee*, June 8, 1970.

42. "Ordinance No. 9439 (New Series)," *San Diego Union and Daily Bee*, June 5, 1966, sec. I.

43. Faderman, "LGBT in San Diego."

44. "Rep. Mike Levin Introduces Bipartisan Bill"; Phil Diehl, "Downtown Oceanside Post Office to Be Named for Local Black Leader," *San Diego Union-Tribune*, October 27, 2023, sec. Oceanside, www.sandiegouniontribune.com

/communities/north-county/oceanside/story/2023-10-27/downtown-oceanside-post-office-renamed; Oceanside Historical Society, "Celebrate Black History in Oceanside," accessed March 24, 2024, https://oceansidehistoricalsociety.org /black-history-in-oceanside/.

45. Taylor and Rupp, "Learning from Drag Queens," 14.

46. Boyd, *Wide-Open Town*, 37.

47. Stryker, "Transgender History," 151.

48. Michels, "Social Scenes," 366–68.

49. Detwiler, *San Diego's Gay Bar History*; Detwiler, "San Diego's Gay Bar History"; Norman Braxton, interview by Jimmie Lovett Jr., mp4, moving image, January 28, 2016, https://archiveorg/details/casdla_000226.

50. Braxton got his start at Bradley's. "At that time there were no black people performing [female impersonation] in the city of San Diego. And all the girls that did perform on stage for Supper Club were all white girls who did black numbers." Braxton interview.

51. Chauncey, *Gay New York*; A. Wilson, "Friedkin's Cruising, Ghetto Politics, and Gay Sexuality."

52. Wittman, "Gay Manifesto"; D'Emilio, *Sexual Politics, Sexual Communities*.

53. Michels, "Social Scenes," 225–26.

54. Michels, "Social Scenes," 125; Michels characterized "trade" and "tricks" as "lonely, sexually deprived, [and those who] have limited funds and are usually at a loss for something to do."

55. This is explicitly discussed in Bernie Michels's thesis and oral history, the oral history of Jess Jessop, and *The Prodigal* newsletters. Michels, "Social Scenes"; Michels interview; David, "Sexploitation"; Jessop interview; A. Smith, "Drag, the Legal Viewpoint," 23; David, "Editor Comments"; Hollenbeck, "On Cruising."

56. Jessop interview.

57. Michels interview.

58. Jessop interview.

59. Regan and Gonzaba, "Mapping the Gay Guides"; *Bob Damron's Address Book*, 1965, 1973: Bradley's was listed in the 1965 Guide as "RT"; the Showbiz Supper Club did not appear until 1970.

60. Regan and Gonzaba, 16.

61. *Bob Damron's Address Book*, 1965.

62. Regan and Gonzaba, "Mapping the New Gay South," 16.

63. Regan and Gonzaba, 16.

64. *Bob Damron's Address Book*, 1965, 1972.

65. Regan, and Gonzaba, "Mapping the New Gay South," 18–19.

66. Regan and Gonzaba, 18.

67. Murray-Ramirez interview; Gove, 72.

68. Bérubé, *Coming Out under Fire*, 116.

69. *Bob Damron's Address Book*, 1972, 1975, 1977, 1980, 1981–1990s.

70. *Bob Damron's Address Book*.

71. *Bob Damron's Address Book*, 2005.

72. A. Smith, "Philadelphia Lawyer."

73. A. Smith.

74. Ancona, "When the Elephants Marched."

75. Shragge and Walshok, *Invention and Reinvention*.

76. Lynch and Appleyard, "Temporary Paradise," 22, 44–45.

77. Trimble, "Making Better Use," 9.

78. Trimble, 4.

79. Trimble, 5.

80. *San Diego Union*, March 29, 1980, B-10; *Los Angeles Times*, April 27, 1980, pt. 6, p. 9.

81. Bernard Hunt, "Gaslamp Quarter's Flame Burns Higher," *San Diego Union-Tribune*, February 5, 1980, B-1.

82. Ervin, "Reinventing Downtown."

83. "Opining."

84. Michels interview.

85. Dillinger, "Hillcrest."

86. Davis, Mayhew, and Miller, *Under the Perfect Sun*, 60; Reft, "Privatization of Military Family Housing"; Eckert, *Unseen Elderly*, 36. Downtown property owners converted the rooming houses of the earlier period into cheap single-room occupancies (SROs)—some of which were federally operated by the US Department of Housing and Urban Development. Many low-income residents relied on SROs because that was their only alternative to living on the street. "Inexpensive" SROs ranged from $12–$14 per night or $120–$249 per week.

87. Eckert, *Unseen Elderly*, 34.

88. Eckert, 42, 50–60.

89. Eckert, 79.

90. Eckert, 80.

91. Eckert, 139.

92. Eckert, 210.

93. Ervin, "Reinventing Downtown."

94. *Bob Damron's Address Book*, 1965, 1972.

95. Ronald W. Powell, "Stubborn Dinosaur: Gaslamp's Only Black Restaurant-Bar Owner Battles to Keep Silver Sands Café in Business," *San Diego Union*, December 8, 1991, B-1; Ronald W. Powell, "It's a Much Brighter World Now for an Old Gaslamp-Area Café," *San Diego Union*, January 11, 1992, B-2; Ozzie Robert, "Don't Mess with Robert Clay Unless You Want a Fight: God, Friends Helping Him Keep his Café," January 13, 1992, B:3.

96. San Diego Police Department, "Tina's Night Club Project."

97. Michels interview.

98. Leroy Harris, "The Other Side of the Freeway"; Vose, *Caucasians Only*; Howard and Gonda, *Unjust Deeds*; Howard, "California Swings for the Fences." For local San Diego history, see the three-part series by Cristina Kim, "The Hidden History of Rracism in San Diego," KPBS, November 17, 2021, and November 18, 2021: www.kpbs.org/news/local/2021/11/19/the-hidden-history-of-racism-in-san-diego-deeds.

99. Campbell and Mallios, "On the Cusp of an American Civil Rights Revolution"; Detwiler, "San Diego's Gay Bar History."

100. Campbell and Mallios, "On the Cusp," 377.

101. Norris, "Logan Heights"; Kevin Delgado, "A Turning Point"; Madyun and Malone, "Black Pioneers in San Diego"; Carlton, "Blacks in San Diego County, 1850–1900."

102. Trotter, "African American Fraternal Associations," 355–6.

103. Liazos and Ganz, "Duty to the Race," 486–87.

104. Liazos and Ganz, 491.

105. Trotter, "African American Fraternal Associations," 358.

106. Trotter, 357.

107. Camp and Kent, "What a Mighty Power We Can Be," 441.

108. Camp and Kent, 445.

109. Camp and Kent, 461.

110. Field notes.

111. Kutty, "Sanctuaries along Streets, 54.

112. Fidelity Lodge No. 10 official website, www.fidelity10.mylodgehelper.com, and Facebook page, https://web.facebook.com/sandiegofidelitylodge10.

113. Bentley Films, "Donisha Hughes 40th Bday Celebration."

114. P. Johnson, "'Quare' Studies," 4.

115. McCune, *Sexual Discretion*.

116. See www.facebook.com/granvally.hughea.

117. See www.facebook.com/granvally.hughea.

118. "Greater Johnson Missionary Baptist Church: African American Heritage Soul Food Dinner," Facebook, accessed April 14, 2024, www.facebook.com/photo.php?fbid=122125913612163596&set=pb.61554907884919.-2207520000&type=3.

119. "Save the Clementine McDuff Elks Lodge."

Chapter 4

Epigraph: M. Corinne Mackey, *The Gathering* playbill, February 11, 1991, at the Lyceum Theatre (San Diego, CA). Marti Corrine Mackey Collection, 1989-1992 (L1997.05), Lambda Archives of San Diego.

1. Adeyemi, *Feels Right*, 125.

2. See SoulKiss advertisement at www.facebook.com/photo/?fbid=118423 5586668&set=a.1152914923671.

3. Miller-Young, *Taste for Brown Sugar*, 63.

4. Bernie Michels interview.

5. Author's interview with Vertez Burks.

6. Lawrence-Wallace and Heathers interview; Michels interview; Detwiler, *San Diego's Gay Bar History*; Gove, 60–61.

7. Davis, *Angela Davis: An Autobiography*, 161.

8. Davis, 161.

9. Lawrence-Wallace and Heathers interview.

10. Lawrence-Wallace and Heathers interview.

11. Walker, *In Search of Our Mothers' Gardens*; also see Collins, "What's in a Name?

12. Lawrence-Wallace and Heathers interview.

13. Lawrence-Wallace and Heathers interview.

14. Michels interview.

15. Davis, *Angela Davis: An Autobiography*. It is unclear if Davis identified as a lesbian in the 1960s, but she did reveal her lesbian identity in a February 1998 interview for *Out* magazine. Lawrence-Wallace and Heathers interview.

16. Davis says that the US organization was "popular"; Davis, *Angela Davis: An Autobiography*, 157–61. See Odom, "From Southern California to Southern Africa."

17. Davis, *Angela Davis: An Autobiography*, 161.

18. Brown, "The Significance of the Newspaper," ix.

19. "Pigs Amuck in San Diego."

20. Davis, *Angela Davis: An Autobiography*, 154–57.

21. "Movement for a Democratic Military."

22. See Moser, *The New Winter Soldiers*; Cortwright, "Black GI Resistance during the Vietnam War"; Parsons, *Dangerous Grounds*; Lewis, *Hardhats, Hippies, and Hawks*.

23. *Attitude Check*, vol. 2, no. 1, California State University San Marcos Special Collections (SC010); see also Lewis, 133.

24. See Chrisman, "Free The Camp Pendleton 14"; Walsh, "Free the Pendleton 14"; Everett R. Holles, "Marines in Klan Openly Abused Blacks in Pendleton, Panel Hears," January 9, 1977, 34; Everett R. Holles, "Suit Defending Klan Causing Dissension in Coast A.C.L.U.," February 27, 1977, 20; Bill Richards, "ACLU Role in Klan Suit against Marines Provokes Dispute," *Washington Post*, January 28, 1977, www.washingtonpost.com/archive/politics/1977/01/29/aclu-role-in-klan-suit-against-marines-provokes-dispute/ae2d433e-cdc5-439e-b197-3a082346a2ac/. The photos are located at the Bancroft Library, Berkeley, CA.

25. See Favara, "Good Black Soldiers."

26. Favara, 1–2.

27. Carby, "White Woman, Listen!"; Wallace, "A Black Feminist's Search for Sisterhood."

28. Hutchison, "Lesbian Blood Drives."

29. *The Gathering* playbill.

30. Burks interview.

31. See "The San Diego LGBT Community Center's Community Wall of Honor," https://thecentersd.org/community-wall-of-honor/.

32. *The Gathering* playbill.

33. "San Diego Women's Show Including Marti Mackey," moving image, ½-inch videotape, 1991, https://californiarevealed.org/do/0577db1b-3ac6-4028-b7b9-8d543e49e66c.

34. Jan Cohen-Cruz, "The Problem Democracy Is Supposed to Solve," 427; seen first in Madison, *Acts of Activism*, 201.

35. Jones, *Is God a White Racist?*; Finley and Gray, "God Is a White Racist"; Blum and Harvey, *The Color of Christ*; and Evans, *The Burden of Black Religion*.

36. K. Brown, "Richard Pryor and the Poetics of Cursing," 67.

37. See remembrance video shot and edited by Vertez Burks: "LAGADU," January 21, 1989, English, ½-inch videotape. https://californiarevealed.org /do/6523ffe1-2556-497a-9f34-fd5413781474.

38. *AAGWA Gayzette*, October 1995, Lambda Archives, San Diego.

39. San Diegans join veterans and active military enlistees from around the country in urging President Clinton to lift the ban against gays/lesbians in the military. The MCC and the San Diego Veterans Association both sponsor post-card-writing campaigns, and community activist Herb King participates in the cross-country Campaign for Military Service bus tour. *San Diego Gay and Lesbian Times*, May 26, 1993, 15. One hundred demonstrators march in Balboa Park on July 4 to protest the ban on gays in the military. All branches of the military are represented. Some march in uniform; some wear paper bags over their heads to conceal their identities. The demonstrators are met by an antiwar end-the-military counter-demonstration by Queer Nation and Act-Up. *San Diego Gay and Lesbian Times*, July 8, 1993, 11–12 photo; update July 7, 1993, A-1.

40. Cohen, *The Boundaries of Blackness*.

41. See https://thecentersd.org/housing-services/#KARIBU.

42. The Lesbian and Gay Center, officially the Center for Social Services, a name taken almost thirty years ago when very few newspapers or telephone directories would print the words *gay* and *lesbian*, changes its name to San Diego Lesbian, Gay, Bisexual & Transgender Community Center, dba, The Center. Update June 6, 2002, 1; *San Diego Gay and Lesbian Times*, June 6, 2002, 14, 18; the San Diego LGBT Center reopens after eight months of renovation. The newly renovated building at 3090 Centre Street is soon to be the site of the Center's thirtieth anniversary celebration. *San Diego Gay and Lesbian Times*, April 24, 2002, 14,18 photo; update April 24, 2003, 7; see also update May 1, 2003, 1, photo.

43. In 1993: Sixth District Council member Valerie Stallings announces the promotion of her council representative Stan Lewis to the post of chief of staff. Lewis is now the highest-ranking openly gay staff person in San Diego city government and the first to hold the position of chief of staff; Chris Kehoe, an openly gay candidate for Third District City Council, officially launches her campaign April 10 in Trolley Barn Park in University Heights. She is endorsed by retiring council member John Hartley, in whose office she worked for over two years. *San*

Diego Gay and Lesbian Times, April 15, 1993, 9 photo. In 2000: Openly lesbian Kehoe and Toni Atkins win in the elections. Kehoe moves to the State Assembly and Atkins replaces her as Third District councilperson. Update November 9, 2000, 1 photo, and November 16, 2000, 1, 14; *San Diego Gay and Lesbian Times*, November 9, 2000, 14, 18 photo; November 16, 2000, 14,18 photo.

44. The redistricting process uses the most recent census data, including statistics on age, race/ethnicity, and gender, to determine new congressional and state legislative district boundaries. Redistricting has given residents tools to challenge gerrymandering—the manipulation of district boundaries by politicians in order to establish an unfair political advantage for one particular group or party. Historically, whites have practiced gerrymandering in order to prevent African Americans and other marginalized communities from electing their own leaders. Therefore, measures like the Voting Rights Acts help to protect minority representation by allowing racialized communities to create their own districts and elect representatives of their choice.

45. Redistricting Commission Archived Videos, City of San Diego, May 2, 2011, http://granicus.sandiego.gov/ViewPublisher.php?view_id=43.

46. Abrajano, "Are Blacks and Latinos Responsible"; Roker, "Stop Blaming California's Black Voters."

47. Coates, "Prop 8 and Blaming the Blacks."

48. This was also a time when President Barack Obama's ideas about gay marriage were "evolving"—from outright opposing gay marriage (2004) to supporting civil unions but not gay marriage (2007), signing the Matthew Shepard and James Byrd Hate Crimes Act (2009), repealing "Don't Ask, Don't Tell" (2010), to eventually being the first president to support same-sex marriage (2012). Steinmetz, "See Obama's 20-Year Evolution."

49. Redistricting Commission Archived Videos, City of San Diego, May 2, 2011, http://granicus.sandiego.gov/ViewPublisher.php?view_id=43.

50. Redistricting Commission Archived Videos, City of San Diego, May 2, 2011, http://granicus.sandiego.gov/ViewPublisher.php?view_id=43.

51. McEntee, "Owners Who Helped Shape the 'Gayborhood.'"

52. Screenshot.

53. Redistricting Commission Archived Videos, May 2, 2011.

54. Conlan, "San Diego Queers Split"; also see Lamb, "End of Round 1."

55. Florido, "Culture Clash."

56. Florido.

57. 2010 Redistricting of the City of San Diego Filing Statement, Final Redistricting Plan for the City of San Diego, August 25, 2011. https://cdn.kpbs .org/news/documents/2016/02/23/2011finalplan.pdf.

58. Yarborough, "Black by Birth"; C. Smith, "Apprehending Black Queer Diasporas."

59. Bailey, *Butch Queens*.

60. Bailey, 246.

61. "An Evening of Jazz and Fashion, Mr. and Miss Black Gay San Diego (Clarence and GiGi)," May 9, 1999, ½ inch videotape, http://archive.org /details/casdla_00006.

62. See www.sandiegoblackpride.org/about.

63. See www.facebook.com/soulkisstheater.

64. "As a profitable organization may not be sustainable, and a sustainable organization may not be profitable"; Adeyemi, *Feels Right*, 124.

65. See Global Male on Facebook, www.facebook.com/GlobalMaleEvents.

66. Adeyemi, *Feels Right*, 129–30.

67. Adeyemi, 92–95.

68. Adeyemi, 122.

69. Ketchum, "All Are Welcome Here?," 604; see also Ketchum, "Say 'Hi' from Gaia."

70. "Coffeehouse Controversy."

71. GPA Consulting, *San Diego Citywide LGBTQ Historic Context Statement*.

72. Garcia and Lopez, "LAGADU Lesbians and Gays of African Descent United."

73. Fofie Bashir, San Diego resident interviewed by Christina Carney, November 26, 2013.

74. See Mackey-Cua Project, www.facebook.com/QTPPOCSanDiego.

Epilogue

1. Va, "Gov. Newsom Signs."

2. Carpenter and Gates, "Nature and Extent of Gang Involvement."

3. Richie, *Arrested Justice*, 107.

4. Stallings, *Funk the Erotic*, 20.

5. Chateauvert, *Sex Workers Unite*, 4.

Bibliography

List of Archives

Bancroft Library, University of California, Berkeley
Lambda Archives of San Diego, San Diego
Martin Luther King, Jr. Research and Education Institute, Stanford University
Maya Angelou Papers, Schomburg Center for Research in Black Culture, New York Public Library
National Archives and Records Administration, Washington, DC
Research Library and Municipal Archives, City of Savannah, Georgia
Rosa Guy Papers, Schomburg Center for Research in Black Culture, New York Public Library
San Diego Historical Society Public Records Collection, San Diego

Newspapers

Attitude Check
Black Panther Community News Service (later the *Black Panther Intercommunal News Service*)
Chicago Defender
Evening Tribune (San Diego)
Huffington Post
Lesbian Connection
Los Angeles Times
San Diego Gay and Lesbian Times
San Diego Reader
San Diego Union
San Diego Union and Daily Bee
San Diego Union-Tribune
San Diego Weekly Union

Published Sources

Abrajano, Marisa. "Are Blacks and Latinos Responsible for the Passage of Proposition 8? Analyzing Voter Attitudes on California's Proposal to Ban Same-Sex Marriage in 2008." *Political Research Quarterly* 63, no. 4 (2010): 922–32.

Abremski, Dennis, and Paul Roben. "UC San Diego, the Military, and Building a Unique, Diversified Economic Growth Ecosystem." *Journal of Commercial Biotechnology* 26, no. 1 (2021), 93–101.

Adeyemi, Kemi. *Feels Right: Black Queer Women and the Politics of Partying in Chicago.* Durham, NC: Duke University Press, 2022.

Allen, Robert L. "Racism, Sexism, and a Million Men." *Black Scholar* 25, no. 4 (1995): 24–26.

Almaguer, Tomás. *Racial Fault Lines: The Historical Origins of White Supremacy in California* (Berkeley: University of California Press, 1994).

Als, Hilton. "Maya in the Mirror." *New Yorker*, July 2022. www.newyorker.com /magazine/2002/08/05/songbird.

Alvarez, Luis. *The Power of the Zoot: Youth Culture and Resistance during World War II.* Berkeley: University of California Press, 2008.

Amero, Richard. "The Making of the Panama-California Exposition, 1909–1915." *Journal of San Diego History* 36, no. 1 (1990): 1–47.

"An Evening of Jazz and Fashion, Mr. and Miss Black Gay San Diego (Clarence and GiGi)," May 9, 1999, ½ inch videotape, http://archive.org /details/casdla_00006.

Ancona, Vincent S. "When the Elephants Marched Out of San Diego." *Journal of San Diego History* 38, no. 4 (1992), https://sandiegohistory.org/journal /1992/october/elephants/.

Andrews, Gregg. "Black Working-Class Political Activism and Biracial Unionism: Galveston Longshoremen in Jim Crow Texas, 1919–1921." *Journal of Southern History* 74, no. 3 (2008): 627–68.

Angelou, Maya. *And Still I Rise.* Boston: Little, Brown, 2013.

———. *The Collected Autobiographies of Maya Angelou.* New York: Random House, 2004.

———. *Conversations with Maya Angelou*, edited by Jeffrey M. Elliot. Jackson: University of Mississippi Press, 1989.

———. *Gather Together in My Name.* New York: Random House, 2009.

———. *I Know Why the Caged Bird Sings*. New York: Bantam Books, 1983.

———. *Just Give Me a Cool Drink of Water 'fore I Diiie: Poems*. New York: Random House, 2013.

———. *Miss Calypso*. Liberty, 1957.

———. *Mom & Me & Mom*. New York: Random House, 2013.

———. *Wouldn't Take Nothing for My Journey Now*. New York: Bantam Books, 1993.

Application of Shepard for Habeas Corpus, vol. 34, criminal no. 759 (California Appellate Decisions, 2nd Appellate District, Division Two, 1921), 272.

Bailey, Marlon M. *Butch Queens Up in Pumps: Gender, Performance, and Ballroom Culture in Detroit*. Ann Arbor: University of Michigan Press, 2013.

Bailey, Marlon M., and Rashad Shabazz. "Gender and Sexual Geographies of Blackness: Anti-Black Heterotopias (Part 1)." *Gender, Place, and Culture* 21, no. 3 (2014): 316–21.

Beam, Joseph, ed. *In the Life: A Black Gay Anthology*. New York: Alyson Books, 1986.

Bellon, Walter. "House Wreckers Reveal Stingaree Secrets." In *Memoirs, 1912–1972*, n.d.

———. "Walter Bellon Manuscript," n.d.

Bennett, Herman L. *Africans in Colonial Mexico: Absolutism, Christianity, and Afro-Creole Consciousness, 1570–1640* (Bloomington: Indiana University Press, 2005).

Benoit, Cecilia, Michaela Smith, Mikael Jansson, Samantha Magnus, Jackson Flagg, and Renay Maurice. "Sex Work and Three Dimensions of Self-Esteem: Self-Worth, Authenticity and Self-Efficacy." *Culture, Health, and & Sexuality* 20, no. 1 (2017): 69–83. https://doi.org/10.1080/13691058.2017.1328075.

Bentley Filmz. "Donisha Hughes 40th Bday Celebration." YouTube, April 21, 2014. https://youtu.be/1ZhS5sAAOKU?si=gyPA_QFXJV_cAISZ.

Berg, Heather. *Porn Work: Sex, Labor, and Late Capitalism*. University of North Carolina Press, 2021.

Bérubé, Allan. *Coming Out under Fire: The History of Gay Men and Women in World War II*. Chapel Hill: University of North Carolina Press, 1990.

BlackPast. "A Brief History of the San Diego NAACP, 1917–2007." December 11, 2007. www.blackpast.org/african-american-history/brief-history-san-diego-naacp-1917-2007/.

Blair, Cynthia. *I've Got to Make My Livin': Black Women's Sex Work in Turn-of-the-Century Chicago*. Chicago: University of Chicago Press, 2018.

Blanchette, Thaddeus Gregory, and Ana Paula Da Silva. "On Bullshit and the Trafficking of Women: Moral Entrepreneurs and the Invention of Trafficking of Persons in Brazil." *Dialectical Anthropology* 36 (2012): 107–25.

Blassingame, John W. "Black Autobiographies as History and Literature." *Black Scholar* 5, no. 4 (1973): 2–9.

Blatchford, E. "Venereal Disease in the Canal Zone." *Social Hygiene* 5 (1919): 259–63.

Blum, Edward J., and Paul Harvey. *The Color of Christ: The Son of God and the Saga of Race in America*. Chapel Hill: University of North Carolina Press, 2012.

Bob Damron's Address Book. San Francisco: Bob Damron Enterprises, 1965.

Bob Damron's Address Book. San Francisco: Bob Damron Enterprises, 1972.

Bob Damron's Address Book. San Francisco: Bob Damron Enterprises, 1973.

Bob Damron's Address Book. San Francisco: Bob Damron Enterprises, 1975.

Bob Damron's Address Book. San Francisco: Bob Damron Enterprises, 1977.

Bob Damron's Address Book. San Francisco: Bob Damron Enterprises, 1980.

Bob Damron's Address Book. San Francisco: Bob Damron Enterprises, 1981.

Bob Damron's Address Book. San Francisco: Bob Damron Enterprises, 1990.

Bob Damron's Address Book. San Francisco: Bob Damron Enterprises, 1991.

Bob Damron's Address Book. San Francisco: Bob Damron Enterprises, 1992.

Bob Damron's Address Book. San Francisco: Bob Damron Enterprises, 1993.

Bob Damron's Address Book. San Francisco: Bob Damron Enterprises, 1994.

Bob Damron's Address Book. San Francisco: Bob Damron Enterprises, 2005.

Bolzenius, Sandra. *Glory in Their Spirit: How Four Black Women Took On the Army during World War II*. Champaign: University of Illinois Press, 2018.

Boyd, Nan. *Wide-Open Town: A History of Queer San Francisco to 1965*. Berkeley: University of California Press, 2005.

Brandt, Allan M. *No Magic Bullet: A Social History of Venereal Disease in the United States since 1880*. 35th anniversary ed. New York: Oxford University Press, 2020.

Bristow, Nancy. *Making Men Moral: Social Engineering during the Great War*. New York: New York University Press, 1997.

Brooks, Siobhan. "Innocent White Victims and Fallen Black Girls: Race, Sex Work, and the Limits of Anti-Sex Trafficking Laws." *Signs: Journal of Women in Culture and Society* 46, no. 2 (2021): 513–21.

Brown, Elaine. "The Significance of the Newspaper of the Black Panther Party," in *The Black Panther*, edited by David Hilliard (Atria Books, 2008).

Brown, Kate E. "Richard Pryor and the Poetics of Cursing." In *Richard Pryor: The Life and Legacy of a "Crazy" Black Man*, edited by Audrey Thomas McCluskey. Bloomington: Indiana University Press, 2008.

Butler, Anne M. *Daughters of Joy, Sisters of Misery: Prostitutes in the American West, 1865–90*. Champaign: University of Illinois Press, 1987.

"California Reports Local Improvements." *Social Hygiene Bulletin* 5, no. 1 (1918): 4.

California State Board of Health. "Between the Devil and the Deep Sea of Deceit." *Monthly Bulletin* 7–8 (December 1911): 43.

Camp, Bayliss J., and Orit Kent. "'What a mighty power we can be': Individual and Collective Identity in African American and White Fraternal Initiation Rituals." *Social Science History* 28, no. 3 (2004): 439–83.

Campbell, Breanna, and Seth Mallios. "On the Cusp of an American Civil Rights Revolution: Dr. Martin Luther King, Jr.'s Final Visit and Address to San Diego in 1964." *Journal of San Diego History* 61, no. 2 (2005): 375–410.

Canaday, Margot. *The Straight State: Sexuality and Citizenship in Twentieth-Century America*. Princeton, NJ: Princeton University Press, 2009.

Carby, Hazel. "White Woman, Listen! Black Feminism and the Boundaries of Sisterhood." In *Black British Feminism: A Reader*, edited by Heidi Safia Mirza, 45–53. New York: Routledge, 1997.

Carlton, Robert L. "Blacks in San Diego County, 1850–1900." San Diego State University, 1977. Bancroft Library.

———. "Blacks in San Diego County: A Social Profile, 1850–1880." *Journal of San Diego History* 21, no. 4 (1975): 7–20.

Carpenter, Ami, and Jamie Gates. "The Nature and Extent of Gang Involvement in Sex Trafficking in San Diego County." United States Department of Justice, 2016. www.ojp.gov/library/publications/nature-and-extent-gang-involvement-sex-trafficking-san-diego-county.

Carrico, Richard L., and Stacey Jordon. "Centre City Development Corporation Downtown San Diego African American Heritage Study." San Diego: Mooney and Associates, 2004.

Chateauvert, Melinda. *Sex Workers Unite: A History of the Movement from Stonewall to SlutWalk*. Boston: Beacon Press, 2015.

Chauncey, George. *Gay New York: Gender, Urban Culture, and the Makings of the Gay Male World, 1890-1940*. New York: Basic Books, 1994.

Chen, Yong. *Chinese San Francisco, 1850-1943: A Trans-Pacific Community*. Palo Alto, CA: Stanford University Press, 2000.

Chrisman, Robert. "Free the Camp Pendleton 14: Black Marines Battle Ku Klux Klan at Camp Pendleton Base," *Black Scholar* 8, no. 6 (1977): 46-49.

Christensen, Catherine. "Mujeres Públicas: American Prostitutes in Baja California, 1910-1930." *Pacific Historical Review* 82, no. 2 (2012): 215-47.

Chuang, Janie A. "Exploitation Creep and the Unmaking of Human Trafficking Law." *American Journal of International Law* 108, no. 4 (2014), 611.

Ciani, Kyle E. "A 'Growing Evil' or 'Inventive Genius': Anglo Perceptions of Indian Life in San Diego, 1850 to 1900." *Southern California Quarterly* 89, no. 3 (2007): 249-84.

Cimino, Eric C. "Safeguarding the Innocent: Traveler's Aid at the Panama-California Exposition, 1915." *Journal of San Diego History* 61, no. 3-4 (2015): 455-74.

Classic San Diego. "Bradley's Puka-Puka." Accessed March 23, 2024. https://classicsandiego.com/restaurants/bradleys-puka-puka-rum-bar/.

Clement, Elizabeth Alice. *Love for Sale: Courting, Treating, and Prostitution in New York City, 1900-1945*. Chapel Hill: University of North Carolina Press, 2006.

Coates, Ta-Nehisi. "Prop 8 and Blaming the Blacks." *The Atlantic*, January 7, 2009. www.theatlantic.com/entertainment/archive/2009/01/prop-8-and-blaming-the-blacks/6548/.

"Coffeehouse Controversy," *Lesbian Connection*, June 1, 1978, 7-8.

Cogeanu, Oana. "Maya Angelou: A Trickster's Tale." *Quarterly of Language, Literature, and Culture* 62, no. 4 (2014): 309-26. https://doi.org/10.1515/zaa-2014-0034.

Cohen, Cathy J. *The Boundaries of Blackness: AIDS and the Breakdown of Black Politics*. Chicago: University of Chicago Press, 1999.

Cohen-Cruz, Jan. "The Problem Democracy Is Supposed to Solve." In *Sage Handbook of Performnce Studies* (2006): 427–45.

Coleman, Willi. "African American Women and Community Development in California, 1848–1900." In *Seeking El Dorado: African Americans in California*, 98–125. Seattle: University of Washington Press, 2014.

Collins, Patricia Hill. "What's in a Name? Womanism, Black Feminism, and Beyond." *Black Scholar* 26, no. 1 (1996): 9–17.

Complaint: Ella J. Gates (Plaintiff) vs. John Gates (Defendant), no. 16871.

Complaint, Irene Shepard v. James Byer, H. H. Kenney, and Bernard Sotomayor (Superior Court of the State of California, County of San Diego, April 1921).

Conlan, Mark Gabrish. "San Diego Queers Split over City Redistricting." *Zenger's Newsmagazine*, May 17, 2011. http://zengersmag.blogspot.com /2011/05/san-diego-queers-split-over-city.html.

Connelly, Mark Thomas. *The Response to Prostitution in the Progressive Era.* Chapel Hill: University of North Carolina Press, 1980.

Cooper, Brittney C. *Beyond Respectability: The Intellectual Thought of Race Women.* Champaign: University of Illinois Press, 2017.

Cortwright, David. "Black GI Resistance during the Vietnam War." *Vietnam Generation* 2, no. 1 (1990): 51–64.

Couto, Pablo, Antonio Gomes, Carle Porcino, Valquíria Rodrigues, Alba Vilela, and Tarcísio Flores. "Between Money, Self-Esteem, and the Sexual Act: Social Representations of Female Sexual Satisfaction for Sex Workers." *Revista Eletronica Enfermagem (REE)* 22, no. 59271 (2020): 1–8.

Cudjoe, Selwyn R. "Maya Angelou and the Autobiographical Statement." In *Black Women Writers (1950–1980:) A Critical Evaluation*, edited by Mari Evans. New York: Anchor Press/Doubleday, 1984.

D'Arcy, Adelyse Marie. "Elderly Hotel Residents and Their Social Networks in Downtown San Diego." Master's thesis, San Diego State University, 1976.

David, Charles. "Editor Comments." *The Prodigal* 3, no. 39 (December 6, 1971).

———. "Sexploitation." *The Prodigal* 5, no. 77 (July 15, 1973).

Davis, Angela Y. *Angela Davis: An Autobiography.* Haymarket Books: 2022.

Davis, Colin J. "'Shape or Fight?' New York's Black Longshoremen, 1945–1961." *International Labor and Working-Class History*, no. 62 (2002): 143–63.

Davis, Mike. "Fortress Los Angeles: The Militarization of Urban Space." In *Variations on a Theme Park*, edited by Michael Sorkin, 154–80. New York: Hill and Wang, 1992.

Davis, Mike, Kelly Mayhew, and Jim Miller. *Under the Perfect Sun: The San Diego Tourists Never See*. New York: New Press, 2005.

DeGout, Yasmin Y. "The Poetry of Maya Angelou: Liberation Ideology and Technique." *Langston Hughes Review* 19 (Spring 2005): 36–47.

Delany, Samuel. *Times Square Red, Times Square Blue*. New York: New York University Press, 1999.

Delgado, Grace Peña. "Border Control and Sexual Policing: White Slavery and Prostitution along the U.S.-Mexico Borderlands, 1903–1910." *Western Historical Quarterly* 43, no. 2 (2012): 157–78.

Delgado, Kevin. "A Turning Point." *Journal of San Diego History* 44, no. 1 (Winter 1998). https://sandiegohistory.org/journal/1998/january/chicano-3/.

D'Emilio, John. *Sexual Politics, Sexual Communities*. 2nd ed. Chicago: University of Chicago Press, 2012.

———. "The Gay Liberation Movement." In *The Social Movement Reader: Cases and Concepts*, 3rd ed., 24–29. Sussex: Wiley/Blackwell, 2015.

Detwiler, Paul, dir. *San Diego's Gay Bar History*. 2018. www.pbs.org/video/san-diegos-gay-bar-history-tgoue6.

———. "San Diego's Gay Bar History: Reflections on Community History and the Documentary Film Process." *Journal of San Diego History* 65, no. 1 (2019).

Dickel, Simon. *Black/Gay: The Harlem Renaissance, the Protest Era, and the Constructions of Black Gay Identity in the 1980s and 90s*. East Lansing: Michigan State University Press, 2012.

Dietzler, Mary M. "Individual Histories of Detention Houses." GPO. "Detention Houses and Reformatories as Protective Social Agencies in the Campaign of the United States Government against Venereal Disease." Washington, DC: United States Interdepartmental Social Hygiene Board, 1922.

Dillinger, Michael E. "Hillcrest: From Haven to Home." *Journal of San Diego History* 46, no. 4 (2000).

Donovan, Brian. *White Slave Crusades: Race, Gender, and Anti-Vice Activism, 1887–1917*. Champaign: University of Illinois Press, 2010.

Dunlap, Leslie K. "The Reform of Rape Law and the Problem of White Men." In *Sex, Love, Race: Crossing Boundaries in North American History*, edited by Martha Hodes, 352–72. New York: New York University Press, 1999.

Eckert, Kevin J. *The Unseen Elderly: A Study of Marginally Subsistent Hotel Dwellers*. San Diego: Campanile Press, 1980.

Eliot, Charles E., and William F. Snow. "1900–1915 Progress." *Social Hygiene* 2 (1916): 37–48.

Ella Gates vs. John A. Gates, no. 16871 (Superior Court of the County of San Diego, California).

Engstrand, Iris H.W. "A Brief Sketch of San Diego's Military Presence: 1542–1945." *Journal of San Diego History* 60, no. 1–2 (2014): 1–26.

———. *San Diego: California's Cornerstone*. San Diego: Sunbelt Publications, 2005.

Enloe, Cynthia. *Bananas, Beaches, and Bases: Making Feminist Sense of International Politics*. Berkeley: University of California Press, 1989.

Ervin, Jordan. "Reinventing Downtown San Diego: A Spatial and Cultural Analysis of the Gaslamp Quarter." *Journal of San Diego History* 53, no. 4 (2007): 188–217.

———. "San Diego's Urban Trophy: Horton Plaza Redevelopment Project." *Southern California Quarterly* 90, no. 4 (December 1, 2008): 419–53. https://doi.org/10.2307/41172445.

Espiritu, Yen Le. *Home Bound: Filipino American Lives across Cultures, Communities, and Countries*. Berkeley: University of California Press, 2003.

Evans, Curtis J. *The Burden of Black Religion*. Oxford: Oxford University Press, 2008.

Evaristo, Bernardine. "Mom & Me & Mom by Maya Angelou—Review." *The Observer*, April 22, 2013, sec. Books. www.theguardian.com/books/2013/apr/22/mom-me-mom-maya-angelou-review.

Faderman, Lillian. "LGBT in San Diego: A History of Persecution, Battles, and Triumphs." *Journal of San Diego History* 65, no. 1 (2019). https://sandiegohistory.org/journal/2019/july/lgbtq-in-san-diego-a-history-of-persecution-battles-and-triumphs/.

Fair, Freda. "Surveilling Social Difference: Black Women's Alley Work." In "Industrializing Minneapolis." *Surveillance and Society* 5, no. 15 (2017): 655–75.

Favara, Jeremiah. "Good Black Soldier: Race, Masculinity, and US Military Recruiting in the 1970s." *Critical Military Studies* 7, no. 1 (2021): 1–22.

Feimster, Crystal N. *Southern Horrors: Women and the Politics of Rape and Lynching.* Cambridge, MA: Harvard University Press, 2009.

Ferguson, Roderick. *Aberrations in Black: Toward a Queer of Color Critique.* Minneapolis: University of Minnesota Press, 2004.

Ferris, Lesley, ed. *Crossing the Stage: Controversies on Cross-Dressing.* New York: Routledge, 2005.

Fikes, Robert, Jr. "Pioneers, Warriors, Advocates: San Diego's Black Legal Community, 1890–2013." *Journal of San Diego History* 60, no. 1–2 (2014): 45–64.

———. "Remarkable Healers on the Pacific Coast: A History of San Diego's Black Medical Community." *Journal of San Diego History* 57, no. 3 (2011): 135–53.

Findlay, John. *Magic Lands: Western Cityscapes and American Culture after 1940.* Berkeley: University of California Press, 1992.

Finley, Stephen C., and Biko Mandela Gray. "God Is a White Racist: Immanent Atheism as a Religious Response to Black Lives Matter and State-Sanctioned Anti-Black Violence." *Journal of Africana Religions* 3, no. 4 (2015): 443–53.

Fischer, Anne Gray. *The Streets Belong to Us: Sex, Race, and Police Power from Segregation to Gentrification.* Chapel Hill: University of North Carolina Press, 2022.

Flores-Villalobos, Joan. *The Silver Women: How Black Women's Labor Made the Panama Canal.* Philadelphia: University of Pennsylvania Press, 2023.

Florido, Adrian. "A Culture Clash Where Three Neighborhoods Meet." *Voice of San Diego,* July 5, 2011. www.voiceofsandiego.org/all-narratives /neighborhoods/a-culture-clash-where-three-neighborhoods-meet/.

Foner, Philip S. "Reverend George Washington Woodbey: Early Twentieth-Century California Black Socialist." *Journal of Negro History* 61, no. 2 (April 1976).

Freedman, Estelle B. *Their Sisters' Keepers: Women's Prison Reform in America, 1830–1930.* Ann Arbor: University of Michigan Press, 1981.

Furlonger, Jaye. "San Diego's Bygone Burlesque: The Famous Hollywood Theatre." *Journal of San Diego History* 51, no. 1–2 (2005): 21–41.

Garcia, Gabrielle and Ethan Lopez. "LAGADU Lesbians and Gays of African Descent United, 1989-1994," Lambda Archives of San Diego, https://

lambdaarchives.starter1ua.preservica.com/uncategorized/IO_f6c2e7e0
-0df0-4311-bbf9-8d6e799f1628/.

Gilmore, Ruth Wilson. *Golden Gulag: Prisons, Surplus, Crisis, and Opposition in Globalizing California*. Berkeley: University of California Press, 2007.

Goluboff, Risa Lauren. *Vagrant Nation: Police Power, Constitutional Change, and the Making of the 1960s*. Oxford: Oxford University Press, 2016.

Goluboff, Risa, and Adam Sorensen. "United States Vagrancy Laws." In *Oxford Research Encyclopedia of American History*. Oxford: Oxford University Press, 2018. https://doi.org/10.1093/acrefore/9780199329175.013.259

Gonzalez, Vernadette Vicuña, and Jana K. Lipman. "Introduction: Tours of Duty and Tours of Leisure." *American Quarterly* 68, no. 3 (2016), 510.

Gove, John. "From the Campus to the Community: The Struggle for Gay and Lesbian Rights in 1970s San Diego." Master's thesis, San Diego State University, 2020.

GPA Consulting. *San Diego Citywide LGBTQ Historic Context Statement: City of San Diego, Department of City Planning*. Third draft, August 16, 2016, www.sandiego.gov/sites/default/files/san_diego_lgbtq_historic_context _august2016_draft.pdf.

Grace, Joshua, Christopher Rhamey, Megan Dukett, Kaylin Gill, and Ricky Bell. "Coming Out Gay, Coming Out Christian: The Beginnings of GLBT Christianity in San Diego, 1970–1979." *Journal of San Diego History* 53, no. 3 (2007).

Gross, Kali N. *Colored Amazons: Crime, Violence, and Black Women in the City of Brotherly Love, 1880–1910*. Durham, NC: Duke University Press, 2006.

Groth, Paul. *Living Downtown: The History of Residential Hotels in the United States*. Berkeley: University of California Press, 1999.

Guevarra, Rudy P., Jr. *Becoming Mexipino: Multiethnic Identities and Communities in San Diego*. New Brunswick, NJ: Rutgers University Press, 2012.

———. "'Skid Row': Filipinos, Race, and the Social Construction of Space in San Diego." *Journal of San Diego History* 54, no. 1 (2008): 26–38.

Halberstam, Judith (Jack). *Female Masculinity*. Durham, NC: Duke University Press, 1998.

Haley, Sarah. *No Mercy Here: Gender, Punishment, and the Making of Jim Crow Modernity*. Chapel Hill: University of North Carolina Press, 2016.

Hallgren, Katherine. "Mothers Raise the Army: Women's Politics, Popular Culture and the Great War in America, 1914–1941." PhD diss., City University of New York, 2012.

Hanhardt, Christina. *Safe Space: Gay Neighborhood History and the Politics of Violence*. Durham, NC: Duke University Press, 2013.

Hannigan, John. *Fantasy City: Pleasure and Profit in the Postmodern Metropolis*. London: Routledge, 2005.

Hardison, Ayesha K. "Why Maya Angelou Partnered with Hallmark." *Humanities* 42, no. 1 (Winter 2021). www.neh.gov/article/why-maya-angelou-partnered-hallmark.

Harris, LaShawn. *Sex Workers, Psychics, and Numbers Runners: Black Women in New York City's Underground Economy*. Champaign: University of Illinois Press, 2016.

Harris, Leroy E. "The Other Side of the Freeway: A Study of Settlement Patterns of Negroes and Mexican Americans in San Diego, California." Carnegie Mellon University, 1974.

Hartman, Saidia. *Wayward Lives, Beautiful Experiments: Intimate Histories of Social Upheaval*. New York: W. W. Norton, 2020.

Hegarty, Marilyn E. "Patriots, Prostitutes, and Patriotutes: The Mobilization and Control of Female Sexuality in the United States during World War II." PhD diss., Ohio State University, 1988.

Hennessey, Gregg R. "San Diego, the U.S. Navy, and Urban Development: West Coast City Building, 1912–1929." *California History* 72, no. 2 (1993): 128–49.

Hennigan, Peter C. "Property War: Prostitution, Red-Light Districts, and the Transformation of Public Nuisance Law in the Progressive Era." *Yale Journal of Law and the Humanities* 16 (2004): 123–98.

Hernández, Bernadine Marie. *Border Bodies: Racialized Sexuality, Sexual Capital, and Violence in the Nineteenth-Century Borderlands*. Chapel Hill: University of North Carolina Press, 2022.

Hernández, Kelly L. *City of Inmates: Conquest, Rebellion, and the Rise of Human Caging in Los Angeles, 1771–1965*. Chapel Hill: University of North Carolina Press, 2017.

Hetherington, Philippa, and Julia Laite. "Editorial Note." Special issue, Migration, Sex, and Intimate Labor, *Journal of Women's History* 33, no. 4, (2021): 7–39.

Hicks, Cheryl D. *Talk with You Like a Woman: African American Women, Justice, and Reform in New York, 1890–1935*. Chapel Hill: University of North Carolina Press, 2010.

Hirata, Lucie. "Free, Indentured, Enslaved: Chinese Prostitutes in Nineteenth-Century America," *Signs* 5 (1979): 3–29.

"A History and a Forecast." *Social Hygiene* 5, no. 4 (n.d.): 553–66.

Hobbs, Allyson. *A Chosen Exile: A History of Racial Passing in American Life*. Cambridge, MA: Harvard University Press, 2014.

Hochschild, Jennifer L., and Brenna Marea Powell. "Racial Reorganization and the United States Census, 1850–1930: Mulattoes, Half-Breeds, Mixed Parentage, Hindoos, and the Mexican Race," *Studies in American Political Development* 22, no. 1 (2008), 59–96.

Hof, Reiner M. "San Diegans, Inc." *Journal of San Diego History* 36, no. 1 (1990). https://sandiegohistory.org/journal/1990/january/sdinc/.

Hollenbeck, C. David. "On Cruising." *The Prodigal* 3, no. 27 (June 27, 1971).

Hong, Grace, and Roderick A. Ferguson. *Strange Affinities: The Gender and Sexual Politics of Comparative Racialization*. Durham, NC: Duke University Press, 2011.

Howard, Lexi Purich. "California Swings for the Fences to Strike Racially Restrictive Covenants from the Public Record." *California Real Property Law Journal* 39, no. 4 (2021).

Howard, Lexi Purich, and Jeffrey D. Gonda. *Unjust Deeds: The Restrictive Covenant Cases and the Making of the Civil Rights Movement*. Chapel Hill: University of North Carolina Press, 2015.

Hua, Julietta. "Telling Stories of Trafficking: The Politics of Legibility." *Meridians* 12, no. 1 (2014): 201–7.

Hua, Julietta, and Holly Nigorizawa. "US Sex Trafficking, Women's Human Rights and the Politics of Representation." In *New Directions in Feminism and Human Rights*, 109–31. New York: Routledge, 2019.

Huff, Karen L. *The Lillian and Ocie Grant Properties: Supplemental Study of the Historical Assessment of the 1431–63 J Street Building*. San Diego: Black Historical Society of San Diego, 2006.

———. *Rebuttal to the Moomjian Reply: The Battle to Save the Clement/Coast Hotel*. San Diego: Gaslamp Black Historical Society, 2001.

Huff, Karen L., and Kathleen Flanigan. *Joe Robison's Place: An Historical Study of the Ideal Hotel and Harlem Locker Club.* San Diego: Gaslamp Black Historical Society, 2002.

Hutchison, Beth. "Lesbian Blood Drives as Community-Building Activism in the 1980s." *Journal of Lesbian Studies* 19, no. 1 (2015): 117–28.

Johnson, Bascom. "Eliminating Vice from Camp Cities." *Annals of the American Academy of Political and Social Science* 78, no. 1 (1918): 60–64.

———. "What Some Communities of the West and Southwest Have Done for the Protection of the Morals and Health of Soldiers and Sailors." [United States] War Department: Commission on Training Camp Activities (1917). Reprinted in *Social Hygiene* 3 (1916): 487–503.

Johnson, Patrick E. "'Quare' Studies, or (Almost) Everything I Know about Queer Studies I Learned from My Grandmother." *Text and Performance Quarterly* 21, no. 1 (2001): 1–25.

Jones, William Ronald. *Is God a White Racist? A Preamble to Black Theology.* Anchor Press, 1973.

Justia Law. "Perez v. Sharp," March 27, 2024. https://law.justia.com/cases/california/supreme-court/2d/32/711.html.

Kahn, Lawrence. "Internal Labor Markets: San Francisco Longshoremen." *Industrial Relations* 15, no. 3 (1976): 333–37.

Ketchum, Alex D. "'All are welcome here?': Navigating Race, Class, Gender, Sexual Orientation, Age, and Disability in American Feminist Coffeehouses of the 1970s and 1980s." *Gender, Work, and Organization* 28, no. 2 (2021): 594–609.

Ketchum, Alexandra "Alex" Diva. "'Say "hi" from Gaia': Women's Travel Guides and Lesbian Feminist Community Formation in the Pre-Internet Era (1975-1992)." *Feminist Media Studies* 22, no. 3 (2022): 502–18.

King, Edith Shatto, and Frederick A. King. *Pathfinder Social Survey of San Diego: Report of Limited Investigations of Social Conditions in San Diego, California.* San Diego: Labor Temple Press, 1914.

King, Jamilah. "Yes, Maya Angelou Was a Sex Worker." *Colorlines.* May 30, 2014, https://colorlines.com/article/yes-maya-angelou-was-sex-worker/.

Kneeland, Marilyn. "The Modern Boston Tea Party: The San Diego Suffrage Campaign of 1911." *Journal of San Diego History* 34 (1977): 35–42.

Kun, Josh. "Tijuana and the Borders of Race." In *A Companion to Los Angeles*, edited by William Deverell and Greg Hise, 313–26. Oxford: Wiley Blackwell, 2010.

Kutty, Asha. "Sanctuaries along Streets: Security, Social Intimacy, and Identity in the Space of the Storefront Church." *Journal of Interior Design* 45, no. 1 (2020).

Lamb, John R. "End of Round 1: San Diego Redistricting Commission Pleases—and Peeves." *San Diego City Beat*, July 27, 2011. http://sdcitybeat.com/article-9333-san-diego-redistricting.html.

Lapp, Rudolph M. *Blacks in Gold Rush California*. Washington, DC: Georgetown University Press, 2013.

Lee, Erica. *America's Gates: Chinese Immigration during the Exclusion Era, 1882–1943*. Chapel Hill: University of North Carolina Press, 2003.

Lewis, Penny W. *Hardhats, Hippies, and Hawks: The Vietnam Antiwar Movement as Myth and Memory*, Ithaca, NY: Cornell University Press, 2013.

Liazos, Ariane, and Marshall Ganz. "Duty to the Race: African American Fraternal Orders and the Legal Defense of the Right to Organize." *Social Science History* 28, no. 3 (2004): 485–534.

Lim, Julian. *Porous Borders: Multiracial Migrations and the Law in the U.S.-Mexico Borderlands*. Chapel Hill: University of North Carolina Press, 2017.

Limoncelli, Stephanie A. *The Politics of Trafficking: The First International Movement to Combat the Sexual Exploitation of Women*. Stanford, CA: Stanford University Press, 2010.

Lindsay, Martin S. "Chi-Chi Club, San Diego." *Classic San Diego*. May 27, 2016. https://classicsandiego.com/restaurants/chi-chi-club-san-diego/.

Lionnet, Françoise. "Con Artists and Storytellers: Maya Angelou's Problematic Sense of Audience." In *Autobiographical Voices: Race, Gender, Self-Portraiture*, 130–66. Ithaca, NY: Cornell University Press, 1989.

Love, Amanda. "My Journey to Finding Maya Angelou in My Life." Center for Culture, Sexuality, and Spirituality. August 13, 2014, https://sacredsexualities.org/2014/08/13/my-journey-to-finding-maya/.

Loza, Mireya. *Defiant Braceros: How Migrant Workers Fought for Racial, Sexual, and Political Freedom*. Chapel Hill: University of North Carolina Press, 2016.

Luker, Kristin. "Sex, Social Hygiene, and the State: The Double-Edged Sword of Social Reform." *Theory and Society* 27, no. 5 (1998): 601–34.

Lynch, Kevin, and Donald Appleyard. *Temporary Paradise: A Look at the Special Landscape of the San Diego Region*. San Diego City Planning Department, 1974.

MacPhail, Elizabeth C. "Shady Ladies in the 'Stingaree District' When the Red Lights Went Out in San Diego." *Journal of San Diego History* 20, no. 2 (n.d.): 2–28.

Madison, D. Soyini. *Acts of Activism: Human Rights as Radical Performance*. Cambridge: Cambridge University Press, 2010.

———. *Critical Ethnography: Method, Ethics, and Performance*. Thousand Oaks, CA: Sage Publications, 2012.

Madyun, Gail, and Larry Malone. "Black Pioneers in San Diego, 1880–1920." *Journal of San Diego History* 27, no. 2 (1981).

Manalansan, Martin. "Race, Violence, and Neoliberal Spatial Politics in the Global City." *Social Text* 23, nos. 3–4 (84–85) (Fall–Winter 2005): 141–55.

"Maya Angelou, Sex Worker and Hero." *Decriminalize Sex Work* (blog), February 23, 2022. https://decriminalizesex.work/maya-angelou-sex-worker-and-hero/.

"Maya Angelou: Sex Worker Is Part of Her Esteemed Legacy." *Old Pros* (podcast), February 2, 2022. https://oldprosonline.org/maya-angelou-sex-worker/.

McCorkel, Jill A. *Breaking Women: Gender, Race, and the New Politics of Imprisonment*. New York: New York University Press, 2013.

McCune, Jeffrey Q., Jr., *Sexual Discretion: Black Masculinity and the Politics of Passing*. Chicago: University of Chicago Press, 2014.

McEntee, Jennifer. "Owners Who Helped Shape the 'Gayborhood.'" *San Diego Magazine* (July 14, 2021), www.sandiegomagazine.com/meet-the-hillcrest-business-owners-who-helped-shape-the-gayborhood/article_a36b2a7e-e0fc-11eb-8855-b7f5bebf535c.html.

McEvoy, Arthur F. "In Places Men Reject: Chinese Fishermen at San Diego, 1870–1893." *San Diego Historical Society Quarterly* 23, no. 4 (1977). https://sandiegohistory.org/journal/1977/october/chinese-2/.

McKanna, Clare V. "Prostitutes, Progressives, and Police." *Journal of San Diego History* 35, no. 1 (1989): 44–50.

McKittrick, Katherine. *Demonic Grounds: Black Women and the Cartographies of Struggle*. Minneapolis: University of Minnesota Press, 2006.

McKittrick, Katherine, and Linda Peake. "What Difference Does Difference Make to Geography?" In *Questioning Geography: Fundamental Debates*, edited by Noel Castree, Alisdair Rogers, and Douglas Sherman, 39–54. Malden, MA: Blackwell, 2005.

McPherson, Dolly A. *Order Out of Chaos: The Autobiographical Works of Maya Angelou*. New York: Peter Lang, 1990.

McWhorter, John. "Saint Maya." *New Republic*, May 19, 2002. https://newrepublic.com/article/66279/saint-maya.

Menchaca, Celeste R. "'The Freedom of Jail': Women, Detention, and the Expansion of Immigration Governance along the U.S.-Mexico Border, 1903–1917." *Journal of American Ethnic History* 39, no. 4 (2020): 27–41.

Meyerowitz, Joanne. *Women Adrift: Independent Wage-Earners in Chicago, 1880–1930*. Chicago: University of Chicago Press, 1988.

Michels, Bernard. "Social Scenes of the Male Gay Community of San Diego." Master's thesis, San Diego State University, 1974.

Miller Hagstrom, Karl. *Segregating Sound: Inventing Folk and Pop Music in the Age of Jim Crow*. Durham, NC: Duke University Press, 2010.

Miller-Young, Mireille. "Putting Hypersexuality to Work: Black Women and Illicit Eroticism in Pornography." *Sexualities* 13, no. 2 (2010): 219–35. https://doi.org/10.1177/1363460709359229.

———. *A Taste for Brown Sugar: Black Women in Pornography*. Durham, NC: Duke University Press, 2014.

Mitchell, Gregory. *Panics without Borders: How Global Sporting Events Drive Myths about Sex Trafficking*. Berkeley: University of California Press, 2022.

Monod, David. *Vaudeville and the Making of Modern Entertainment, 1890–1925*. Chapel Hill: University of North Carolina Press, 2020.

Montelongo, Irma Victoria. "Illicit Inhabitants: Empire, Immigration, Race, and Sexuality on the U.S.-Mexico Border, 1891–1924." PhD diss., University of Texas, El Paso, 2014.

Moore, H. H. "Four Million Dollars for the Fight against Venereal Diseases," American Social Hygiene Association, 1919, 15–26.

Moore, Shirley Ann Wilson. *To Place Our Deeds: The African American Community in Richmond, California, 1910–1963*. Berkeley, University of California Press, 2000.

Morrison, Toni. *Sula*. New York: Knopf Doubleday, 2007.

Moser, Richard R. *The New Winter Soldiers: GI and Veteran Dissent during the Vietnam Era* (New Brunswick, NJ: Rutgers University Press, 1996).

"Movement for a Democratic Military." *The Black Panther* (San Francisco) 4, no. 13 (February 28, 1970): 19.

Mulroy, Kevin, Lawrence B. de Graaf, and Quintard Taylor, eds. *Seeking El Dorado: African Americans in California*. Seattle: University of Washington Press, 2014.

Mumford, Kevin J. *Interzones: Black/White Sex Districts in Chicago and New York in the Early Twentieth Century*. New York: Columbia University Press, 1997.

Murib, Zein. "Lgbt." *TSQ: Transgender Studies Quarterly* 1, no. 1–2 (May 1, 2014): 118–20. https://doi.org/10.1215/23289252-2399776.

Murray-Ramirez, Nicole interview by Frank Nobiletti. Audio Cassette, February 8, 1990. https://californiarevealed.org/do/b36dddeo-3dd5 -459c-af61-dd3dea6e48be.

Nagel, Toni. "San Diego's Chinatown and Stingaree District." Archaeological Report. University of San Diego, 1985.

Nash, Gerald. *The American West Transformed: The Impact of the Second War*. Lincoln: University of Nebraska Press, 1985.

Nash, Jennifer. *Birthing Black Mothers*. Durham, NC: Duke University Press, 2021.

Nealon, Christopher. "Invert-History: The Ambivalence of Lesbian Pulp Fiction." *New Literary History* 31, no. 3 (2000): 745–64.

Nishikawa, Kinohi. "Reading the Street: Iceberg Slim, Donald Goines, and the Rise of Black Pulp Fiction." PhD diss., Duke University, 2010.

Norris, Frank. "Logan Heights." *Journal of San Diego History* 29, no. 1 (1983). https://sandiegohistory.org/journal/1983/january/logan/.

Northrup, Herbert R. "The New Orleans Longshoremen." *Political Science Quarterly* 57, no. 4 (1942): 526–44.

Odom, Mychal Matsemela-Ali. "From Southern California to Southern Africa: Translocal Black Internationalism in Los Angeles and San Diego from Civil Rights to Antiapartheid, 1960 to 1994." PhD diss., University of California, San Diego, 2017.

Official California Negro Directory and Classified Buyers' Guide. Los Angeles: New Age Publishing, 1941.

Onkst, David H. "'First a Negro . . . Incidentally a Veteran': Black World War Two Veterans and the G.I. Bill of Rights in the Deep South, 1944–1948." *Journal of Social History* 31, no. 3 (1998): 517–43.

"Opining: Gay Center for Social Services." *The Prodigal* 4, no. 66 (February 4, 1973): 2.

Paligutan, James. "American Dream Deferred: An Oral History of Filipino Servants in the US Navy and Coast Guard, 1952–1974." *Pacific Historical Review* 90, no. 2 (2021): 233–60. https://doi.org/10.1525/phr.2021.90.2.233.

Parascandola, John. "Presidential Address, Quarantining Women: Venereal Disease Rapid Treatment Centers in World War II America." *Bulletin of the History of Medicine* (2009): 431–59.

Parker, Eunice B., and Minnie Gay. *The Official California Negro Directory and Classified Buyers' Guide*. Los Angeles: New Age Publishing, 1941.

Parsons, David. *Dangerous Grounds: Antiwar Coffeehouses and Military Dissent in the Vietnam Era*. Chapel Hill: University of North Carolina Press, 2017.

Pascoe, Peggy. "Miscegenation Law, Court Cases, and Ideologies of 'Race' in Twentieth-Century America." In *Sex, Love, Race: Crossing Boundaries in North American History*, edited by Martha Hodes (New York: New York University Press, 1999), 464–90.

———. *Relations of Rescue: The Search for Female Moral Authority in the American West, 1974–1939* (Oxford: Oxford University Press, 1990).

Pastras, Philip. *Dead Man Blues: Jelly Roll Morton Way Out West*. Berkeley: University of California Press, 2001.

Peiss, Kathy. *Cheap Amusements: Working Women and Leisure in Turn-of-the-Century New York*. Philadelphia: Temple University Press, 1986.

The People of the State of California (Plaintiff) vs. Anna Barnett (Defendant), no. 15926 (Superior Court of the County of San Diego, State of California, 1910).

Perry, Imani. *Looking for Lorraine: The Radiant and Radical Life of Lorraine Hansberry*. Boston: Beacon Press, 2018.

"Pigs Amuck in San Diego." *The Black Panther* (San Francisco) 3, no. 4 (July 26, 1969), 6.

Pleasant, Keri. "Honoring Black History World War II Service to the Nation." US Army, February 27, 2020. www.army.mil/article/233117/honoring_black_history_world_war_ii_service_to_the_nation.

Pliley, Jessica R. "Claims to Protection: The Rise and Fall of Feminist Abolitionism in the League of Nations' Committee on the Traffic in Women and Children, 1919–1936." *Journal of Women's History* 22, no. 4 (2010): 90–113.

———. "Prostitution in America." In *Oxford Research Encyclopedia of American History*, 2018. https://doi.org/10.1093/acrefore/9780199329175.013.121.

———. "The Sex Wars: Prostitution, Carceral Feminists, and the Consolidation of Police Power." *Journal of Urban History* (2024): 979–82.

Redburn, Kate. "Before Equal Protection: The Fall of Cross-Dressing Bans and the Transgender Legal Movement, 1963–86." *Law and History Review* 40, no. 4 (2022): 679–723.

Reddy, Chandan. "Time for Rights? Loving, Gay Marriage, and the Limits of Legal Justice." *Fordham Law Review* 76, no. 6 (n.d.): 2849–72.

Reft, Ryan. "The Privatization of Military Family Housing in Linda Vista, 1944–1956." *California History* 92, no. 1 (2015): 53–72.

Regan, Amanda, and Eric Gonzaba. "Mapping the Gay Guides," 2019. www.mappingthegayguides.org.

———. "Mapping the New Gay South: Queer Space and Southern Life, 1965–1980." *Southern Quarterly* 58, no. 1 (2020): 11–25.

Remembering Dr. Maya Angelou. "Maya Angelou: Teacher." Accessed April 7, 2024. https://mayaangelou.wfu.edu/story/.

"Rep. Mike Levin Introduces Bipartisan Bill to Name Oceanside Post Office to Honor Local Trailblazer Charlesetta Reece Allen." Press release, October 19, 2023. https://levin.house.gov/media/press-releases/rep-mike-levin-introduces-bipartisan-bill-to-name-oceanside-post-office-to-honor-local-trailblazer-charlesetta-reece-allen, accessed March 24, 2024.

Richie, Beth. *Arrested Justice: Black Women, Violence, and America's Prison Nation*. New York: New York University Press, 2012.

Rodríguez, J. "Pornographic Encounters and Interpretative Interventions: Vanessa Del Rio, Fifty Years of Slightly Slutty Behavior." *Women and Performance: A Journal of Feminist Theory* 25, no. 3 (2016): 315–35.

Roker, Raymond Leon. "Stop Blaming California's Black Voters for Prop 8." *Huffington Post*. December 7, 2008. www.huffingtonpost.com/raymond-leon-roker/stop-blaming-californias_b_142018.html.

Rosen, Ruth. *The Lost Sisterhood: Prostitution in America, 1900–1918*. Baltimore: Johns Hopkins University Press, 1982.

Ross, Becki, and Rachael Sullivan. "Tracing Lines of Horizontal Hostility: How Sex Workers and Gay Activists Battled for Space, Voice, and Belonging in Vancouver, 1975–1985." *Sexualities* 15, no. 5–6 (September 1, 2012): 604–21. https://doi.org/10.1177/1363460712446121.

Rousseau, Nicole. "Morons, Mental Defectives, Prostitutes, and Dope Fiends: Restrictive Reproductive Policies." In *Black Woman's Burden: Commodifying Black Reproduction* (New York: Palgrave Macmillan, 2009), 103–12.

Rubin, Henry S. "Phenomenology as Method in Trans Studies." *GLQ: A Journal of Lesbian and Gay Studies* 4, no. 2 (April 1, 1998): 263–81. https://doi.org/10.1215/10642684-4-2-263.

Russell, Thaddeus. "The Color of Discipline: Civil Rights and Black Sexuality." *American Quarterly* 60, no. 1 (2008).

"Sad Stories: A Reflection on the Fiction of Ann Bannon," *Gay Community News* 7, no. 43 (May 24, 1980): 8–12.

Saito, Leland. "African Americans and Historic Preservation in San Diego: The Douglas and the Clermont/Coast Hotels." *Journal of San Diego History* 54, no. 1 (2008): 1–15.

Salmon, Marylynn. *Women and the Law of Property in Early America*. Chapel Hill: University of North Carolina Press, 2016.

San Diego Police Department (Mid City Division). "Tina's Night Club Project." Arizona State University for Problem-Oriented Policing. https://popcenter.asu.edu/sites/default/files/library/awards/goldstein/2011/11-32.pdf.

San Diego's Gay Bar History. Documentary, 2018. www.pbs.org/video/san-diegos-gay-bar-history-tgoue6/.

Sánchez, George J. *Becoming Mexican American: Ethnicity, Culture, and Identity in Chicano Los Angeles*. New York: Oxford University Press, 1993.

"Save the Clementine McDuff Elks Lodge." Accessed March 21, 2024. www.cbs8.com/video/news/local/save-the-clementine-mcduff-elks-lodge/509-f459171b-01c0-45a0-ac22-5296d92dfefd.

Sawyer, Wilbur. "Report of the Bureau of the Hygienic Laboratory for January." *Monthly Bulletin, California State Board of Health* 7–8 (1911): 197–207.

Schwartz, Henry. "The Mary Walker Incident: Black Prejudice in San Diego, 1866." *Journal of San Diego History* 19, no. 2 (Spring 1973). https://sandiegohistory.org/journal/1973/march/mary-walker-incident-black-prejudice-san-diego-1866/.

Shabazz, Rashad. *Spatializing Blackness: Architectures of Confinement and Black Masculinity in Chicago*. Urbana: University of Illinois Press, 2015.

Shragge, Abraham. "'A New Federal City': San Diego during World War II." *Pacific Historical Review* 63, no. 3 (1994): 333–61. https://doi.org/10.2307/3640970.

Shragge, Abraham J., and Mary Lindenstein Walshok. *Invention and Reinvention: The Evolution of San Diego's Innovation Economy*. Stanford, CA: Stanford University Press, 2013.

Shigematsu, Setsu, and Keith L. Camacho. *Militarized Currents: Toward a Decolonized Future in Asia and the Pacific*. Minneapolis: University of Minnesota Press, 2010.

Smith, Alan. "Drag, the Legal Viewpoint." *The Prodigal* 4, no. 50 (May 28, 1972): 23.

———. "Philadelphia Lawyer." *The Prodigal* 4, no. 50 (May 28, 1972): 12.

Smith, Barbara. "Toward a Black Feminist Criticism." In *All the Women Are White, All the Blacks Are Men, But Some of Us Are Brave*, edited by Gloria T. Hull, Patricia Bell Scott, and Barbara Smith, 157–75. New York: Feminist Press, 1982.

Smith, Christopher Gary. "Apprehending Black Queer Diasporas: A Study of Black Pride Festivals and Their Emplacements." PhD diss., University of Toronto, 2020.

Smith, Jeff. "The Douglas Hotel: The Harlem of the West." *San Diego Reader*, August 5, 1999. www.sandiegoreader.com/news/1999/aug/05/douglas-hotel/.

Snorton, Riley C. *Black on Both Sides: A Racial History of Trans Identity*. Minneapolis: University of Minnesota Press, 2017.

Snow, William F. "December Bulletin: Impending Health Legislature." *Monthly Bulletin, California State Board of Health* 7–8 (December 1911): 89–96.

Stallings, L. H. *Funk the Erotic: Transaesthetics and Black Sexual Cultures*. Champaign: University of Illinois Press, 2015.

"A State Health Department and a City Department Prepare for Action." *Social Hygiene* 3, no. 4 (1917): 447–48.

Steinmetz, Katy. "See Obama's 20-Year Evolution on LGBT Rights." *Time*, April 10, 2015. https://time.com/3816952/obama-gay-lesbian-transgender-lgbt-rights/.

Stern, Scott W. *The Trials of Nina McCall: Sex, Surveillance, and the Decades-Long Government Plan to Imprison "Promiscuous" Women*. Boston: Beacon Press, 2018.

Stewart-Winter, Timothy. *Queer Clout: Chicago and the Rise of Gay Politics*. Philadelphia: University of Pennsylvania Press, 2016.

Storey, Thomas. "Evaluation of Governmental Aid to Detention Houses and Reformatories." In *Detention Houses and Reformatories as Protective Social Agencies in the Campaign of the United States Government against Venereal Diseases*, by Mary Dietzler, 3–9. GPO. Washington, DC: United States Interdepartmental Social Hygiene Board, 1922.

Storm, Claire. "Controlling Venereal Disease in Orlando during World War II." *Florida Historical Quarterly* 91, no. 1 (2012): 86–117.

Stryker, Susan. "Transgender History, Homonormativity, and Disciplinarity." *Radical History Review*, Queer Futures, 100 (2008): 145–57. https://doi.org/10.1215/01636545-2007-026.

Taylor, Lawrence D. "The Wild Frontier Moves South: US Entrepreneurs and the Growth of Tijuana's Vice Industry, 1908–1935." *Journal of San Diego History* 48, no. 3 (2002): 204–29.

Taylor, Verta, and Leila J. Rupp. "Learning from Drag Queens." *Contexts* 5, no. 3 (2006): 14.

Teaiwa, Teresia K. "bikinis and other s/pacific n/oceans." *The Contemporary Pacific* 6, no. 1 (Spring 1994): 87–109. www.jstor.org/stable/23701591.

Thompson, Loyd, and Lyle Kingery. "Syphilis in the Negro." *American Journal of Syphilis* 3 (1919): 384–97.

Toombs, Charles P. "Harlem Renaissance in San Diego: New Negroes and Community." In *The Harlem Renaissance in the American West: The New Negro's Western Experience*, edited by Bruce A. Glasrud and Cary D. Wintz (London: Routledge, 2011), 226–36.

Travers, Chris. "The Norman Baynard Photograph Collection: Three Perspectives." *Journal of San Diego History* 57, no. 3 (2011). https://sandiegohistory.org/journal/v57-3/v57-3travers.pdf.

Trimble, Gerald. "Making Better Use of Urban Space: Local Redevelopment Initiatives, the New Downtown San Diego: Horton Plaza." San Diego: Centre City Development Corporation, 1984.

Trotter, Joe W. "African American Fraternal Associations in American History: An Introduction." *Social Science History* 28, no. 3 (2004): 355–66.

"United States of America, Bureau of the Census. Fifteenth Census of the United States, 1930. Washington, DC: National Archives and Records Administration, 1930. T626, 2,667 Rolls. Ancestry.com.

Va, Stina. "Gov. Newsom Signs the Safer Streets for All Act (SB 357)." ACLU California Action, July 1, 2022, https://aclucalaction.org/2022/07/gov-newsom-signs-the-safer-streets-for-all-act-sb-357/.

Valentine, David. *Imagining Transgender: An Ethnography of a Category*. Durham, NC: Duke University Press, 2007.

Vijayakumar, M., and Ruth Neyah. "Unwinding the Identity and Racial Saga in Maya Angelou's *Gather Together in My Name*." *Theory and Practice in Language Studies* 12, no. 7 (2022). https://doi.org/10.17507/tpls.1207.12.

VisionaryProject. "Maya Angelou: Gather Together in My Name." YouTube, https://youtu.be/59cS6T)4IdQ, accessed March 12, 2023.

Vose, Clement E. *Caucasians Only: The Supreme Court, the NAACP, and the Restrictive Covenant Case*. University of California Press, 1967.

Walker, Alice. *In Search of Our Mothers' Gardens: Womanist Prose*. San Diego: Harcourt Brace Jovanovich, 1983.

Wallace, Michele. "A Black Feminist's Search for Sisterhood." In *All the Women Are White, All the Blacks Are Men, but Some of Us Are Brave*, edited by Gloria T. Hull, Patricia Bell Scott, and Barbara Smith, 5–12. New York: CUNY Feminist Press, 1982.

Walsh, Steve. The podcast series "Free the Pendleton 14," https://freethependleton14.wordpress.com/.

Weitzer, Ronald. *Legalizing Prostitution: From Illicit Vice to Lawful Business*. New York: New York University Press, 2011.

Wheeler, B. Gordon. *Black California: The History of African-Americans in the Golden State*. New York: Hippocrene Books, 1993.

Williamson, Terrion L. *Scandalize My Name: Black Feminist Practice and the Making of Black Social Life*. New York: Fordham University Press, 2016.

Wilson, Alexander. "Friedkin's Cruising, Ghetto Politics, and Gay Sexuality." *Social Text* 4 (1981): 98–109.

Wilson, Charla. "Why the Y? The Origin of San Diego YWCA's Clay Avenue Branch for African Americans." *Journal of San Diego History* 62, no. 3–4 (2016): 303–22.

Wilson-Buford, Kellie. *Policing Sex and Marriage in the American Military: The Court-Martial and the Construction of Gender and Sexual Deviance, 1950–2000*. Lincoln: University of Nebraska Press, 2018.

Wittman, Carl. "A Gay Manifesto." In *Feminism and Masculinities*, edited by Peter Murphy, 28–40. Oxford: Oxford University Press, 1970.

Women Marines Association. "MCRD WRBN 1943–1946—'Serving the Nation and Making a Difference.'" June 17, 2016. www.womenmarines.org/mcrd-wrbn-1943-1946-serving-the-nation-and-making-a-difference/.

Wood, Louis Lee, III. "Almost 'No Negro Veteran . . . Could Get a Loan': African Americans, the GI Bill, and the NAACP Campaign against Residential Segregation, 1917–1960." *Journal of African American History* 98, no. 3 (2013): 392–417.

Yarborough, Orilonise C. D. "Black by Birth, Gay by God, Proud by Choice: The Origins and Spread of DC Black Pride, 1991–2015." Master's thesis, North Carolina Central University, 2022.

Young, Yolanda. "From Prostitute to Professor: The Lessons in Maya Angelou's Messy Life." *Medium.* December 12, 2016, https://medium.com/@yolandayoungesq/from-prostitute-to-professor-the-lessons-in-maya-angelous-messy-life-d827d1e31b9d.

Index

Angelou, Maya *(continued)*
President Bill Clinton (1993), 109;
as patriot, 109; seventieth
birthday celebration and "Maya
Celebrates 70" book (hosted by
Oprah Winfrey), 104–5; as
unhoused in San Diego, 79–80;
visit to her father (Daddy Bailey)
in SD, 78–80
—MOTHER OF (VIVIAN BAX-
TER): Defoe's *Moll Flanders* as
fictional counterpart, 73–74; in
Gather, as sex worker and sexually
liberated woman, 72, 74–75, 82; in
Gather, MA leaving and returning
to San Francisco house of, 80–82,
98–99; Hallmark Life Mosaic card
honoring, 107–8; resolution of
complex relationship with, 107–8;
as supporting MA's decision to
disclose sex work, 103
—WORKS: "Aunt Sukie" (unpublished), 95–97, 102; "Getting Up
Stayed on My Mind," 72; Hallmark
collection (Life Mosaic) (1991), 77,
107–8; *I Know Why the Caged Bird
Sings* (1969), 71, 72, 78–80; *Just
Give Me a Cool Drink of Water 'fore
I Diiie* (1971), 106–7; *Mom & Me
& Mom* (2013), 108; "Still I Rise"
(1978), 106–7; "They Go Home"
(1971), 106; *Wouldn't Take Nothing
for My Journey Now* (1993), 108. *See
also* Angelou, Maya, *Gather
Together in My Name* (1974)
Angelou, Maya, *Gather Together in
My Name* (1974): overview, 17,
66–71; black vernacular and folk
traditions (Br'er Rabbit) and, 73,

76; decision to disclose her sex
work, 103; disreputability used to
achieve respectability, 17, 69, 71,
74–75, 103–10; limited interiority
access in (as trickster we will
never truly know), 70–71, 104–6;
as literary autobiography, 69–73,
223n5; as source, 223n; "strong
women" element (Defoe's *Moll
Flanders*) and, 73–74; trickster
framing avoided for herself, as
protection of her image, 102,
103–4; trickster framing of sex
workers, 66–67, 75–76, 77, 95–97,
102, 103; and uplift of the race,
African American autobiography
and literature conventions for, 70,
72–73, 103–4
—AS BLACK/LESBIAN PULP
GENRE FICTION: cautionary
tale framing of, 103–4; as
confirming the value of lives of
marginalized subjects, 76–77;
literary critics meaning to insult
MA's writing as pulp, 77–78,
224n26; MA as fan of (reading
Street and Smith pulp magazine),
76; melodramatic and exaggerated prose, 76; trickster-troping
(subversively embedding desire
and queerness), 75–78
—STORYLINE: overview, 67–68;
application for the WACS, 74–75,
98–99; "Are you in the life?,"
89–90; contempt for others, 69,
93, 95, 102–3; employment
opportunities limited to domestics
and cooks, 80–81, 90–92, 94, 99;
ending by framing herself as

victim of coercion and manipulation, 104; maternal side of family rejecting, 82; mother's house in San Francisco, leaving and returning, 80–82, 98–99; performance of reputability for employment and child care, 78, 80–81, 88–90, 94, 97; pregnant and completing high school, 80; return to her grandmother's (Momma) in Arkansas, and racial violence threat against her, 97–98
—STORYLINE: AS BROTHEL WORKER IN SAN JOAQUIN VALLEY: overview, 68, 99–100; contempt for others in the brothel, 69, 102–3; ending by framing herself as victim of coercion and manipulation, 104; exploited in similar way to her exploitation as pimp, 68; first trick, 101–2; interracial contact policed for black sex workers, 100–101; as patriotic service, 109; pay inequalities for black sex workers, 100–101; and pimp (L. D. Tolbrook), 68, 100, 101, 102–3; state surveillance as less worrisome, 68, 99; Stockton (CA) setting among Bracero farmworkers, 68, 99–101
—STORYLINE: AS PIMP IN SAN DIEGO (BEATRICE AND JOHNNIE MAE): overview, 67–69, 75–76; and choice to pimp vs. tricking herself, 94, 95; contempt for the women, 69, 93, 95, 102; exploitative pimp arrangement made by MA, 67–69, 93–95;

historic and economic context of, 67–68, 69; male intermediaries employed in syndicate (Hank and the cab driver), 68–69, 94–95; prices and split of money, 68, 94–96; pride in her role as pimp, vs. defensiveness of role as brothel worker, 104–6; threat by Johnnie Mae to call the vice squad, and sudden departure from SD, 95; titillation by lesbian couple she imagines are trying to seduce her, 75, 91–92, 93; tricksters, sex workers framed as, 66–67, 75–76, 77, 95, 102

Anita Hotel (rooming house), 55, 59, 62

antigay violence, safe space activists and discursive use of, 18, 31, 227–28n13

antiwar activism: demonstrations against campaign to allow gays/lesbians in the military, 235n39; Movement for a Democratic Military inspired by, 172; of Vietnam War, as annihilated in the military ranks by national and local authorities, 173

antiwork politics: sex work as form of, 8–9, 10, 211–12; work culture and capitalism as perpetuating the demand for human trafficking, 9–10, 211–12

Appleyard, Donald, 135

archives and knowledge production, methodology of critical engagement with, 15–16

Armed Services YMCA, 118, 119, 133

play) as questioning, 179–84; as
sidelining HIV/AIDS epidemic,
185–86. *See also* Fidelity Lodge No.
10 (black Masonic lodge,
Logan)—Greater Johnson
Missionary Baptist Church;
storefront churches

black clergy, demanding obliteration
of transactional sex, 24–25, 26, 63

Black/Ebony Prides, 198

black family and community
acceptance of queer family
members: Fofie Bashir's experience as black lesbian, 207, 209; the
black church and history of, 208; as
contrast to safe space activists'
refusal to extend, 146, 154, 159,
209; and the false narrative of
inherent black homophobia, 208,
209. *See also* Bubba (Granville
"Bubba" Omega Hughes)—family
acceptance and mutuality; Fidelity
Lodge No. 10 (black Masonic
lodge, Logan)—Greater Johnson
Missionary Baptist Church

black feminist framework: black
women's liberatory practices in
disreputability as necessary for, 8;
as methodology, 5; and refusal as
form of activism and practice of
freedom, 7. *See also* the disreputable, politics of (black women's
liberatory practices)

black fraternal orders: black female
auxiliaries to, 147–48; as enduring
institutions, 115–16, 146, 159–60;
mutual-benefit spatial practices of,
148, 149, 150–51, 159–60; as
racially segregated secret societies

paralleling white fraternal orders,
146; rituals and initiations of,
accessibility to working-class men,
147; sexual economy housed by,
created in response to displacement of black people, 18, 160; as
understudied, claimed to not be a
worthy subject of scholarly study,
146, 148; white fraternal orders
challenging legal status of, by civil
and criminal means, 146–47. *See
also* Elks Lodge (black fraternal
order); Fidelity Lodge No. 10
(black Masonic lodge)

black lesbians: Hillcrest social scene
not welcoming, 164, 197–98; racism
experienced organizing in safe
space activist spaces, 163–64,
165–66, 167; sexism in black
nationalist spaces, 164, 169–70, 175;
sexism in safe space activist spaces,
163, 165–66, 175, 176; "Where
Sistahs Hang" listing of resources
for (AAGWA), 186, *187, 188–89. See
also* Afrikan American Gay Women
Association (AAGWA); black
lesbian separatism; Davis, Angela;
LAGADU (Lesbians and Gays of
African Descent United); Lawrence-Wallace, Cynthia—as
cofounder of the Center; lesbian
parties ("for women by women");
Mackey-Cua Project (Queer
Progressive People of Color)

black lesbian separatism: black
nationalism as misunderstood
by white men and women,
166; embraced as necessary
community-building project,

black trans queens: and quareness, 154–57; safe space activists as vehemently opposed to acceptance of, 146, 159; sex-working after gigs, 125–26; Silver Sands Café as haven for, 115, 122; statistics on disproportionate enforcement of California Penal Code Section 653.22 (loitering with intent to commit prostitution), 210; in straight clubs, 124. *See also* Bubba (Granville "Bubba" Omega Hughes); drag queens

black women: black female auxiliaries to fraternal orders, 147–48; the Chinese District as only option to rent rooms (early 20th c.), 12, 25, 31; hesitancy to align with second-wave feminism, 166; medical bias toward ("hypersexuality"), 50; mobility in public space curtailed due to Progressive Era antiprostitution laws, 68, 93–94; not involved in sex work, targeted by police in interzones (early 20th c.), 4, 20–22, 25; population statistics of disproportionate arrests (and fines) for prostitution and vagrancy (1910–1930), 25; "promiscuous," 41. *See also* black lesbians; the disreputable, politics of (black women's liberatory practices)

Blanchesi, Anna, 32

Blue Jacket (bar), 118, 119

Boggs, James, 8–9

Bolzenius, Sandra, 99, 225n39

Bonzaba, Eric, 132

Booby Trap (Logan bar), 125

Bottom Line (SRO), 59

Boyd, Nan, 117, 127

Bradford, Cheryl, and AAGWA, 184

Bradley's (bar), 118, 122, 133, 230n50

Brass Rail (bar): in *Damron's Address Book*, 133; as first and longest-lived gay bar in SD, 117, 133; fundraising for the Center, 138; Global Male parties, 199; Latino nights, 197–98

Braxton, Norman, 128–29, 230n50

Brent, Linda, 72

Bristow, Nancy K., 50–51

Brooks, Siobhan, 10

Brown, Anna B., 55, 62

Brown, Elaine, 170

Brown, Kate, 183

Bubba (Granville "Bubba" Omega Hughes): overview, 115–16; on arrests for cross-dressing, 1, 123–24; arrival in San Diego (1965), 2, 111; death, tributes, and celebration of life, 156, 157–59; and "the DL," 156; in male drag, as performance, 152–54; Phoenix AZ as hometown, Bubba named "Mother of Phoenix," 124–25; Phoenix origins and life, 111, 143, 155–56; preference for diverse working-class institutions vs. white middle-class Hillcrest options, 111, 140, 143; quareness as appropriate understanding of, 154–57; "queer" rejected as term by, 154; on Silver Sands Café, the atmosphere and importance of, 122; on Silver Sands Café being

(banning gay marriage), black and
Latine population falsely accused
of being responsible for passage
of, 191–94; Rumford Housing Fair
Housing Act (1963), and repeal by
Prop 14 (1964), 145; Safer Streets
for All Act (2022), 210, 211. *See also*
decriminalization of sex work;
incarceration; miscegenation
laws; Red Light Abatement Act
(1914)

California Negro Directory, 83

California Real Estate Association,
meeting at gay bar to decide
whether to sponsor Prop 14 (1964
attempt to repeal fair housing
law), 145

California State Board of Equalization (liquor control): corruption
scandal, 88; focus on liquor vs.
vice, and expansion of queer
institutions, 117

California State Board of Health:
credited for detention of
(disproportionately black) women
suspected of venereal disease, 48,
49; letter outlining steps to
eliminate vice (from SD Health
Department), 47–48

California Supreme Court, black
woman denied inheritance, 39–42,
219n79

Camarillo, Mateo, 196

Camp, Bayliss J., 147–48

Camp Pendleton Marine Base
(Oceanside): anti-black violence
in, 173–74; KKK and other
white-supremacist groups
permitted to organize on bases,

173–74; Marines taking the bus to
Armed Forces YMCA downtown,
118, 119; Movement for a
Democratic Military formed by
marines at, 172; and the Pendleton
14 prosecution, 173–74; systematic
mistreatment of black servicemen
in, 173–74. *See also* Oceanside

capitalism and work culture, as
perpetuating the demand for
human trafficking, 9–10, 211–12

Carey, Thom: in common cause with
Lawrence-Wallace as black
partner of a white activist (Bernie
Michels), 167–68; identity of, as
attached to white partner, 167–68;
labor of, as critical to development
of the Center, 168; as MCCSD
member, 167; as military veteran,
167

Caribbean black population:
migration to San Diego, 16;
women migrants in Panama,
detention if suspected of venereal
disease, 49

Casino Theatre, 26

Catholic Charities, development of
new YMCA, 196–97

the Center (LGBT Community
Center of San Diego): buildings
and their locations, 139, 190,
235n42; fundraising for, 113,
138–39, 144; fundraising strategy,
antiprostitution activism
mobilized as, 18, 112–13; Bernie
Michels resignation, 144; name
changes of, 190, 235n42; public
funding, 190; sponsored programs
of, 186; support meetings for

Clark, Reginald Eugene, 122

Clay, Robert. *See* Silver Sands Café (Robert Clay, owner)

Clermont Hotel (SRO), 59, 62, *62*

Clinton, Bill: Maya Angelou as inaugural poet for, 109; Defense of Marriage Act (1996), 192; political pressure to lift ban against gays/lesbians in the military, 235n39

the Club (bar), 138

Coates, Ta-Nehisi, 191–92

Cohen, Cathy, 185

Cohen-Cruz, Jan, 179–81

COINTELPRO, 173

Collective Voice of San Diego: An African American Coalition for Progressive Change, 185

College Grove, 118

coming out. *See* visibility politics and "coming out" as focus of safe space activists

Commission on Training Camp Activities (CTCA), 48, 50–51

Consolidated Aircraft, 14

Convair, 82

Creole Palace Café (interracial cabaret): military designating off-limits, 53; morals charges brought against, 52–53

Creole Palace nightclub. *See* Douglas Hotel and Creole Palace

cribs (stables), 28

critical studies of tourism and militarism, 15, 215n46

cross-dressing Ordinance 9439 (Section 5619) (1966): overview of history of cross-dressing laws in general and late passage in SD, 2;

court appearance of queen, description of, 134; MCCSD advice on how to avoid arrest under, 134; and police claim of "men posing as women" targeting servicemen and robbing them, 2, 123, 134; redevelopment of downtown as motive for passing, 1–2, 3, 112; safe space activists not fighting, 12, 13, 133–34; selective arrests of street queens using, 1–2, 122–24; vice officers' claim they only arrest if crimes or endangerment present, 134

cruising. *See* gay cruising

CTCA (Commission on Training Camp Activities), 48, 50–51

Cua, Jim: cofounder of Gay/Lesbian Asian-Pacific Islander Social Support group and LAGADU, 205; Mackey-Cua Project named for, 165, 205

Cudjoe, Selwyn, 69, 72, 223n5

Damron Address Book (1965–2021): classification of gay friendly bars, businesses, and cruising areas, 131–33, 142; cruising areas in SD not listed after 2005 due to aggressive policing, 133; lesbian sites (and map), 186, *188–89*; map of gay men's sites, *120–21*; as productive of difference, 132

dance halls (temperance saloons) as interracial meeting place: outlawed in the cleanup for Panama-California Exposition, 26, 30, 33–34, 63; transactional sex occurred in nearby rooming

50–51; as California state plan, 48, 49; challenges in the courts, 20–22; de-housing in process of, 22, 53–54; and eugenics discourse of black women as particularly sexually perverse, 50, 53; Health Department of San Diego as recommending, 48; interracial contact as primary target, 52–53; Bascom Johnson's enthusiasm for, 48, 52; length of detentions, 52; military (federal) funding of, 20, 51, 52; military officials' supporting and implementing, 48, 49–50; nationwide implementation, 52, 53–54; number of women detained, 52; in Panama, 49, 53; the prostitute created as new gendered class of criminals, 48–49, 53. *See also* Mission Valley Isolation Hospital (San Diego)

Detwiler, Paul, *San Diego's Gay Bar History* (documentary), 117

Diablo's (bar), 138

Dillinger, Michael E., 112, 113–14, 139

Dilno, Jeri, 178

discrimination. *See* housing—racial discrimination in; military (United States)—black soldiers' differential treatment; racial segregation; racial violence; racism

disreputable: as analytical category, 16; as term in early 20th-century reformism, 5

the disreputable, politics of (black women's liberatory practices): overview, 4–6; Angelou's limited interiority access, 70–71, 104–6; Angelou's trickster-troping

(subversively embedding desire and queerness), 75–78; Angelou using disreputability to achieve respectability, 17, 69, 71, 74–75, 103–10; black feminism and lesbian and queer activism as only possible due to, 8; definition of disreputability, 19; liberative subjecthood produced through, 5; non-normative behaviors, vagrancy charges for, 8; as place-based act of refusal, 6–8; reconceptualizing the domestic sphere, 6–7; refusal as form of activism and practice of freedom, 6–8, 19, 42–43, 142–43; refusal to leave neighborhood places and spaces, 6–8, 142–43; scavenger methods of, defined, 5–6; sex work as antiwork politics, 8–9, 10, 211–12

"the DL" as epistemology, 156

domestic work: black women as relegated to low-paying work as domestics and cooks, 80–81, 90–91, 94, 99; classified ads placed by California employers in black newspapers, 34–35; white women leased out for, vs. incarceration, 11

Douglas Hotel and Creole Palace (black hotel and cabaret): cost to build, 55; location of, 55, 56; military designating off-limits, 64; George Ramsey and Robert Rowe as developers of, 54; Mabel Rowe/Ramsey (née Tyler) as actively involved in, 54–59, 57, 222nn142–143; in the Zoot-Suit Riots (1943), 65–66. *See also* Ramsey, George

Douglas Hotel *(continued)*
—THE CREOLE PALACE (BLACK CABARET): black stage and screen acts booked by, 55; Bubba's Pluton's playing, 125; Creole Cuties Chorus, 118; interior and staff, 57; location inside the Douglas Hotel, 55, 56; reputation for prostitution and gambling, 55; vaudeville acts, 118
Douglass, Frederick, 72
downtown San Diego: the Community Concourse (1963), 118–19; early twentieth-century queer culture, 117–18; ghettoization of black communities in, 12; suburban shopping malls and economic decline of, 118. *See also* downtown vice district (postwar era); Gaslamp Quarter; Panama-California Exposition (1915–1916)—cleanup of downtown ordered in preparation; redevelopment of downtown (postwar era); red-light district (Health Department defined); red-light district, police-protected (Stingaree)
downtown vice district (postwar era): overview of the necessity of sex tourism for the military economy, 3; Bubba's performance circuit of primarily straight clubs, 125–27; businesses accommodating servicemembers, 118; the Community Concourse (1963) as unofficial dividing line from central business district, 119; drag queen performance circuit, 125;

early-twentieth century queer culture in theater districts, 117–18; the gay Tenderloin (interracial servicemen's bars), 63, 118, 133; map of, 120–21; peep shows, court declaring "not obscene," 119, 122; racial and class divisions among poor and housing-precarious people in SROs, 141–42; racial and class divisions between Hillcrest and, 111, 112, 140–41, 143; refusal of queer sex-working people to leave after redevelopment to Gaslamp Quarter, 142–43; servicemen renting civilian clothes for a night out, 119; servicemen taking the bus to Armed Services YMCA, 118, 119; as sex-working queens' central place, 125–26. *See also* drag queens; Gaslamp Quarter; gay bars; gay cruising; redevelopment of downtown (postwar era); safe space activists (gay neighborhood development)—antiprostitution activism of; Silver Sands Café (Robert Clay, owner); SROs (single-room occupancies)
—POLICING OF: of cruising areas, and *Damron* listings, 133; designation of vice districts and maintenance of white heteropatriarchal status quo, 3–4; military "off limits" mandates businesses, declared unconstitutional but still used, 119, 122; renovation into Gaslamp Quarter and, 138. *See also* cross-dressing Ordinance 9439 (Section 5619) (1966)

drag queens: disrupting the gender binary for straight audiences, 126–27; female impersonators, as more respectable, 112, 117, 127–29, 230n50; lesbians' discomfort with, 114; performance circuits of mostly straight clubs, 125–27; racial and class divisions among, 111–12; safe space activists seeking to differentiate themselves from, 112, 114; San Diego Imperial Court, 112; "street drag" as disreputable, 127–28; "taking dates" for sex work after gigs, 125–26. *See also* black trans queens; cross-dressing Ordinance 9439 (Section 5619) (1966); Latine queens; white queens (low-capital)

Du Bois, W.E.B., 7

East African residents, 192
East San Diego, 145
Ebony/Black Prides, 198
Eckert, Kevin J., 141–42, 231n86
El Cortez Hotel, 118; Sky Room (bar), 117, 118, 145
Eliot, Charles, 50
Elks Lodge (black fraternal order, Logan): among black-owned businesses in Logan, 83; black vaudeville "chitlin circuit" performances at, 160; Bubba and the Plutons performing at, 115–16, 125, 159, 160; continuing entertainments (e.g., weekly "Reggae Saturdays" promoted by Lady Princess), 160; as enduring institution, 115–16, 146, 159–60; queer history of, 160; sexual

economy housed by, created in response to displacement of black people, 18, 160. *See also* black fraternal orders

Ellington, Duke, 55
El Morocco Club (Logan), 83, 86–87, *86*

Emerald, Marti, 196
employment: Angelou's job searches and working as cook and waitress, 80–81, 90–92, 94, 99; black women as relegated to low-paying work as domestics and cooks, 80; defense industry in SD, black workers mostly left out of, 67; postwar difficulties for black workers, and turn to disreputable informal economies, 67–68; white women's opportunities, 80. *See also* antiwork politics; defense industry and California; domestic work; sex tourism industry in San Diego; sex work

Ensenada, Mexico, Angelou's visit with Father (Daddy Bailey), 78–79
Equal Suffrage Association, 24
Ervin, Jordan, 137–38, 142
eugenics discourse: black women posited as particularly sexually perverse, 50, 53; prostitutes as "feebleminded" and therefore incompetent, 42. *See also* detention of (disproportionately black) women suspected of venereal disease

family. *See* black family and community acceptance of queer family members federal laws: Chamberlain-Kahn Act (1917), 48–49; Chinese Exclusion Act (1882), 12, 34; Defense of Marriage Act (1996), 192; Matthew Shepard and James Byrd Hates Crimes Act (2009), 236n48; racially restrictive covenants outlawed (1948), 145; repeal of "Don't Ask, Don't Tell," 236n48

female impersonators, as more respectable drag queens, 112, 117, 127–29, 230n50

feminists and feminism: positionality of the researcher in bias about Bubba's religious life, 150; second-wave, hesitancy of black women to align with, 166; supporting policies criminalizing sex work, 10. *See also* black feminist framework

feminists and feminism, first-wave: and creation of same-sex women's prisons, 11; demanding closure of the Stingaree, 24, 63; moral crisis about sex work mobilized by, 13, 26; suffragists noting the disproportionate cruelty of black women's treatment in prison, 11. *See also* white slavery (sex-trafficking moral panic about interracial intimacy)

Fidelity Lodge No. 10 (black Masonic lodge, Logan): among black-owned businesses in Logan, 83; birthday party at venue, description of, 150–51; and black queer storefront masonic theology, 148; as enduring institution, 115–16, 146, 159–60;

establishment of, as first and oldest operating black fraternal order, 148; event rentals, 149; mutual-benefit spatial practices of, 148, 149, 150–51, 159; organizational meetings of, 148–49, *149–50*; positionality of the researcher and, 148; sexual economy housed by, created in response to displacement of black people, 18, 160; as transformed into a storefront church on Sundays, 18, 148. *See also* black fraternal orders

—GREATER JOHNSON MISSIONARY BAPTIST CHURCH: overview, 18; and black queer storefront masonic theology, 148; Bubba as black trans elder in, 152–54, 159; Bubba joining (1991), 148, 153–54; Bubba's Kitchen named in her honor, 153; as chosen family, 154, 156, 159; educators, relationships with (e.g., "African American Heritage"), 159; as enduring institution, 159, 160; establishment as storefront church (prior to 1991), 148; establishment at Fidelity Lodge, 149; Pastor D. R. Anderson, and Mrs. Anderson, 149, 153–54, 156; sexual economy housed by, created in response to displacement of black people, 18, 160

Fifth Ward claimed to be haven for black disreputable women, 32

Filipino immigrants, 12, 100

Fischer, Anne Gray, 4, 11–12

Fitch, Owen Alonzo, 87, 224–25n34

Fitch, Sylura, 87, 224–25n34. *See also* Barron, Sylura Richardson

Flame (bar), 186, 198

floaters, as analytical category, 16

Flores-Villalobos, Joan, 49

Frazier, E. Franklin, 147

Friends Unlimited, 185

funeral repast traditions, 158–59

Ganz, Marshall, 146–47

Garvey, Marcus, 169

Gaslamp Quarter: black club scene as not welcoming to lesbians, 198; Bubba (black trans queen) on emptiness of, 143; policing of, 138; refusal of queer sex-working people to leave after redevelopment, 142–43. *See also* redevelopment of downtown (postwar era)—Gaslamp Quarter project

Gaslamp Quarter Merchants Association, forced closure of the Silver Sands Café, 115, 143

Gates, Ella, 38, 39–42, 219n79

The Gathering (1991 Marti Mackey play), 163, 175–76, 179–79, *180*, 190

gay bars: community of, as leery of the high visibility of safe space activists, 131; early twentieth century, 117–18; "extra carding" practices to exclude disreputables, 164; fundraising for the Center, 138–39; of Hillcrest, black lesbians not welcomed in, 164, 197–98; lesbian bars, map showing, *188–89*; map showing, *120–21*; meeting of real estate association at, to sponsor Prop 14 (1964

attempt to repeal fair housing law), 145; mid-century urban redevelopment and attacks by authorities on, 119, 122; number of, 117; in Oceanside, 119, 122; as racially segregated, 118; repeal of Prohibition and proliferation of, 117; safe space activists' view of, as detriments to gay liberation, 130–31; support for redistricting plan cutting off City Heights, 194; World War II mobilization and proliferation of, 116–17. *See also* downtown vice district (postwar)

Gay Center for Social Services. *See* the Center (LGBT Community Center of San Diego)

gay cruising: *Damron Address Book* listings for, 133, 142; *Damron's* listings, and policing of, 133; defined as non-gay-identified men discreetly seeking out other men for casual sex, 130; map showing areas, *120–21*; and refusal to leave Horton Plaza after redevelopment, 142–43; safe space activists condemning as dangerous and perpetuating antigay violence, 130–31

Gay/Lesbian Asian-Pacific Islander Social Support, 205

Gay Liberation Front (SDGLF), safe space activists as members of, 113–14

gender binary: drag queens as disrupting, for straight audiences, 126–27. *See also* cross-dressing Ordinance 9439 (Section 5619) (1966); drag queens

Heathers, Peggy: in black/white interracial lesbian couple with Cynthia Lawrence-Wallace, 114, 165–66, 167; as cofounder of the Center, 114, 165; discomfort with drag queens, 114; and the HIV/AIDS crisis blood drives, 176; as inductee of Community Wall of Honor, 178; and racism experienced by her black partner, 167; on sexism in organizing, 165–66; as sometimes not included in black lesbian gatherings, 166. *See also* Lawrence-Wallace, Cynthia

Henderson, Emma, 32, 33

Hennigan, Peter C., 44

Hernandez, Carlotta, 203–4

Hernández, Kelly Lytle, 214n31

Hi Ho Club (Logan), 90

Hillcrest Brewing Company, 194

Hillcrest neighborhood: antigay violence used discursively in gentrification of, 18, 31, 227–28n13; Balboa Park proximity, 140; bars and clubs, "extra carding" practices to exclude certain racialized bodies, 164; black lesbians not welcomed in social scene of, 164, 197–98; demographic change to white middle-class gay men and lesbians, 139–40; lesbian parties ("for women by women") held in, 198, 202–3; lesbian population in, 140; map of public spaces frequented by lesbian and queer women, *188–89*; originally a diverse working-class and older-persons neighborhood, 13, 18, 139–40;

racial and class divisions between downtown queer culture and, 111, 112, 140–41, 143; redevelopment/gentrification by safe space activists, 13, 18, 113–14, 139–40; and redevelopment of surrounding neighborhoods, 139, 140. *See also* the Center (LGBT Community Center of San Diego); safe space activists (gay neighborhood development)

—REDISTRICTING CAMPAIGN BY SAFE SPACE ACTIVISTS: overview, 164–65, 190–91; accusations (false) that Proposition 8 (banning gay marriage) passed due to homophobia of black and Latine residents of City Heights, 191–94; argument to exclude City Heights based on "flow" of visual/economic spatial imaginary, 194–95; Balboa Park claimed by, 191, 192, 195; Catholic Charities stepping in to thwart wealthier white residents' plan to redevelop City Heights, 196–97; demographics of the new districts, 197; the Latino Redistricting Committee and, 196, 197; legal basis for redistricting, 236n44; new District 9 argued as better representation for the lower-income, highly diverse City Heights community, 192, 195–96; new District 9 as reinforcing the idea that poverty, race, and immigration are not relevant LGBT topics, 197; new District 9 boundaries proved to reinforce

Hillcrest neighborhood *(continued)* wealthier white property owners, 196–97; protected neighborhood status as "special interest" group argued for, 191; racialized metaphors about safety used in, 191; as racist and classist, media coverage of the proposed map as, 192, 195

Hines, Fannie B., 33

HIV/AIDS crisis: the black Christian churches as sidelining, 185–86; Blood Sisters blood drive program by SD lesbians, 176; Jesse Jessop's death (1990), 144; Karibu support group for black men, 185–86; Little Brothers of the Blood Sisters, 176; solidarity between lesbians and gay men during, as networks unavailable to black men, 175

Hobbs, Allyson, 56

Holiday, Billie, 55, 224n26

homophobia: false narrative of black people as inherently homophobic, 191–94, 207–8, 209; of security personnel in rented venues for lesbian parties ("for women by women"), 200–201. *See also* black family and community acceptance of queer family members

Horton Plaza: *Damron's Address Book* on bars and cruising in, 133, 142; refusal to leave neighborhood, as resistance to redevelopment, 142–43; selective arrests of black queens for cross-dressing code violations (1960s), 1–2, 122–24. *See also* cross-dressing Ordinance

9439 (Section 5619) (1966); downtown vice district (postwar)

Horton Plaza Redevelopment Plan: Lynch and Appleyard's report on the ethics of preserving public space in downtown, 135; signed off by Pete Wilson, 134–35. *See also* redevelopment of downtown (postwar era)

Horton Plaza Shopping Center, 120–21, 136; *Damron's Address Book* on cruising in, 142

Horton-Stalling, LaMonda, 8–9

House Un-American Activities list, 98–99

housing: in Logan Heights, 83; permanent housing program for LGBT youth (Center as sponsor), 186; public housing opposition, 141; refusal to provide due to Progressive Era antiprostitution laws limiting all women's mobility, 93–94; waterfront shacks, demolition of and de-housing of residents, 45–46, 46. *See also* de-housing of black women accused of prostitution; rooming houses; SROs (single-room occupancies)

—RACIAL DISCRIMINATION IN: attempt to overturn the state Rumsford Fair Housing Act (1964 Prop 14), 145; the Chinese District as only option for black women to rent rooms (early 20th c.), 12, 25, 31; as consequence, Logan Heights as one of few places black and Latine residents could own property, 83, 145; as displacement of black residents in tandem with four-decades urban redevelopment, 144–45; on military bases, 83, 169; restrictive covenants, as preventing black and Latine residents from owning property (despite being illegal), 83, 144–45; SROs charging black guests more, 142

Hubert, Ella, 51

Hughes, Donisha, 150–51

Hughes, Granville "Bubba" Omega. *See* Bubba (Granville "Bubba" Omega Hughes)

Human Dignity Ordinance Task Force, 178

human trafficking laws (antitrafficking laws): capitalism and work culture as perpetuating the demand for human trafficking, 9–10, 211–12; used to subject sex-working people of color to police harassment and incarceration, 9–10, 210–11

Hutchinson, Beth, 176

Imani Worship Center, 185

immigrant communities: and City Heights, 192, 196–97; in interzones of vice districts, 2, 12. *See also* Chinese District

incarceration: mutually constitutive role of race and gender in policies for, 10–11. *See also* detention of (disproportionately black) women suspected of venereal disease
—IN EARLY 20TH-CENTURY CALIFORNIA: black women as disproportionately sentenced and subjected to gender violence, 11; black women imprisoned in men's penal institutions, 11; black women's population statistics showing disproportionate arrests and fines, 25; feminist reforms of, 11; and prostitution as newly created crime, 48–49, 53; same-sex women's prisons, as reform, 11, 53; white women leased out as domestics as alternative to, 11; white women less subject to harsher forms of labor in, 11

indigenous lands, sale by SD to US military below market value, 14

indigenous people: communities in interzones with vice districts, 2, 12; farmworkers, and interracial policing of sex work, 100; un-housed by the Red Light Abatement Act, 45–46

inheritance, court finding for denial of, 40–42, 219n79

Inside Out (bar), 194

International Guild Guides, 132

interracial intimacy as focus of policing: among indigenous and mestizo farmworkers, 100; in California's Chinese Districts, and moral panic of "yellow slavery," 34, 218n53; and denial of inheritance, 39–41; gentrification processes and, 11–12; and military enforcement against prostitution, 52–53; and selective policing campaign ahead of Panama-California Exposition, 25, 26, 30, 35–39, 41–42; vagrancy charges for, 8.

176–77; committees of, 177–78; disbanding of, 184; *The Gathering* (1991 group production of Marti Mackey play), 163, 175–6, 178–79, *180*, 190; as interracial group, 205, 209; and intersectional queer black nationalist activism, 18, 176–77, 178–79; Marti Mackey as cofounder and leader of, 177, 186, 209; meetings held at black-dominated spaces due to racism experienced in the Center, 177, 186; and separatism as necessity for community building, 163–64. *See also* Mackey, M. Corinne ("Marti")

Lambda Archives of San Diego (formerly Lesbian and Gay Historical Society): M. Corinne "Marti" Mackey play archive, 184, 190; Mr. and Miss Black Gay San Diego (video), 198; organizing Marlon Riggs Film Festival, 185

Langley, Sara, 39

Las Hermanas coffee shop, expansion to wider audience, 203–4

Latine queens: Bradley's and Chee Chee Club as preferred venues for, 112; hanging out at Horton's Plaza after closing time, 122; and racial and class divisions among drag queens, 111–12. *See also* drag queens

Latine residents: accusations (false) that Proposition 8 (banning gay marriage) passed due to homophobia of black and Latine residents of City Heights, 191–94;

Central American population in SD, 16; in City Heights diverse population, 192, 196–97; housing discrimination and racial covenants as preventing home ownership by, 83, 144–45; lesbian coffee shop, expanding to wider audience, 203–4; Logan Heights emerging as one of few places property ownership was possible for, 145. *See also* Hillcrest neighborhood—redistricting campaign by safe space activists; Latine queens; Logan Heights; Mexican/Mexican Americans

law and policy. *See* California laws; federal laws; San Diego law and policy

Lawrence, Larry, 177

Lawrence-Wallace, Cynthia: as black lesbian coupled with white lesbian Peggy Heathers, 114, 165–66, 167; and black lesbian separatism, need for, 166; as cofounder of LAGADU, 177; as County Human Relations Commission appointee, 190; discomfort with drag queens, 114; and the HIV/AIDS crisis blood drives, 176; as inductee of Community Wall of Honor, 178; and lesbian separatism, need for, 166; racial issues as focus of, 168; sexism experienced in black nationalist activism, 176; white woman partner as sometimes limiting, 166. *See also* black lesbian separatism; Heathers, Peggy

—AS COFOUNDER OF THE CENTER: overview of experience

Lawrence-Wallace, Cynthia *(continued)* as black lesbian, 114, 165; as both invisible and hypervisible, 165; and common cause with Thom Carey as black partners of white gay and lesbian activists, 167–68; identity attached to white partner, 167; racism experienced by, 165–66, 167; sexism experienced by, 165–66, 175, 176; tokenization of, 166; white colleagues wanting her to educate about racism, 165–66

Lesbian and Gay Historical Society. *See* Lambda Archives of San Diego

lesbian cofounders of the Center: overview, 144; black, and absence of black lesbians from Hillcrest, 18; discomfort with drag queens, 114; as four of fifteen-person planning committee, one of whom was black, 165; gay men upset that lesbians wanted a women's night, but frequently had events that didn't include women, 165–66; Bernie Michels resignation citing disagreements with, 144; and racism (*See* Lawrence-Wallace, Cynthia—as cofounder of the Center); sexism experienced by, 163, 165–66, 175, 176. *See also* black lesbian separatism; Center (LGBT Community Center of San Diego); lesbian separatism

lesbian parties ("for women by women"): atmosphere and dancing, 198–99; expanding events to appeal to wider audience as alienating original

(black) audience, 202–3, 205; map of places events were hosted, *188–89*; as meeting space for casual sex and long-term dating, 162; as national trend, 204–5; problems between queer black patrons and homophobic male security in rented venues, 200–201; Soulkiss parties, 162, 198–99, 200, 205

—Passage Playground (Cabaret Passage): advertising and marketing, and racialized queer spatial practices, 162, 163; advertising in Hillcrest and UCSD campus, 201–2, 202; advertising through visual economy of black queer joy, 199; as autoethnography, 18–19; burnout as problem for promoters, 162, 199, 204–5; and context of the redistricting process as racial exclusion, 164–65, 190–91, 197, 209; and the dance floor as site of activism, 191, 198–99; lack of building ownership as issue, 200–201, 205; longevity of companies offering, 199; map of places events were hosted, *188–89*; motivations of promoters, 199; promotion as hard work with little profit, 161–62, 199, 201–3, 204; teaming up with other promoters, 163, 199, 200; themed nights and nonclub events, 202–3; in the tradition of monetizing black women's bodies in the militarized sex tourism industry, 19, 161, *201*; as undermining

critical studies of tourism and militarism, 15, 215n46; "scavenger methodology," 5–6. *See also* positionality of the researcher

Metropolitan Community Church of San Diego (MCCSD): in campaign to end the ban on gays/lesbians in the military, 235n39; instructing cis gay men on avoiding conflation with drag queens, 13, 134; members of, as safe space activists, 17–18, 113, 167; Bernie Michels and, 18, 113; on policing of "plaza drag queens," 133–34. *See also* the Center (LGBT Community Center of San Diego); safe space activists (gay neighborhood development)

Mexican/Mexican Americans: migrant workers, and policing of interracial sex work, 100–101, 225n48; servicemen, the Zoot-Suit Riots and solidarity with black servicemen, 65. *See also* Angelou, Maya, *Gather Together in My Name* (1974)—storyline: as brothel worker in San Joaquin Valley; Latine queens; Latine residents; Logan Heights

—W O M E N : detention on suspicion of venereal disease, 51–52; and interracial sex work among migrant workers, 100

Mexico: American black masculinity in, 79–80; Baja California, migration of white prostitutes to, 47; colonial, African-descended people and fluidity of race and interethnic relationality, 220n87;

Ensenada, 78–79; prostitution as legal in, 47. *See also* Tijuana, Mexico

Michels, Bernie: background of, 227n6; characterization of lesbian and/or black groups as "separatist," 163, 176; as cofounder of the Center, 112; as complicit in policing of black queens congregating in Horton Plaza, 13; on downtown as "skid-rowish" and not comfortable for middle-class lesbians and gays, 112; on female impersonators, 128; fundraising for the Center, 18, 113, 138–39, 144; on gay bars and cruising as detrimental to gay liberation, 130–31; in interracial relationship with Thom Carey, 167–68; MCCSD involvement of, 18, 113; resignation, citing disagreements with lesbian cofounders of the Center, 144; working together with Jess Jessop, and parting of ways, 113–14, 143–44

migration of African Americans. *See* black migration to California

military (United States): all-volunteer force transition, marketing campaigns replacing the ideal figure of the white soldier with the "good black soldier," 174–75; annihilation of antiwar activism among the ranks, 173; critical studies of tourism and militarism, 15, 215n46; "don't ask, don't tell" and political pressure to lift ban on gays/lesbians in, 190, 235n39; "don't ask, don't tell,"

military (United States) *(continued)*
repeal of, 236n48; KKK and other
white supremacist groups
permitted to organize on bases,
173–74; mobilization for World
War II, 116–17; officials as
members of American Social
Hygiene Association, 48, 49–50;
professionalization and moves
toward racial equity in the 1980s,
174–75; women's branches
established (1942), 225n39. *See also*
defense industry and California;
detention of (disproportionately
black) women suspected of
venereal disease; military
economy of San Diego; Women's
Army Corps (WAC); World War II
—BLACK SOLDIERS' DIFFEREN-
TIAL TREATMENT: GI Bill
benefits denied to, 67; systematic
mistreatment, 169, 173–74, 175;
unable to live on base, 83, 169;
venereal disease surveillance and
quarantine, 50–51
—MILITARY POLICE: CTCA force,
venereal disease protection, 48,
50–51; Movement for a Democratic Military (MDM), raids to
dismantle, 172, 173; off-limits
designations for businesses, 53,
64, 119, 122; policing cruising
around the Armed Services
YMCA, 133
military economy of San Diego:
annual contribution to the
regional economy (current), 14;
annual economic contribution of
sex tourism industry as second

only to (2016 report), 3; and black
migration postwar, 14, 82; black
workers mostly left out of defense
industry, 67; downturn in
immediate aftermath of WWII,
82; indigenous land sold below
market value to attract, 14; as
insulating SD from economic
crises and downturns, 14; safe
space activism of SD as uniquely
influenced by, 114–15; sex tourism
industry as requirement for, 3; The
Panama-California Exposition as
project of, 2, 14, 16, 22; threats by
military to leave town (1972), 135;
World War II and growth of
defense industry, 14. *See also*
defense industry and California
military in San Diego: black and
Mexican servicemembers unable
to live on base, 83, 169; black and
Mexican servicemen systematically mistreated, 169, 173–74, 175;
black sailors, scams against, 87;
black servicemembers staying on
after World War II, 116–17; court
martial of black sailor Edward
Lynn for highlighting racism on
base, 169; "don't ask, don't tell"
and political pressure to lift bans
on gays/lesbians in, 190, 235n39;
funding Mission Valley Isolation
Hospital, 20, 51; gay pornography
rings, 115; KKK and other
white-supremacist groups
permitted to organize on bases,
173–74; loss of employment by
partners of women accused of
prostitution, 22; servicemembers

living in SROs downtown, 141; taking the bus to the Armed Forces YMCA downtown for recreation, 118, 119; and the unique racial-sexual geography of the city, 16; Zoot-Suit Riots (1943), 63–65. *See also* Johnson, Bascom (director of Army Sanitary Corps)

—MILITARY POLICE: attacks on gay bars and institutions, 119, 122; Movement for a Democratic Military (MDM), raids to dismantle, 172, 173; off-limits designations for businesses, 53, 64, 119, 122; off-limits mandates by, declared unconstitutional in several courts but continued into the 1980s, 119, 122

Miller-Young, Mireille, 9, 95–96

miscegenation laws: as antiprostitution charges, 38, 94, 95; consequences facing black women accused of disobeying, 21–22; and early gay bars as racially segregated, 118; military camps ignoring, 222n130; postwar SD arrests on antiprostitution pretexts, 95; presence of black woman with a white man as violation of, 94; repeal of California state laws (1948), 118; and twenty-first century queer spatial practices, 162. *See also* racial segregation

misogyny. *See* sexism

Mission Hills, 140, 145

Mission Valley Isolation Hospital (San Diego detention facility for women suspected of venereal disease): overview, 20–21; arrests and detention in, 51–52; de-housing of women detained, 22; detention of black women in, despite court dismissal for lack of evidence, 21; length of detentions, 52; military (federal) funding, 20, 51; number of women detained, 52. *See also* detention of (disproportionately black) women suspected of venereal disease

Mission Valley shopping center, 118, 139

modern-day slavery abolitionism, 9–10

Modern Hotel (SRO), 59

Moll Flanders (Defoe), 73

Monod, David, 118

Monte Carlo Club (bar), 125

Montelongo, Irma Victoria, 51–52

moral panics (narratives of sex work as moral crisis): first-wave feminism and, 13, 26; interraciality of California's Chinese Districts, and moral panic of "yellow slavery," 34, 218n53; sex-work activists as reinforcing, and obscuring the issues of work, 211–12. *See also* interracial intimacy as focus of policing; white slavery (sex-trafficking moral panic about interracial intimacy)

Morton, Jelly Roll, 55

Mo's Bar & Grill, 194

Mo's Universe ("bar-and-restaurant empire"), 194

Mountain View Estates (SRO), 59

Mountain View Park: police-provoked attack (July 1969), 170–71;

of Times Square, 227–28n13; San
Diego safe space activism
differentiated from, 114–15; World
War II and proliferation of gay
bars and enclaves, 116
"The Nigger God" (Marti Mackey
play), 179–84
Nishikawa, Kinohi, 76
Nixon, Richard: Angela Davis's
critique of, 172–73; and removal of
Republican National Convention
from SD (1972), 134–35
nonmarital sex: as "promiscuous,"
41; vagrancy charges for, 8
Normal Heights, 140
North Park, 140

Obama, Barack: evolution of views
on gay marriage, 236n48;
Matthew Shepard and James Byrd
Hates Crimes Act (2009), 236n48;
repeal of "Don't Ask, Don't Tell,"
236n48
Obelisk the Bookstore, 186
Oceanside, California: Bubba and
the Plutons playing in, 125; Bubba
"taking dates" for sex work after
the gigs, 125; Camp Pendleton
Defense Fund rally (1977), 174;
gay bars near, map of, 120–21; gay
bars near, military and other
authorities attacking, 119, 122;
KKK cross-burning incident
(1976), 174; People's Armed
Forces Day (1969), 172–73. See also
Camp Pendleton Marine Base
(Oceanside)
Odom, Mychal, 159

Orpheum Theatre, 117
Oyos, Teresa, 203–4

Pacific Hotel (rooming house), 59, 62
Panama: detention of (disproportionately black) women suspected
of venereal disease, 49, 53;
General Order No. 20 (1918) to
outlaw prostitution, 49
Panama-California Exposition
(1915–1916): 1909 as turning point
year in preparation for, 16, 22; as
first major redevelopment project
of SD, 14; Panama Canal
completion as motive for, 16, 22;
as project of militarization, 2, 14,
16, 22

—CLEANUP OF DOWNTOWN
ORDERED IN PREPARATION:
overview, 2–3, 16, 22–23; black
syndicates, attempts to thwart,
42–43; black women challenging
arrests in court, 35, 37–38; black
women disproportionately
targeted in, 2–3, 11, 12; dance halls
(temperance saloons) outlawed,
26, 30, 33–34, 63; de-housing black
women and other marginalized
persons, 23, 30–31, 38–39, 45–46,
47; demolition of buildings and
rooms, 22–23; interracial contact
as basis for arrests, 25, 26, 30,
35–39, 41–42; police campaign of
selectively policing sex resorts
outside the Stingaree (police-
protected vice district), 12, 25, 30,
33–34; police resistance to cleanup
in Stingaree, 12, 23–25; the Red

Bubba by closest friends and family members, 156–57; and perception of Bubba's male drag, 152–54; and "queer" as term, 154; and redistricting of City Heights and Hillcrest, 164–65. *See also* lesbian parties ("for women by women")—Passage Playground (Cabaret Passage); methodology

Pride Parade: Black/Ebony Prides, 198; gay and lesbian police officers march in (1991), 190

prisons. *See* incarceration

privacy rights: black women demanding, by challenging arrests in court, 20–22, 35, 37–38, 215n1; black women in rooming houses and, 16; LGBT identity based in, and erasure of race and class as limits on access to, 227–28n13; police violation of, as clearance technique, 42; white upscale parlors affording patrons exercise of, 28, 30

private property, and Red Light Abatement Act, 44

Prodigal (periodical of MCCSD), 13, 133–34, 138

Progressive Era reformers: and disreputability as threat to be managed, 19; eradication of prostitution as goal of, 24–25, 46; male intermediaries needed by sex workers due to laws limiting mobility of women, 68, 93–94; pressure to close Stingaree (police-protected vice district), 12, 24–25; and the Red Light Abatement Act (1914), 44–45, 46; and

the tenement, view of vs. black women's experience of, 7. *See also* safe space activists (gay neighborhood development)

Prohibition repeal, and expansion of queer institutions, 117

Project Unity, 185

"promiscuous" black women, 41

prostitution: eugenics' conclusion of prostitutes as "feebleminded" and therefore incompetent, 42; as newly created crime, 48–49, 53. *See also* de-housing of black women accused of prostitution; detention of (disproportionately black) women suspected of venereal disease; moral panics (narratives of sex work as moral crisis); Progressive Era reformers; red-light district(s), as places of marginalization; safe space activists (gay neighborhood development)—antiprostitution activism of; sex work; *entries at* redevelopment

Provost, Louis H., 117–18

Pryor, Richard, 179, 183

Purity League of the WCTU, 24, 26

quarantining. *See* detention of (disproportionately black) women suspected of venereal disease

quare studies and quareness, 154–57

"queer" as identity, 208

"queer" as term, 154

queer communities, and racial and class divisions: among drag queens, 111–12; attempts to defeat

queer communities *(continued)*
   fair housing law (1964), 145; the
   Damron Address Book as producing difference, 132–33; between
   downtown and Hillcrest, 111, 112,
   140–41, 143; "extra carding"
   practices in Hillcrest bars to
   exclude disreputables, 164; spatial
   practices, 162, 163. *See also* safe
   space activists (gay neighborhood
   development)—racism and
queer culture: Black/Ebony Prides,
   198; early twentieth-century,
   117–18; lesbian coffee shops,
   expansion to wider audiences,
   203–4; Marlon Riggs Film Festival,
   185; proliferation with mobilization for World War II, 116–17. *See
   also* Afrikan American Gay
   Women Association (AAGWA);
   black lesbians; black trans queens;
   downtown vice district (postwar
   era); drag queens; gay bars; gay
   cruising; Hillcrest; LAGADU
   (Lesbians and Gays of African
   Descent United); lesbian parties
   ("for women by women"); safe
   space activists (gay neighborhood
   development)
Queer Nation, 235n39

race: colonial Mexico and fluidity of,
   220n87; essentialized and rigid
   constructs of, challenges to,
   42–43, 220n87. *See also* technologies of race
racial capitalism: black sex workers
   make less money, 69, 95–96, 97,
   100–101; false claim of undesirabil-

ity of black women ("myth of prohibition"), 95–96, 110, 163. *See also*
   mutual aid projects organized by
   black queer women as respite from
   racial capitalism and exploitation
racial segregation: criminalization of
   sex workers as central to
   enforcement of, 4; desegregation
   and closure of black bars and
   clubs in Logan, 143; downtown
   ghettoization of black communities, 12; of early gay bars, 118;
   ghettoization of black communities to southeast of the city, 65,
   160; policing of sex workers and
   interracial sex as key to gentrification processes, 11–12; spatialized
   blackness and, 11–12; of twenty-
   first century queer spatial
   practices, 162, 163. *See also*
   Hillcrest neighborhood—
   redistricting campaign by safe
   space activists; housing—racial
   discrimination in; interracial
   intimacy as focus of policing;
   miscegenation laws
racial violence: against black
   servicemen at Camp Pendleton,
   173–74; gender violence against
   incarcerated black women, 11;
   mayor of SD blaming black
   parents for, 65; for refusal to be
   subservient (in Arkansas), 98;
   Zoot-Suit Riots (1943), 63–65
racism: among poor and housing-
   precarious residents in downtown
   SROs, 141–42; gerrymandering to
   prevent representation by
   marginalized communities,

236n44; land-use and zoning policies, storefront vacancies resulting from, 145–46; medical bias, 50. *See also* eugenics discourse; Hillcrest neighborhood—redistricting campaign by safe space activists; housing—racial discrimination in; interracial intimacy as focus of policing; queer communities, and racial and class divisions; racial segregation; racial violence; safe space activists (gay neighborhood development)—racism and; white supremacy

Ramsey, Abbie, 38. *See also* white supremacy

Ramsey, Alfred "Sunny," 38

Ramsey, George: Anita Hotel, 55, 59, 62; arrival in SD, 52–53, 55; brothel and other investments in Logan, 88, *89*; and corruption scandal of state and local officials, 88; Creole Palace Café (interracial cabaret), 52–53; death of, 59; and Mabel Tyler/Rowe/Ramsey, marriages and racial passing as strategic choices to support her active business life, 54–59, 57, 222nn142–143; Yesmar Hotel, 55, 59, 62. *See also* Douglas Hotel and Creole Palace

Ramsey, Mullen, 88, *89*

rape, of black women by white prison guards, 11

Reconstruction, 7

redevelopment, gay-led. *See* safe space activists (gay neighborhood development)

redevelopment of downtown (early twentieth century). *See* Panama-California Exposition (1915–1916)—cleanup of downtown ordered in preparation

redevelopment of downtown (postwar era): overview, 63; and attacks on gay bars and institutions by local, state, and military authorities, 119, 122; black residences as the first targeted in, 11; Community Concourse (1963), 118–19; cross-dressing Ordinance 9439 passed to aid removal of black "plaza queens," 1–2, 3, 112; ethics report on preserving public space in downtown (Lynch and Appleyard), 135; red-light districts as justifying the violent removal of a (criminalized) class of people to make way for, 4; refusal to leave neighborhoods, as form of activism and practice of freedom, 7–8, 142–43; removal of queens as priority in, 1–2, 3, 112, 113; sign-off by Pete Wilson (1972), 135–36; and the Silver Sands Café and Horton Plaza as last remaining spaces for black queens to congregate, 1, 115, 143. *See also* Horton Plaza Shopping Center; safe space activists (gay neighborhood development)—antiprostitution activism of

—GASLAMP QUARTER PROJECT: black club scene as not welcoming to lesbians, 198; Bubba (black trans queen) on emptiness of, 143; bus stops removed, 138,

redevelopment of downtown (continued) 142; characterized as act of war to produce "safe zones," 136–37; charitable organizations and adult entertainment outlawed in, 138, 142; cleanup and criminalization of marginalized residents, 136–38, 142; defined in redevelopment plan, 136; the last black-owned business (Clay's Silver Sands Café) forced to close, 115, 143; policing of, 138; private security and, 138; public benches removed, 137–38, 142; public parks closed at night, 138; public restroom closures, 142; refusal to leave neighborhood, as form of activism and practice of freedom, 142–43; SRO closures, 136, 142; visibility of "disreputables" in public space, measures taken to conceal as failing to address social problems, 142; zoning ordinances, 137, 138

redistricting. See Hillcrest neighborhood—redistricting campaign by safe space activists

Red Light Abatement Act (1914 California): American Social Hygiene Association handling challenges to, 44–45; de-housing of women under, 21–22, 45–46; as erosion of common law principles, 44–45; housing refused to women in general due to, 94; informal notice might be given, 44; keeping a "disorderly house" charges under, 20, 21, 44; notice of raids not required, 44; and the Panama-California Exposition cleanup in SD, 44–46; Progressive Era reformers and passage of, 44, 46; property owners threatened with forfeiture of property for renting to (suspected) prostitutes, 21, 44

red-light district(s), as places of marginalization: black women targeted in, regardless of whether sex-working, 4, 25; as justifying the violent removal of a (criminalized) class of people for urban renewal and gentrification, 4; obliteration of prostitution not the goal in, 4; as separating sexual deviancy to protect the virtue of respectable white women, 4; subjugation practices and, 6; as supporting the imagined need for police and expansion of discretionary powers, 4; white heteropatriarchal status quo reproduced via, 3–4; white women's sex work decriminalized in, 4, 12, 33–34

red-light district (Health Department defined): overview, 23; map of, 60–61; men prohibited from living in section of, 30; politicians and prominent men owning and profiting off properties in, 3, 23; population of black women in (less than 200), 11. See also Panama-California Exposition (1915–1916)—cleanup of downtown ordered in preparation; red-light district, police-protected (Stingaree)

red-light district, police-protected (Stingaree): overview, 3–4, 60–61;

black (and other marginalized) people placed on the outskirts of, 12; black women restricted from working in, 12, 212; black women warned by police chief to stay within boundaries of, or leave the city, 2–3, 30; boundaries of, 23; bribery, graft, and syndicates of police in, 3, 23, 34; campaign to selectively police sex resorts outside of, undertaken to divert attention from, 12, 25, 30, 33–34; Health Department order to clean up for Panama-California Exposition, 22–23, 45; interracial houses in, 27–28; interracial stables (cribs) in, 28; map of, 60–61; mutual aid networks among entrepreneurial black women as direct challenge to police, 38; and no incentive for police to obliterate prostitution, 23, 30; political campaigns financed with excess monies from, 3, 30; Progressive Era reformers pressuring police to shut down, 12, 24–25; upscale and racially segregated parlor houses in, 28; white brothels left alone, 12, 33–34. *See also* Panama-California Exposition (1915–1916)—cleanup of downtown ordered in preparation; Wilson, Keno (police chief)

Red Scare, 98–99

refugees, in City Heights, 165, 197

refusal, as form of activism and practice of freedom, 6–8, 19, 42–43, 142–43

Regan, Amanda, 132

Republican National Convention, moved from San Diego (1972), 134–35

Republican Party and San Diego, black participation in, 224–25n34

Richie, Beth, 211

Richmond, California, black history of, 14

Rich's, 186

Riggs, Marlon: *Anthem*, 185; *Black Is . . . Black Ain't*, 185; Marlon Riggs Film Festival, 185; *Tongues Untied*, 185

robbery and assault: authorities claiming sex workers endanger the lives of men for, 37; police claim that "men posing as women" were targeting sailors, and criminalization of cross-dressing, 2, 123, 134; sex workers as most likely to be victims of, 37; trial of Anna Barnett for (1910), 35, 37–39; vice officers' claim their interest lies in preventing sex-worker victimization, 134

Robinson, Joe and Belle, 62

Rodríguez, Juana María, 104

Rolland Hotel (rooming house), 59, 62

rooming houses: black-women owned or managed, 31, 32–33, 45; black women using for sex work (because shut out of red-light district access), 6, 12, 212; Chinese immigrant-owned, as only option for black women, 12, 25, 31; dance hall as interracial meeting place, with transactional sex in nearby, 26, 27–28, 30, 35; interior room arrangements, 31; licensing

rooming houses *(continued)*
requirement imposed on, and
de-housing of residents, 45; in
Logan, housing black population,
83; map of, 60–61; mixed gender,
black migrants and, 31; police raids
on, while white brothels left alone,
12; and privacy, right to, 16; sharing
rooms, as mutual aid between
black women, 30–31. *See also* SROs
(single-room occupancies)
Rosenberg, Nate, 117–18
Ross, Becki, 13, 112
Roundtable. *See* Tina's Night Club
(Logan)
Rowe, Robert: as a developer of the
Douglas Hotel and Creole Palace,
54; background of, 55, 56–57; and
Mabel Tyler/Rowe/Ramsey,
marriages and racial passing as
strategic choices to support her
active business life, 54–57, 222n143
Rupp, Leila J., 127
Russell, George, 38–39

safe space activists (gay neighborhood development): overview,
112–15; and antigay violence,
discursive use of, 18, 31, 227–28n13;
as architects of disreputable
zones, 12–13; black trans queens,
vehement opposition to inclusion
of, 146, 159; definition of, 114–15;
gay bars and cruising viewed as
detriments to gay liberation,
130–31; gay bars fundraising for the
Center, 138–39; gay political power
as investment of, 13, 190,
235nn39,43, 236nn44,48;

intermingling of gay-identified
men with straight non-gay-
identified men as condemned by,
130–31; and militarized gay culture,
114–15; military veterans as, 115,
167, 227n6; property politics as
focus of, 12–13, 145; and redevelop-
ment/gentrification of Hillcrest, 13,
18, 113–14, 139–40; as seeking to
differentiate themselves from
gender-nonconforming people, 13,
112; sexism experienced by lesbian
organizers in, 163, 165–66, 175, 176;
visibility and "coming out" as
focus of, 130, 131, 156; visibility
politics, bar patrons as leery of, 131;
visibility politics, Bubba (black
trans queen) and, 143, 156;
visibility politics, "the DL" as
different epistemology, 156. *See
also* the Center (LGBT Community
Center of San Diego); Hillcrest
neighborhood; Hillcrest neighborhood—redistricting campaign by
safe space activists
—ANTIPROSTITUTION
ACTIVISM OF: disreputability as
threat to be managed, 19; as
driven by the need to be seen as
morally upright citizens and
community leaders, 13, 112;
mobilized as fundraising strategy
for the Center building, 18, 112–13;
predatory policing of black
queens, silence on, 13, 112, 133–34;
queens downtown as especially
targeted by, 130–31, 146, 159
—RACISM AND: differences of
class and race between downtown

queens and, 111, 112, 140–41, 143; experienced by black lesbian and gay organizers, 163–64, 165–66, 167–68, 175; experienced by black partners of white activists, 167–68, 175; meetings of LAGADU not held in the Center due to, 178, 186. *See also* Hillcrest neighborhood—redistricting campaign by safe space activists; Lawrence-Wallace, Cynthia—as cofounder of the Center

Salisbury, Gertrude, 51

saloons. *See* dance halls (temperance saloons)

same-sex marriage: accusations (false) that Proposition 8 (banning gay marriage) passed due to homophobia of black and Latine residents of City Heights, 191–94; Defense of Marriage Act (1996), 192; Barack Obama's evolution on topic of, 236n48

Samuel, Emma, 32–33

San Diego: as "All American City" (National Municipal League), 118–19; Compton Riots (1965), 168–69; as "patriotic" city compared to "lawless" Tijuana, 137; Zoot-Suit Riots (1943), 63–65. *See also* anti-war activism; black nationalism; black population of San Diego; City Heights; downtown San Diego; Hillcrest neighborhood; housing; Logan Heights; military economy of San Diego; Oceanside, California; Panama-California Exposition (1915–1916); queer culture; San

Diego law and policy; sex tourism industry in San Diego; US-Mexico border and San Diego

San Diego Black Pride (formerly San Diego Black Coalition), 198

San Diego Blood Sisters, 176

San Diego Democratic Club, 176, 190, 235n43

San Diego Down Association, 112

San Diego Equality Business Association, 113

San Diego Imperial Court, 112

San Diego Inc.: and construction of the Community Concourse (1963), 118–19; formation to sanitize the downtown vice district, 112

San Diego law and policy: dance halls (temperance saloons) outlawed (Ordinance 3985), 26, 30, 33–34, 63; hotel/rooming house license requirement, 45; public housing opposed, 141; redistricting, 236n44; zoning ordinances, 137, 138, 145. *See also* California laws; cross-dressing Ordinance 9439 (Section 5619) (1966); federal laws; Health Department of San Diego; housing—racial discrimination in; miscegenation laws; police department of San Diego (SDPD); prostitution; racism; vagrancy laws; *entries at* redevelopment

San Diego Negro Directory, 1926 (revised), 58

San Diego Race Relations, 65

San Diego State University: area incorporated into new District 9, 196; Black Student Council, 168

impersonation venue, 128–29, 230n50; fundraising for the Center, 138; as Rosenberg and Provost property, 117–18

Silver Sands Café (Robert Clay, owner): as black bar that served as queer space, 122, 200; Bubba on the atmosphere of, 122; Bubba's drag revue group (The Plutons) playing regularly at, 115, 125; as downtown "monument," 122; the Gaslamp Quarter Merchants Association forcing closure of via expensive lease, 115, 143; as haven for black queens, 115, 122; as holding on despite redevelopment of downtown, 1; as last black-owned business downtown, 115, 143; map showing location, 120–21; matchbook illustration, 123; opening and location (1964), 115, 122; and selective arrests of black queens in raids, 1, 122–24

single-room occupancies. See SROs (single-room occupancies)

Sister Pee-Wee's Soul Food (Logan), 125, 126

Sky Room (bar), 117, 118, 145

slavery, in colonial Mexico, 220n87

Smith, Alan, 133–34

Snorton, Riley, 43

Snyder, Doug, 194

Soulkiss (parties "for women who love women"), 162, 198–99, 200, 205. See also lesbian parties

southeast San Diego. See Logan Heights

South Seas Room, 118

spatial acts, practices of subjugation as, 6

spatialized blackness, 11–12

Spectrum, 185

Sportsman Club (Logan), 125

SROs (single-room occupancies): overview, 63; black guests charged more, 142; at constant risk of being demolished, 62–63; cost of, 231n86; elderly residents, serving as communal support and alternative to nursing homes, 141; federally operated (HUD), for low-income residents, 231n86; military servicemen as residents of, 141; police claim that "men posing as women" were targeting sailors and robbing them in, 2, 123; racial and class differences among residents of, 141–42; redevelopment (1980s) and demolition of, 136, 142; rooming houses of early twentieth-century converted to, 59–62, 63, 212, 231n86. See also rooming houses

stables (cribs), 28

Stallings, L. H., 75, 211–12

Stallings, Valerie, 235n43

State Health Officers' Association of the United States, 48

Stern, Scott, 49, 222n130

Stingaree. See red-light district, police-protected (Stingaree)

Stockton, California. See Angelou, Maya, Gather Together in My Name (1974)—storyline: as brothel worker in San Joaquin Valley storefront churches: black migration from the South and establishment of, 148; as enduring institutions, 148; racist policies and disinvestment creating overabundance of vacant storefronts (for use) in postwar era, 145–46. *See also* Fidelity Lodge No. 10 (black Masonic lodge, Logan)—Greater Johnson Missionary Baptist Church

structural violence: antiwork politics of sex work as retreat from, 8–9. *See also* Hillcrest neighborhood—redistricting campaign by safe space activists; housing—racial discrimination in; incarceration; queer communities, and racial and class divisions; racism; sexism; *entries at* redevelopment

Stryker, Susan, 127–28

substance use or sale, arrests for, 38, 42–43

suburban shopping centers, 118, 139

suffragists, on disproportionate cruelty to black women in prison, 11

Sullivan, Rachael, 13, 112

Supper Club. *See* Show Biz Supper Club

Taylor, Verta, 127

Teaiwa, Teresia, 215n46

technologies of gender (cross-dressing): as access to other informal work, 43–44; as longstanding practice among black people, 43; refusal to provide police with information

sought, 42; transgender interpretation of historical documents, 43

technologies of race: as challenge to essentialist racialized discourse, 42–43, 220n87; passing and marriages chosen by Mabel Tyler/Rowe/Ramsey to facilitate her life as active businesswoman, 54–59, 57, 222nn142–143; refusal to provide police with information sought, 42–43

temperance saloons. *See* dance halls (temperance saloons)

Thompson, Lloyd, 50

Tijuana, Mexico: as black musicians' circuit, 79; as hub of blacks from the American West, 79; migration of white prostitutes to, 47; "patriotic" San Diego compared to "lawless" Tijuana, 137; social hygienists' blaming for prostitution in SD, 52. *See also* Mexico

Tina's Night Club (Logan), 143, 144

tourism. *See* sex tourism industry in San Diego; white tourists

Townhouse (Oceanside club), 125

transgender people: black trans elder, Bubba's transition to, 152–54, 159; interpretation of historical technologies of gender, 43; safe space activists seeking to differentiate themselves from, 112, 114; social scientists' acceptance of homosexuals but not transfolk, 114. *See also* black trans queens; Bubba (Granville "Bubba" Omega Hughes)

Trotter, Joe W., 146, 147

women, mobility in public space curtailed due to Progressive Era antiprostitution laws, 68, 93–94

Women's Army Corps (WAC): application by Angelou, 74–75, 98–99; black women's mistreatment in, 99; establishment of (1942), 225n39; veterans of, 92

Women's Christian Temperance Union (WCTU), 24, 44

Woodworth, Douglas R., 134

World Beats Center, 185

World War I. *See* detention of (disproportionately black) women suspected of venereal disease

World War II: black migration to Stockton CA, 100; and defense industry growth in SD, 14; establishment of women's military service branches (1942), 225n39; and proliferation of gay bars and enclaves, 116–17

—POSTWAR PERIOD: black migration increases to the West, 14, 82; defense industries closed to black workers in SD, 67; defense industry downturn, 82; disreputability as a way for black women to survive and thrive, 67–68, 73; GI Bill systematically denied to black soldiers, 67; white (and federal) disinvestment in Logan Heights, 145–46. *See also* downtown vice district (postwar era); military economy of San Diego; redevelopment of downtown (postwar era); safe space activists (gay neighborhood development)

Wright, Richard, 76

X, Malcolm, 169

yellow slavery (sex-trafficking moral panic about interracial intimacy), 34, 218n53

Yesmar Hotel (rooming house), 55, 59, 62

YMCA: Armed Services YMCA, 118, 119, 133; Catholic Charities development in City Heights, 196–97

Yokum (rooming house), 32–33

Young, Roxanna, 163

YWCA (Young Women's Christian Association, San Diego), women of color prohibited from, 31

YWCA Clay Avenue Branch (Logan), black women accommodated in, 83

Zebra Club (bar), 125

Zenger's Newsmagazine, 195

Zoot-Suit Riots (1943), 63–65

zoot suits, as resistance against white supremacy, 64–65

Founded in 1893,
UNIVERSITY OF CALIFORNIA PRESS
publishes bold, progressive books and journals
on topics in the arts, humanities, social sciences,
and natural sciences—with a focus on social
justice issues—that inspire thought and action
among readers worldwide.

The UC PRESS FOUNDATION
raises funds to uphold the press's vital role
as an independent, nonprofit publisher, and
receives philanthropic support from a wide
range of individuals and institutions—and from
committed readers like you. To learn more, visit
ucpress.edu/supportus.

www.ingramcontent.com/pod-product-compliance
Lightning Source LLC
Jackson TN
JSHW022149240525
84995JS00001B/1